VOICES OF
DECLINE

VOICES OF DECLINE

The Postwar Fate of U.S. Cities

Second Edition

ROBERT A. BEAUREGARD

Routledge
New York • London

Published in 2003 by
Routledge
29 West 35th Street
New York, NY 10001
www.routledge-ny.com

Published in Great Britain by
Routledge
11 New Fetter Lane
London EC4P 4EE
www.routledge.co.uk

10 9 8 7 6 5 4 3 2 1

Library of Congress Cataloging-in-Publication Data

Beauregard, Robert A.
    Voices of decline: the postwar fate of U.S. cities/Robert A. Beauregard.—
Rev. ed.
    p. cm.
  Includes bibliographical references and index.
  ISBN 0-415-93237-8—ISBN 0-415-93238-6 (pbk.)
    1. Cities and towns—United States. 2. Urban policy—United States. 3.
  Metropolitan areas—United States. 4. Inner cities—United States. 5. United
  States—Social conditions—1945- I. Title.

HT123.B33 2002
307.76′0973—dc21

                                                                    2002069661

Contents

Preface

I grew up as the cities were dying. Trips to the movie theater and the library, Saturday morning breakfasts with my mother at the coffee shop downtown, meanderings through the sole department store at Christmas time, and frequent visits to the factory where my father worked just blocks from City Hall uncovered few signs, at least for those youthful and untrained eyes, that our small city of the 1950s would soon be less busy, less prosperous, and less attractive. Later, I watched as an interstate highway transformed Providence and Pawtucket; their commercial areas, once busy with shoppers, turned desolate and shabby. More recently, I wandered through Detroit's derelict landscape of downtown office buildings and observed outer-borough neighborhoods in New York City bypassed by the soaring real estate values and personal wealth of Manhattan.

After World War II, the large industrial cities of the United States entered a period of profound collapse. Factories closed and manufacturing jobs disappeared. Local tax revenues plummeted and governments faced bankruptcy. Slums and blight engulfed retail districts and neighborhoods alike. For twenty-five years, conditions relentlessly worsened and even the most optimistic of observers began to lose hope that the cities would ever regain their former glory.

In the worst of times, the cities continued to offer numerous opportunities for people to prosper. Signs of vitality were visible and have been throughout the postwar period. Particularly in the late 1980s and 1990s, such images became clichés: gleaming office towers, festival marketplaces, gentrified neighborhoods, historically restored train stations, waterfront marinas, and multipeaked skylines.

Nonetheless, the problems of the cities, like some ecological Night of the Living Dead, always return to haunt us. Potholed streets jolt our automobiles while boarded-up stores dampen our urge to linger and consume. The homeless appear on residential sidewalks, immigrants crowd into the house next door. Our suburban neighbors deal drugs, a pornographic bookstore opens on Main Street. Escape is only temporary, or a delusion.

The proclaimed decline of large cities framed the lives of those who came of age in the United States in the last half of the twentieth century. People who grew up in these cities confronted the difficulties of urban life on a daily basis: riding the subway, attending a concert in the park, walking to work, shopping at the neighborhood supermarket. Even people who moved to the suburbs watched stories of arson and crime on the nightly news and debated whether to shop downtown during the holidays. On the way to their offices in the city, they drove through physically devastated neighborhoods. No matter where people were living and working—declining cities, prosperous suburbs, booming Sunbelt communities, or sparsely populated countrysides—their lives were touched by the spreading consequences and anxieties of urban decline.

The postwar traumas of the large cities thereby traveled beyond the actual sites of deterioration and neglect. By doing so, they exacerbated the ambivalence toward cities that Americans have embraced for over a century. In turn, postwar urban decline fused urban ambivalence to widespread anxieties about racial relations, prosperity, national identity, upward mobility, and personal safety. The city became the discursive site for society's contradictions, and anxiety emerged as the discourse's dominant quality.

Since the late 1800s, the cities have enabled large numbers of people to live well—some to become quite wealthy—and have been the sites of a national economy of global dimensions. They have nurtured a vibrant popular culture and supported endless intellectual ferment. At the same time, and for over one hundred years, cities have served as the focal point of the nation's collective anxieties, the object around which to debate injustice and inequalities, and the scapegoat for social ills not of their making. Whether commerce was expanding or impoverishment deepening, the cities have been viewed as places of decay, moral turpitude, and social disorganization.

Not surprisingly, the obsession with decline has been fickle. Gripped by a foreboding sense of crisis in the late 1960s, public commentary turned optimistic in the late 1970s when evidence of gentrification surfaced. It remained buoyant throughout the late 1980s and 1990s as a booming economy lured investors and households to the cities. Few observers focused on the cities' problems. Data from the national census of 2000 seemed to confirm the change of fortunes. Population decline had ebbed (and reversed in some cities), job growth was robust, and even those cities—Cleveland, Detroit—that had been most devastated seemed, at least, to have stabilized.

Why have Americans devalued their cities? Why do they view them as problems rather than opportunities? The answer to these questions lies in the wide-ranging and national debate concerning the ills of the country's industrial cities, a debate that began in the late nineteenth century. To present this discourse on urban decline, I draw on the words of those who wrote and spoke publicly about cities and did so mainly in mass-market magazines, national newspapers, government reports, and various public forums. My goal is to capture how urban decline was represented to a national audience.[1] Here is where popular anxieties and aspirations were expressed for all to consider. This is the discourse as it was heard and read by people who lived during those times.

Most scholarly writings on postwar urban decline have aimed to capture its objective circumstances. Social scientists have analyzed decline's causes and consequences, interviewed its victims, and searched for explanations that might make sense of what happened. Urban historians have drawn on the historical evidence to construct narratives of the city that are grounded in factual conditions. The way in which the city has been represented has rarely figured in their investigations.[2]

Attempts to capture a single reality of the city strike me as useful and important but ultimately insufficient for understanding the city as a place of lived experience. When we discuss urban decline or read how others perceive it, we engage with highly charged stories built-up of layers of subjective impressions, not emotionally flat renditions of objectively specified conditions. Decline involves personal and collective loss, and that loss constitutes a symbolic alienation from the city. Something valuable has been misplaced, and it is not simply a matter of fewer people, diminished job opportunities, or a shrinking housing stock.

Certainly, social and cultural historians of the city have attended to how people experience the city. Their work has helped us to understand daily life, popular culture, and the vibrancy of the public realm.[3] Representation, though, is treated as unproblematic, and decline as merely background.

In fact, few urban historians have embraced urban decline as an object of study. Chronological syntheses and city biographies, particularly as they extend through the late twentieth century, recognize postwar decline but often use it as an excuse to shift the narrative focus to the suburbs. Historians who resist that urge retain the city at the core of their story only by finding an optimistic ending in the prosperity of the 1980s and 1990s.[4] Historians whose work has direct relevance for urban decline generally have a narrower agenda: the ghetto, economic collapse, public housing, or redevelopment.[5] Scholars have generally neglected the place of decline in the popular imagination and thus its role in shaping the decisions made by countless households and institutions.

This book is my response. *Voices of Decline* makes two contributions. First, it documents the popular and national discourse on postwar urban decline, a documentation absent prior to the first edition of this book in 1993. Second, it offers an interpretation of postwar urban decline that centers on issues of representation. How is it that people negotiate their understandings of the city?[6]

My premise is that the discourse on urban decline is more than objective reporting. It functions ideologically to shape our attention, provide reasons for our actions, and convey a comprehensible, compelling, and consistent story of the fate of the twentieth-century U.S. city. Operating in a diverse society burdened by social, economic, and political contradictions, the discourse draws on, even as it transcends, the conditions that govern current realities and future prospects. At the same time, the fears and anxieties engendered by a precarious world become attached to the city. Geographically confined and rationalized, these fears and anxieties are subsequently diminished.

Voices of Decline unfolds chronologically. My intent is to reveal the continuities, interruptions, and cumulative understandings of the discourse that make it both rich and conflicted. An introductory chapter establishes my thematic and intellectual point of view, and a final chapter reflects on how the discourse has mediated the ways we interpret the prospects and problems of the cities and negotiate its— and society's—conflicts.[7]

Acknowledgments

This second and much revised edition of *Voices of Decline* owes its existence to the perspicacity of David McBride at Routledge. Dave saw the "history book" that was partially submerged in the first edition. He then helped me to think through how it might be extracted, updated, and made better. I am in his debt.

Many people contributed both to the earlier version and my rewriting of it. Four friends—Susan Fainstein, Bob Lake, Daphne Spain, and Iris Young—read the full manuscript for the first edition, and I thank them again. Since then, their comments on my work—and their work—have been both insightful and encouraging. In addition, various book reviews and presentations after the book's first publication (specifically a symposium at the meetings of the Association of American Geographers in 1995) helped me to rethink my approach, as did all those people who over the last year unsuspectingly asked, "What are you working on?" and received a long (even if hurried) commentary on the flaws of the first edition and the magic I expected to perform to create its successor. Having the book not just cited but used by other scholars—in the classroom and in their own work—has also been important for the reasons all authors know too well.

I will always be grateful to George Levine and the Center for the Critical Analysis of Contemporary Culture at Rutgers University for the fellowship year that shaped the initial text. More recently, I benefited greatly from the three-year seminar (1998–2001) on cities that Thomas Bender held at the International Center for Advanced Studies at New York University.

Most of the research was conducted while I was living in Philadelphia. There, I was a frequent visitor to the main libraries at Temple University and the University of Pennsylvania. Bobst Library at New York University enabled me to make the story current.

The production of this second edition went smoothly thanks to the talents and efforts of Stephanie Forster and Dave McBride at Routledge and Peg Latham at Colophon.

On a more personal note, Debra Bilow contributed her usual emotional support as we both negotiated the difficult personal terrain that borders scholarship.

"To imagine a language means to imagine a form of life."

Ludwig Wittgenstein
Philosophical Investigations

Framing the Discourse

CHAPTER 1

Foundational Urban Debates

In the years just after World War II, only the most isolated of the country's residents could avoid the trauma afflicting the large, central cities. The returning veteran looking to house a new family, the automobile manufacturer considering whether and where to expand production, the department store executive contemplating a move to the suburbs, and the big-city mayor scrutinizing next year's budget all acted under the influence of problems increasingly associated with declining cities.

Urban problems were real and well known. The decline of cities was widespread, and its causes were said to extend rootlike throughout American society. Few were spared its consequences. No wonder it became a topic for popular debate.

What had happened, what was happening, and what might happen were questions addressed by public commentators on almost a daily basis. An intricate national discussion ensued around the nature and condition of the country's cities, a discussion in which commentators, speaking and writing in a variety of forums and from diverse perspectives, pursued an elusive prey—the significance of urban decline.

The pivotal issue of that debate, then and now, has been the rapid fall from prosperity of large, industrial cities, a drastic turnabout that seemingly began as World War II drew to a close. Population loss; the physical deterioration of housing, factories, and shops; the collapse of urban land values; rising city property taxes and soaring crime rates; deepening poverty and unemployment; and the growing concentration of minorities have all, at one time or another, been dominant themes. Conditions were shocking, not just because they brought hardship to households, investors, and local governments but also because they seemed to presage the demise of the cities that had made the United States one of the world's most prosperous countries.

Decade after decade, the cities of the United States had grown in population. Production facilities had expanded. Employment opportunities, despite cyclical and thus temporary setbacks, had been abundant. Harland Bartholomew's comments in 1940 before the Mortgage Bankers Association of America were indicative of the expectations of experts and non-experts alike: "From 1870 to 1930 American cities experienced the most rapid growth ever before known. We came to accept growth as a matter of course."[1]

The cities had been the sites for great factories that catapulted the United States into its role as a world power able to fight global wars and to dominate international markets. Cities had been the welcoming ports for thousands upon thousands of immigrants in search of freedom and opportunity, and had subsequently served as the cauldrons within which foreigners and natives forged an American culture. Natives, too, had migrated to the cities in search of wealth, power, and fame. For decades, the progress of the nation had been inseparable from the growth and prosperity of its cities.

In 1944, Louis Wirth, the country's most famous urban sociologist, presented a pessimistic diagnosis, one tinged with less wonderment and more resignation than Harland Bartholomew had mustered a few years earlier: "The seemingly limitless growth of our cities has come to an abrupt end. This is all the more important because . . . we took it for granted that our cities would continue to grow at what now appears a fantastic rate."[2] The finality of his assessment related less to the depths to which cities had plunged—conditions would certainly worsen—than to the sharp and shocking break with historical trends. This new phenomenon affected not only how people lived but also their image of America and of themselves. One could no longer expect that past patterns of residential location, industrial development, and retail activity would continue, nor was it safe to assume that uninterrupted growth would spread evenly across the landscape.

Of course, the country adapted. People found new places to build their homes, industrial and commercial investors uncovered previously overlooked opportunities, and our understandings of growth and progress changed to accommodate quite different communities. Urban decline remained, and though its salience waxed and waned, its persistence could not be denied.

The history of the United States after World War II is thus incomplete without reference to the fate of its once-mighty cities. Urban decline lurks behind every postwar story, appears in analyses of national and local economies, figures prominently in the evolution of federal, state, and municipal governments, and even surfaces as a major event in the history of the American family. Of the many traits that distinguish postwar America from the nearly two hundred years of history that preceded it, urban decline is one of the most salient.

For centuries, societies—and historians—have grappled with the tension between progress and its absence, growth and its immanent other—decay. From at least the early eighteenth century, observers have portrayed Western civilization as under threat or in the throes of decomposition. Historical pessimists have bemoaned the malignant forces attacking civilization's virtues while cultural pessimists have pointed to the rot within. The former dreads the collapse and loss of civilization, the latter hopes for a new beginning in its ruins.[3] Variations on "the rise and fall" and "the end (or crisis) of" abound in the titles of broad histories and cultural commentary. (Oswald Spengler's *The Decline of the West* (1918) and Edward Gibbon's *The History of the Decline and Fall of the Roman Empire* (1896–1900) are two of the most famous examples.) Their authors wield the metaphor of decline to anchor interpretations and tap contemporary anxieties.

These anxieties are rooted in the modernist fascination with and quest for progress. When achievement fails to keep pace, when progress wanes, decline is the symptom. History is seemingly stalled, with prognostications becoming more and more pessimistic. Not just stasis has taken hold, but a weakening as previous accomplishments deteriorate and literally disappear. Decline is a "falling away" from the modernist ideal of uninterrupted human advance.[4]

A sense of lagging behind has surfaced most recently around globalization. What matters for nations, it seems, is global competition and the consequences this has for political and economic dominance in the international system. Global competitiveness is unavoidable and slippage in the world rankings is tantamount to decline. Progress is not absolute, but relative. The United States might remain accomplished in many ways yet—and this is the fear—follow Britain along the trajectory from global superpower to second-rate nation—less powerful, less influential, and less affluent.[5]

A nation (or city) falls away relative to its peers, relative to the paths on which growth is measured, relative to the promise of civilization, and relative to its own progress. Such comparisons give meaning to the fate of cities. Consequently, and out of this perspective, urban historians craft a basic and powerful plot. Its narrative arc is the life-cycle metaphor.[6]

Historians of urban development in the United States usually begin with the colonies of Massachusetts, Rhode Island, Pennsylvania, and Virginia in the seventeenth century. They trace the evolution from protective forts and farming communities to commercial towns that become integrated with adjacent regions and engage, later, in trade with far-flung ports. The story is one of increasing size, prosperity, and complexity. Up to the early 1800s, the dominant themes are ones of progress and conquest, internal development, and external expansion. As cities progress, the wilderness recedes and settlers displace natives.

In this narrative, the nineteenth century becomes the era of the industrial city. Proto-industrialization is subordinate to agriculture and trade in the first half-century. In the second half-century, large-scale manufacturing drives economic growth and rural-to-urban migration. The industrial city ascends to economic, political, and cultural supremacy and drastically shifts the balance between town and country that was envisaged by the first colonists. Plagued by numerous ills—unsafe and overcrowded housing, labor unrest, impassable streets, rudimentary public sanitation, woefully inadequate governmental services, relentless poverty, political corruption, and religious and ethnic conflicts—the industrial cities are portrayed as vibrant engines of expanding prosperity and social mobility, harboring in their midst the potential to overcome their shortcomings.

Up until the 1920s and as factories expand and immigrants flock to them for work, these cities become bigger and bigger. Social problems become more and more intransigent as the industrial cities reach their limits. During the 1930s and 1940s, growth is arrested, first by an economic depression and then by a world war. Amid signs that the trajectory of growth is not only about to slow but to turn downward, optimism prevails and cities are celebrated despite their ills.

By the 1950s, U.S. cities—particularly the central cities of the industrial heartland—have clearly entered a period of decline. Growth flees to the suburbs and abandons the manufacturing regions of the country for the open spaces of the west and south. Cities decay and in the mid-1970s seemingly touch bottom; racial unrest and fiscal distress combine with weakened urban economies to portend a dismal future. Historians turn their attention to new types of settlements, not just suburbs and metropolitan areas, but also nonmetropolitan counties, exurban communities, and edge cities. The central city is no longer the pivot of urban history.

Surprisingly, the precipitous fall of cities is a prelude to recovery. The 1980s bring growth, at least to some people in certain parts of selected cities. Cities once again become attractive, and historians note the resurgence of urban neighborhoods, office and retail districts, and livable waterfronts.[7] People and capital flow inward, and historians laud cities as places of excitement and opportunity. A brief downturn occurs in the early 1990s, but the "renaissance" subsequently resurfaces.

Essentially, cities ascend to economic, political, and cultural dominance only to mature and decay as the burdens of rapid growth and large size outstrip institutional capacities. Manufacturing, an industry that had concentrated investment and workers in the cities, is replaced by a service economy. Widespread prosperity, moreover, enables households to purchase automobiles and live in the metropolitan periphery. Yet, cities are ultimately redeemed, saved from their fall, by new growth. Each stage in the plot emerges from the one before. Decline follows maturity, maturity is the price of growth, and growth is the consequence of youthful vitality. The plot of urban history orders events and conveys moral significance and forward momentum.[8]

The theme of urban decline fits comfortably into this story line. It provides the degeneracy and fall that are so important to a second ascension. Redemption follows. Moreover, because urban decline is an ever-present possibility, growth becomes even more meaningful and progress even more apparent. In this way, decline turns any history of cities into a celebration of American initiative, either by reference to the city's rebirth or to the rise of suburbs, edge cities, and Sunbelt metropolises.

This "ur" plot of U.S. urban history relies only partially on the historical facts. It draws from an organismic analogy that casts the city as a life-form, a metaphor encountered frequently in the discourse. And, it utilizes the tension inherent to the modernist notion of progress. That version is best captured in the economist's Joseph Schumpeter's concept of creative destruction, whereby advances occur over the ruins of previous and now out-moded accomplishments.[9] Progress has overwhelming benefits but also significant costs. That the former outweighs the latter makes progress desirable and confers value on the modernist city.

MODERNISM AND THE CITY

Our twentieth-century ruminations about the city have revolved around its relation to modern society. This became even more apparent beginning in the 1980s when a number of scholars reported the demise of the modern city in the face of society's postmodern transformation. Their claim partially displaced, but also highlighted, a more specific concern: the nation's supposedly anti-urban disposition. Those proposing that Americans inherently dislike cities, however, are frequently challenged by others who argue that Americans have made a pragmatic adaptation, albeit one tinged with deep ambivalence. Central to any interpretation of urban decline, and establishing the context for reading its discourse, are these two foundational debates—the one on modernism and the city and the other on anti-urbanism.

More than a few commentators have argued that the city sits at the center of modernist sensibility.[10] The spirit of the age of science and industry, a time extending from the mid-nineteenth century to the present, was crystallized in the city by the scale and complexity of buildings and structures, the vibrancy and diversity of social life, the concentration of wealth, and the emergence of mass culture.

The modern era severed many of the environmental and technological strictures that had dampened the possibilities for economic growth and physical expansion, and that had confined the population to isolated rural communities and small towns dominated by localized agricultural and commercial elites.[11] No longer did the frontier, the sea, or the plantation confine economic advancement and cultured society. Opportunities for financial and artistic success were concentrated in the cities. Migrants looked to them for jobs, entrepreneurs for capital, inventors for investors. Erstwhile novelists and playwrights went to find like-minded spirits. By the twentieth century, the most successful painters, dancers, musicians, photographers, and actors followed careers that led them to the large urban centers. Only there could fame and fortune be found.

The pace of economic growth, social and technological advances, and the expansion of opportunities defined only one part of the modern era. The other was the enhanced potential for oppression, alienation, and destruction. The city became a metaphor for the personal estrangement and collective angst so central to the modernist sensibility. The city depersonalized by enveloping the individual in a mass society.[12] Densely packed neighborhoods, large bureaucracies, and indomitable economic forces buffeted those without political or economic power. Institutions now mediated the link between work and daily existence. Family life was made perilous by the uncertainty of the economy and the undermining of a civic morality. A pervasive disaffection ensued. Technological advances raised the potential for large-scale human catastrophes: massive fires reducing neighborhoods to ashes, factory explosions, worldwide wars, chemical spills, and nuclear holocaust. Economic prosperity, though, made it possible for the rising middle class to attend to its individual and collective needs, even as that prosperity caused its alienation. Life might not have been any more fragile than it had been before the rise of the modern city, but how people lived was certainly more pronounced as an object of scholarly, governmental, popular, and business concern.

Urban decline, of course, changes the terms but not the equation that juxtaposes modernism with the city. With decline, growth flees the city. Culture becomes brittle, and innovation and creativity no longer mesh so well with an urban vision. Yet, a projection from the decline of cities to the demise of modernism and the undermining of American prosperity and opportunity is too simplistic. Modernity itself is a paradoxical unity: "[I]t pours us all into a maelstrom of perpetual disintegration and renewal, of struggle and contradiction, of ambiguity and anguish."[13]

Commentators with a dyspeptic inclination viewed urban decline as the end of a way of life that had provided the political, financial, and intellectual foundations for modernity. As they shifted their gaze to the expanding suburbs, though, many discovered a cultural wasteland that clung parasitically to the now-weakened economic and social core of the cities. One reaction was to wax romantic and focus on the "urban villages" within the declining cities, marveling at the tenacity of the human spirit. In the 1990s, a number of commentators attached this nostalgia to mid-twentieth-century small towns on the urban fringe, places friendly and secure.[14] Like many who had come before them, they went in search of community outside the cities.

Decline was the physical manifestation of the alienation and insecurity of the modern era. The dismal conditions of the cities thus served as a stark reminder of the distance between modernist promise and realized realities. One would expect an outburst of moral outrage and a call for reform to follow such recognition. Reaction to postwar urban decline, however, produced flight and denial as often as it did attempts at amelioration. By the postwar period, the alienation of the city was so pronounced, the ties of community so eroded, and the desirability of social and spatial mobility so ingrained that commentators' efforts to link urban decline with a celebratory modernism were mounted in vain. Rather than confront its problems, the white middle class fled the cities, and the country's economic and political leaders joined them in spirit if not body. Urban modernity was thrown into disarray. Alienation *and* belonging were relocated to the suburbs, along with prosperous families and new industries. Modernism increasingly became associated not with a place of economic opportunity and intellectual activity—the city—but with a nonplace realm of rootless individuals and nonspatial communities.

Throughout the postwar period, urban decline never drifted far from public scrutiny, but it frequently became disconnected from intellectual currents. Over time, it had less and less impact on the daily lives of the majority of the population.[15] Modernists found it increasingly difficult to integrate urban decline into either the celebration of growth or the alienation of spirit characteristic of the modernist sensibility. It was better to forget the city. On a more practical level, those who could not segregate themselves within the city could always, unless they were black, flee to the suburbs. Urban decline thus became nicely contained symbolically and physically, though still discussed with great passion.

In the 1980s, a new sensibility emerged—postmodernism—to attest that such sea changes were part of the economic and cultural restructuring of capitalism.[16] Like the modernism that ostensibly preceded it, postmodernism had a conflicted approach to the city.

One strain of the postmodern discourse focused on the play of images and the severance of cultural from material practices.[17] Their gaze fixed on the affluence of the 1980s and 1990s and "[t]he domestication of fantasy in visual consumption."[18] For them, the postmodern city was gentrified neighborhoods awash in young, middle-class professionals; waterfronts of upscale apartment complexes and marinas; festival marketplaces; office buildings tenanted by financial, business, and legal services; and retail streets catering to the status-conscious consumer and impulse buyer.

The emphasis was on the transition of the city from a place of industry, commerce, and ethnic neighborhoods to one of spectacle and consumption, financial machinations, and global corporate decision making. The postmodern city was a city of advanced services arranged around banking, financing, and administration. Its workers were affluent and urbane professionals taking their leisure at sidewalk cafes. At its apogee, the postmodern city was a global city, with Los Angeles, New York City, Tokyo, and London serving as the models. From this perspective, urban decline is invisible.

Other postmodern observers were more critical.[19] They recognized the striking affluence and glittering urban landscapes but set them against a background of persistent and deepening poverty, the solidification of a permanent underclass, and the continued existence of slum neighborhoods. To this is added the rise of new immigrant neighborhoods (mostly Asian and Latin American) that provided cheap labor for small-scale manufacturing firms and informal economic activities, unrelenting decline of the white population, the deepening of fiscal problems, the emergence of a dangerous drug culture, growing numbers of homeless, and the erosion of civic commitment. The postmodern city was cast as a city of sharp contrasts—a dual city.[20] To be postmodern was to be in the throes of deepening contradictions.

Postmodern urban theory thus built on the conflicts and tensions that gave rise to the economic growth, cultural ferment, and new physical realms of the late twentieth century. At the same time, it acknowledged the oppression, suppression, exploitation, or neglect of those who lacked political influence and economic power, access to educational opportunities, and professional positions. Like the alienation of modernism, the postmodern city liberated conspicuous consumption, worsened the exploitation of the underclasses, and severed individuals from ethical constraints and communal bonds. If the postmodern city was the leading edge of civilization, taking up where the modern city left off, it was less a city that advances prosperity and the good life to all than one that builds affluence for a few on the exploitation of the many. This all sounded suspiciously like the modernist city.

Infatuation with the postmodern city echoed, but did not revive, an earlier debate centered on the modernist city's displacement of an agrarian and pastoral society. For the most part, postmodernists celebrated the city, standing in awe of the new city of conspicuous consumption, international corporate power, and self-referential architecture. They also condemned its deepening social and economic disparities. Commentators in the eighteenth and nineteenth century who witnessed the rise of the modern city were more fearful and less accepting.

ANTI-URBANISM REVISITED

The postwar decline of cities posed an interesting cultural and ideological problem for Americans. I know of no observer who has claimed that Americans love their cities, though certainly many live within them. To the contrary, Americans are supposed to cling tenaciously to a deep-felt dislike of large urban places. As one recent commentator wrote, "To become urban is to break the spirit of man."[21]

The roots of this purported anti-urbanism lie in the large commercial cities—New York, Philadelphia, Boston—of the eighteenth century that forged links with both an expanding hinterland and other nations. The anti-urban story is about the nurturing in these cities of values and practices antithetical to those held and followed by people living in the countryside. The commercial world substituted cash transactions between strangers for personal relationships. Size produced anonymity, and density bred indifference. Rural values were quite the opposite: bartering, interpersonal respect, and self-sufficiency ruled. That rural farmers would subsequently feel alienated from and exploited by cities comes as no surprise. It is only a short journey from that feeling to a broader condemnation.[22]

This tension between the countryside and the city was exacerbated by the rise of the industrial city in the nineteenth century. The contrast between rural and urban became even more pronounced. Multitudes left rural areas for the economic and social opportunities offered by the big cities. In part, their migration was set in motion by the mechanization of agriculture, an extension of big-city values and practices. By draining the countryside of its people, the industrial city displaced rural sensibilities and the rural pace of life. It integrated the country into the economy of the city and championed values that appalled rural inhabitants.

Such a story is essentially about the emergence of capitalism during the nineteenth century and its subsequent entrenchment in a system of industrial production.[23] The full flowering of capitalism created a landscape of prosperity and control that privileged the city and left country dwellers feeling overwhelmed by the reach of the industrial colossus. Here was also a clash of interests: Frontier yeoman and farmers pushed further west only to be engulfed by a capitalism that promised affluence and security but only made them less secure.

American anti-urbanism, though, resulted from more than simply the forces that joined large cities to an agrarian countryside. It is also about a collective image of American society that took shape during the formative years of the nation. Here the debate about values is even more pronounced.

For this story we must turn to the romantic juxtaposition of nature and society, one pure and the other corrupt, in the seventeenth and eighteenth centuries. Romanticism contrasts the simple life of the countryside with the artificiality of the city. Country folk are deemed closer to nature, more in touch with basic human values, and less driven by selfish desires. Those in the city are out of step with the rhythms of rural life. They exist in a world without innocence. No longer in a state of nature, the inhabitants of cities are driven by selfish motives, distrust of others, and a severing of ties to the basic human values that anchor a moral existence.[24]

The nature–society debate extends out of the seventeenth and eighteenth centuries through to the nineteenth and into the twentieth century. There, it depicts city life as intrinsically immoral and the countryside as the bastion of morality. In the city, moral strictures were cast aside. Religion lost its grip and people's values atrophied. Intemperance, crime, prostitution, and other vices thrived. Youthful rural migrants were corrupted and, as the cities spread, that corruption threatened to invade the countryside. Even city dwellers condemned the loose morals of their fellow citizens and yearned for a lost pastoral ideal. However powerful was the commitment to religious and moral values in the countryside, it did not take hold in the cities.

Those who were politically inclined viewed the immorality and deviance engendered in cities as dangers to governance. The threat that cities posed to democracy was articulated most forcefully by Thomas Jefferson. For him, democracy could flourish only where individuals lived freely and worked independently, and this could take place only in the countryside. City people were forced to work for others and thus to enter into hierarchical relations that undermined their good judgement. In turn, the city engendered and then juxtaposed inequalities, thereby making individuals susceptible to the crowd; the individual voices of free men paled against the power of mobs and their inclination toward insurrection. The solution was a landowning elite that would protect American democracy from the urban masses.[25]

Given these long-standing sentiments, one can build a case for Americans being anti-urban. Drawing on the writings of philosophers and novelists, Morton and Lucia White in 1962 published their examination of the "intellectual roots of anti-urbanism and the ambivalence toward urban life in America." *The Intellectual versus the City* probed the "persistent distrust of the American city."[26] Focusing on intellectual discourse from the eighteenth to the first decades of the twentieth century, their analysis placed anti-urbanism at the center of American culture. Although the Whites included caveats that noted the difficulty of neatly summarizing American ideology, pointed to a possible gap between what intellectuals were writing and what the masses were thinking, and even exposed the equivocation of many of these intellectuals, their broad conclusions made the book into the seminal statement on America's anti-urban prejudices.

Critics were quick to attack the weaknesses to which the caveats had only alluded. One line of attack focused on the relation between the rise of cities in the United States and the emergence of a civilized society. The city, it was claimed, had the potential to lead the way to an American civilization of unprecedented technological and cultural advances. The city was both a challenge and a hope even if it did not always live up to its promises. Even the Whites suggested that intellectuals condemned the city not because it was too civilized, too obverse to the values of the countryside, but rather because it was not civilized enough.[27]

Many commentators were ambivalent. They vacillated between condemning the city for its weaknesses and lamenting its failure to contribute to a more civilized society. Their lament was often wrapped in a hope that the city was the key to prosperity and cultural advancement. The city was not being castigated and abandoned in line with a pure anti-urban ideology. Rather, it was being criticized by those who saw in it a potential for greatness that was not being achieved.

Evidence for this ambivalence can be found in the rise of industrialization. Although large factories were the impetus behind industrialization and urbanization in the late eighteenth century, many of the early factories were built in the countryside. In Lowell, Massachusetts, the factory system directly confronted agrarian society: "[T]raditional New England ideals and patterns of life" entered an "especially sharp and revealing confrontation with the modernizing forces of the industrial city."[28] The response to this "crisis of belief" was to search for a contrapuntal relation between the values of the city and those of the countryside. The issue was how to adapt behaviors and reconcile antagonistic values so as to preserve what was important and good about rural communities while adapting to the imperatives of industrialization. The resulting balance of cultural forces created an urban vision unique to the nineteenth century.

This righteous anti-urbanism has its counterpart in the postwar discourse on urban decline. In imitation of the dialectic of the urban and the pastoral, that discourse contrasted the decay and incapacity of cities with the growth and prosperity of suburbs. The asymmetry worked to define decline and shape the discourse. Postwar cities were places of crime, poverty, fiscal irresponsibility, idleness, drugs, family breakdown, and a loss of community. The suburbs functioned as the opposite; deviance, immorality, and illegality were much less pronounced, while the nuclear family and a sense of community thrived. Sub-urbanites were anti-urbanites.

The discourse looks quite different, though, if one begins with the ambivalence that Americans bring to their judgment of cities. To read the discourse on urban decline from this perspective is to confront the conflicted nature of American culture. Just as city growth established a tenuous cultural accommodation between rural and urban life, urban decline reopened those debates. In one sense, the decline of cities reduced their threat. Yet, decline also provided more fuel for popular scorn.

THE ROOTS OF AMBIVALENCE

The antagonisms between cities and the countryside in the nineteenth century were generated, in part, by the greater number of employment opportunities in the cities and the subsequent migration of rural youth. Rural areas were losing population, rural economies were being absorbed into urban networks, rural families were losing their children, and ostensibly rural values were being marginalized. The contemporary counterpart is the tension between suburbs and large central cities during the 1970s. Then, many big city governments were mired in fiscal crises. They looked toward suburban commuters for tax revenues and suburban state legislators for increased financial aid.

American society is replete with such tensions. Indeed, they give the United States its particular character, generating both political struggle and public controversy: "Americans have managed to be both puritanical and hedonistic, idealistic and materialistic, peace-loving and war-mongering, isolationist and interventionist, conformist and individualistic, consensus-minded and conflict prone."[29]

Investors and producers compete with each other or with consumers, and the economy produces unemployment, inflation, and environmental degradation as a matter of course. Governments are nested in complex relations and hardly agree on how to solve shared problems, or with whose resources. Ethnic and religious groups clash over social norms and whether behavior should be tolerated, regulated, or condemned. Households form neighborhoods of exclusion, individuals and organizations discriminate on the basis of race or sexual orientation, and elected officials engage in "dirty tricks" to defeat their opponents. Taken together, such incongruities undermine the legitimacy of dominant institutions and mock the values of equal treatment and national consensus.[30]

Throughout the twentieth century, poverty has characterized cities and rural areas alike. Except during times of war, unemployment has persisted, despite widespread governmental programs to eliminate it. At no time has the economy, even with the help of government, been able to house adequately all those in need of shelter. Education is widely available, but good education for advancement to the most economically successful occupations is not universally accessible, particularly for racial minorities and those in the working and lower classes. Discrimination on the basis of race and gender prevails in the face of numerous antidiscrimination and equal opportunity laws. In addition, neighborhoods with a high quality of public and private amenities are "open" only to those able to buy their way into them.

Labor unrest has ebbed and flowed since the mid-1800s, but has never disappeared for long periods of time. Racial, ethnic, and religious confrontations are more common than unique, ranging from disputes over neighborhood boundaries to riots in response to police brutality and to attacks on places of worship. Public protests have been a common occurrence: antiwar rallies, marches for gay and lesbian rights, and demonstrations for and against abortion, for and against equal rights for women, for and against environmental preservation, and for and against nuclear power. Individual acts of violence are equally prevalent, many of which are related to the poverty, unemployment, and the wretched living conditions of those cast aside by a capitalism whose interests do not extend beyond the "bottom line."

One would thus be hard-pressed to admit this evidence and then cast America as a country in which values are universally shared, with widespread consensus around social goals and private wants, and people live in harmony. Within such a milieu, it would be astonishing to find that people were not themselves conflicted about their social positions and the conditions under which they live. Antagonisms and ambivalences are rational responses to inequality, exploitation, and oppression.[31]

The discourse on urban decline is rooted in these tensions. The pivotal issue is space. Under capitalism, the growth and decline of cities and regions require that individuals and investments be mobile, and that the landscape experience incessant building up, tearing down, and renewal. A constant movement of people, jobs, and capital characterizes development, a process that includes not only the construction of new buildings and places and the preservation of existing ones, but also the decay, destruction, and abandonment of buildings and locations no longer useful in the relentless pursuit of prosperity. The decline of cities, the rise of suburbs, and the redevelopment of urban neighborhoods are all part of an unending and uneven development of space. Growth and decline feed off each other as households, businesses, and capital switch incessantly from one place to another in search of the "good life" and political and economic rewards.[32]

To avoid the competition that threatens profits and to maintain appropriate levels of growth, investors are constantly looking for new markets and moving capital from one investment outlet to another. Capital pursues a "spatial fix" to problems of too little consumption and shrinking markets.[33] Spurred on by population growth, investors and governments expand into new locations and abandon existing ones when opportunities for investment are no longer as attractive because they are no longer so profitable. Postwar suburbanization followed this pattern. Mass suburbanization was an opportunity to multiply consumption and production in housing, automobiles, land, appliances, furniture, and public schools at a time when the cities had become less desirable. Later, neighborhoods adjacent to central business districts became ripe for redevelopment as investors spotted opportunities for a rapid expansion of retail activities and housing. Capital, often with the support of government, literally creates space.

Targets of investment and disinvestment are also created through the decisions of consumers, demographic trends over which investors have little control, and government initiatives designed to work sometimes in concert with and sometimes against prevailing patterns of development. Nevertheless, power lies with those who control the capital available for investment. Granted, they must "read" consumer preferences and encourage other investors to join them, but urban development in the United States is, in its first instance, a process of capital investment. Intrinsic to its workings, moreover, is an ideology of development, which legitimizes trends, fosters trust, and produces a modicum of acquiescence. Here is where the discourse on urban decline becomes important.

An ideology that celebrates newness and growth, and portrays investors as risk-takers bringing prosperity to all and strength to the nation, legitimizes the uneven geography of growth and decline. By hailing restlessness as a positive virtue and by focusing attention on the creative rather than the destructive aspects of urban development, or at least portraying them much differently—the former as desirable and the latter as unfortunate but necessary and inevitable—new patterns of investment and disinvestment are justified. Urban renewal in the 1960s, with its displacement of businesses and families, becomes necessary to save the city from total decay, while federal aid to fiscally strapped urban governments in the 1970s is viewed as senseless. Growth no longer characterizes these cities, and their governments must shrink accordingly.

Legitimation is fragile and seldom wholly successful, however. Disinvestment from the central cities generates significant burdens on numerous groups. Many households and businesses are directly encumbered: they are displaced, their property vandalized or opportunities for employment or sales denied to them. Minority groups find themselves in inadequate housing, locked into low-wage jobs or commuting long distances, lacking access to neighborhood amenities or public services because of shrinking government expenditures, or threatened by crime. Multitudes of city dwellers struggle to maintain a sense of community and to believe in a better future in the face of a discourse that touts the decay and the demise of their homes and neighborhoods. Residents of and investors in the city must reconcile their hopes with their experiences, and the conditions under which they live and work with the promises of an affluent society proclaiming widespread opportunity.

American ambivalence about cities, then, is inseparable from, though loosely tied to, the realities that existed when commentators made their observations. These realities were inseparable from cultural attitudes, moreover. In order to understand urban decline, we need to do more than respect the historical background. We must additionally account for the ways in which discursive tensions and tendencies were filtered through events and conditions in the cities. This influenced how the discourse was formed, disseminated, and received.

SHAPING ATTENTION

How do households know where to live and whom to have as their neighbors? How do investors know where to place their factories, erect office buildings, and open retail stores? On what basis do governments decide to build infrastructure, subsidize neighborhood-based housing programs, or provide fiscal relief to city governments?

These are not simply technical decisions or instinctive responses. Neither are they idiosyncratic; common perceptions are frequently transformed into shared inclinations. How does this happen?

The answer is public discourse. In a variety of social settings— citizen meetings, barroom monologues, street corner arguments, over-the-fence conversations, dinner-table debates, academic colloquia— people come together and assess how they are living, where they should live, with whom, and at what costs and with what benefits. Similarly, employees of business firms, nonprofit organizations, and governmental bodies participate in a variety of forums designed to help them consider appropriate responses to changing urban conditions. In all of these instances, people share their preferences and intentions. Consequently, they develop, modify, and defend their understandings of cities.

The media provide the background for these encounters. On radio and television and in magazines and newspapers, commentators reflect on the state of urban America. Special reports, editorials, documentaries, and daily articles probe the depths of the city's poverty, the revival of urban retailing, and the successful struggles of neighborhood groups. Governmental officials speak out and consultant reports are summarized and evaluated. The information and impressions that readers and listeners glean from these presentations reappear in their discussions with friends, neighbors, colleagues, and strangers. People verbalize their place in the world and the world of places, and by talking together form a sense of what they should do. The discourse makes "it possible for people to live with themselves, with their moral dilemmas, and with chronic failures to resolve the dilemmas and contradictions."[34]

Of central importance is public assessment of whether what commentators speak and write fits our sense of what is plausible.[35] People ask if the discourse accurately describes an objective reality and clearly conveys its cause-and-effect relationships. Is the discourse credible? Does it portray truthfully the actual conditions of cities?

If the discourse is not credible, then the practical advice is likely to be ignored or viewed with skepticism. The public "voices" I use to present the discourse on urban decline, however, are unlikely to make factual errors. What is most often contested is the appropriateness and sensibility of their interpretations. People decide how to respond on the basis of meanings, not facts.

Consequently, the discourse is not merely an objective reporting of an incontestable reality but a collection of contentious interpretations. The "real world" provides material for discourse, but these understandings are then mediated socially through language.[36] The ways in which urban decline is represented are always problematic. Representations of decline are grounded only tenuously in an empirical reality. Although a commentator might claim privileged access to a "self-evidently solid ground of meaning," no commentator can successfully defend that position.[37]

All representations are indeterminant; their meanings depend not only on strategic juxtapositions with other understandings but also on shifting empirical references. The discourse is disorderly and thematically unstable; it is a collective representation of shared and contested meanings. Thus, we must reject a "straight" story about postwar urban decline that dismisses diverse perspectives and asserts seamless and coherent knowledge of a world external to the storyteller's craft.[38]

As "an abstract receptacle for displaced feelings about other things," the city is used rhetorically to frame the precariousness of human existence in a modern world.[39] Urban decline serves as a symbolic cover for more wide-ranging fears and anxieties. In this role, it discursively precedes the deteriorating conditions and bleak future of the city. The genesis of the discourse is not the entrenchment of poverty, the spreading of blight, the fiscal weakness of city governments, and the ghettoization of African Americans, but society's deepening contradictions. To this extent, the discourse sites decline in the cities. Urban decline provides a spatial fix for our more generalized insecurities and complaints and the discourse forestalls their evolution into a more radical critique of American society.

The discourse on urban decline, then, is not simply a negotiable but practical guide to how to act; it is also replete with moral considerations. Whether as individuals or heads of households, corporate executives or elected officials, policy consultants or government bureaucrats, we are enmeshed in a matrix of unavoidable social obligations.

Essential are the specific social obligations we have toward others—not just to our families but also to those trapped in inner-city ghettos, discriminated against in employment, deprived of quality education, or living in substandard housing. Compared to most, these people have fewer options from which to choose. How do we reconcile our affluence with their poverty, our safe neighborhoods with their fear, our range of choices with their constricted lives? What are we obliged to do?[40]

People need to make sense of their lives in a way that allows them to live comfortably and with purpose. They do so by engaging with others and by reacting to the ways in which realities and possibilities are portrayed in national and local media. And while it is simply not possible to establish an explicit link between the discourse and how people react, the discourse is the medium through which their actions are filtered.[41] After World War II, it was the discourse on urban decline that brought these understandings of the city into sharp relief.

Prelude to Postwar Decline

The World of 1937 by Hendrik Willem Van Loon: A masterpiece of technical perfection but rather perilously balanced and therefore easily upset. *Survey Graphic* 26, 12 (December 1937). Photograph by kind permission of the Library of Congress, Washington.

CHAPTER 2

The Cities Wholesome and Good

The discourse on urban decline began in the latter decades of the nineteenth century when massive urban population growth combined with industrial capitalism to create urban slums, environmental degradation, municipal corruption, and moral danger. Numerous urban ills characterized the industrial city, and reformers, with the help of progressive local governments, attacked the city's problems with the new tools of city planning, public administration, and social research. Though progress had been achieved by the 1920s, the unprecedented and rapid expansion of cities overwhelmed the ability of reformers to keep pace. As the size and influence of cities extended beyond earlier boundaries, the inhabitants of the country-side perceived them as threats to the rural origins and values of American society. Up to the 1930s, the discourse dwelled on the ominous consequences of urban growth and prosperity, and the inevitability of big, vibrant, and dangerous cities.

Until the 1930s, Americans had not experienced large numbers of big cities shedding households, jobs, and businesses. Extensive disinvestment during the Great Depression and the impacts of mobilization during World War II, however, signaled the beginning of widespread urban decline. Later, stagnant population growth, anemic urban economies, and fiscally strapped city governments pointed to structural weaknesses in the urban fabric.

The Depression and war could have been—and many contemporary observers viewed them as—anomalies. Optimists argued that these events had stifled the development of cities and opportunities had only been postponed. Urban growth and national prosperity had been the norm since the mid-1800s. With the end of the war, investors, households, and governments would rededicate money and spirit to renewal.

From the Progressive Era through the 1920s, the discourse occurred in a context of city growth and economic expansion coupled with unparalleled government intervention into private affairs, local Progressive reform, and a virtual invasion of the country by wave after wave of immigrants. The only significant interruption was World War I. Even then, direct American involvement lasted less than two years, and the postwar recession was brief.

Compare this with the historical milieu in which the post–World War II discourse unfolded—a long wave of political and economic expansion that led to U.S. dominance throughout the "free world." Yet, two major military actions also occurred—Korea and Vietnam—and the Cold War shaped both domestic and foreign policy. In the 1960s, African Americans rioted in the cities, and social activists called for a resurgence of grassroots politics and community control over daily life. The cities themselves were faced with middle class flight, industrial decay, and a deepening and spreading poverty. All of these conditions had racial overtones and were set within shifting governmental priorities that marginalized cities and their inhabitants. In part, urban decline was so emotionally wrenching to the United States as a nation because cities had been a defining element in America's industrial prosperity. The postwar discourse on cities confronted the seeming anomaly of national fortune coupled with urban decay.

The structure and substantive themes of the discourse on postwar urban decline thus cannot be separated from the precedents established in the century's first forty-five years. Those times continued to influence ideas about and perceptions of the city and established perspectives that had to be reworked or abandoned in the light of novel conditions, attitudes, and possibilities.

During the first two decades of the twentieth century, public commentators were characteristically ambivalent about big cities but did not reject them. Fear and panic were absent. Rather, what most concerned these observers was the undesirable consequences of growth, not the existence of or potential for decline.

Dominating their view was the rapid growth and large size of industrial cities, an ecological concern that easily turned into moral alarm as the cities became bigger, more attractive, and politically more powerful than the countryside. In quest of expanding urban opportunities, people flocked to the cities, particularly from rural areas. These migrants needed to be warned. Cities were sinful places, their streets congested and housing overcrowded, and their municipal governments corrupt. To travel to the city was to risk destitution and tempt damnation as well.

The warnings were tempered by a spirit of reform and the belief that the problems increasingly concentrated in large cities should be and could be solved. Government officials and reformers were committed to bringing order to the unruly city of industrial capitalism. Ironically, the great majority also opted to leave intact the basic economic relationships that simultaneously created great wealth and, through exploitation, brought poverty. Civic responsibility embodied in "scientific" government and compassionate welfare agencies was the preferred path, and optimism the dominant mood. The problems of the industrial city were viewed as opportunities for reform, not harbingers of decline or collapse.

ENVISAGED AND ATTACKED

The latter decades of the nineteenth century and the first two decades of the twentieth century occupy a privileged position in American urban history. Then, the high modern city, the city of corporate cap-

italism and mass democracy, came into existence. The industrialization of the mid-1800s had laid the foundation, but the modern city's
full flowering had to await the rise of national corporations and the
urban factory system, the arrival of large numbers of rural migrants
and foreign immigrants, the formation of an urban middle class, the
establishment of the local government as a purveyor of public services
and provider of infrastructure, and the spatial segregation of groups
and activities by class, gender, and race. Consequently, this period
represents a turning point, a unique juncture, in the nation's urban
development.[1]

Our image of the turn-of-the-century industrial city is composed
of numerous fragments: immigrants huddled in slum neighborhoods,
large factories spewing dirt and grime, streets clogged with horsecarts
and vendors, elected officials with their hands deep in the public till,
overcrowded and unsanitary tenements, widespread poverty amidst
exploited and sweated labor, and buildings strewn across the landscape in visible disarray. Juxtaposed against this collage is the growing white and professional middle class and its cadre of reformers
assailing the robber barons and the ills of the modern city and offering
numerous cures to governments and citizens.

Framing both the ills and the possibilities were growth and prosperity. Industrial cities contained within them much human suffer-
ing, corruption, exploitation, and inefficiencies, but these problems
were deeply colored—rose-tinted, in fact—by an expanding urban
population, economic vitality, technological advances, and institutional innovations. Walter Weyl, writing in *Harper's Magazine*
in 1915, could thus proclaim, "Everywhere in America city problems are being envisaged and attacked. City poverty, city crime, city
carelessness, city misgovernment, are being studied, analyzed and
combatted."[2]

It was not urban decline that propelled this discourse, and that
of the 1920s that followed, but the burdens of growth and the potential for reform. In general, the pre-Depression discourse extols current accomplishments and is optimistic about the future. Living and
investing in the cities are distinct possibilities, if not inevitabilities.
Of course, this did not stop commentators from reflecting on the

immorality of the industrial city and the fate of those who struggled to live there.

Despite falling urban population growth rates from the 1880s to the 1890s, an editor of *Current Literature* in 1900 was still encouraged enough to comment that "[i]f we take our largest centers of population, the rate of growth seems little short of phenomenal."[3] In fact, Adna Weber, one of the pioneers of urban statistical analysis, argued that the decline in the rate of urban expansion was not likely to be permanent. He offered the thesis that the spatial concentration of population in the United States followed a rhythmical pattern, rising and falling in each alternate decade. Such logic suggested that cities would never shrink but only experience temporary periods of deceleration regularly followed by renewed growth.[4]

In 1901, *McClure's Magazine* published an article sub-titled "The Wonderful Story of the Census of 1900." It praised the rise of the American city: "[N]othing like the metamorphosis that has come over this vast expanse of country was ever dreamed of, much less actually equalled, in the activities of the ancients or of other moderns than ourselves."[5] Virtually a confirmation of this belief, the country by 1910 contained three of the ten largest cities in the world—New York, Chicago, and Philadelphia—and had nearly fifty cities with populations exceeding 100,000 people.

Urban growth was viewed as permanent, inevitable, and even desirable. The Reverend Josiah Strong, Protestant leader and publicist, wrote in 1897 that man's gregarious instinct coupled with the mechanization of agriculture, the rise of manufactures in the city, and the railway have "always made the city as large as it could well be." He evoked Engel's Law: While the world's demand for food was limited, its demand for factory goods was insatiable. As a result, an increasing proportion of people must live in cities. Strong's analysis did not allow for a reversal of trends: "[A]s this instinct and these causes are all permanent, it is obvious that this tendency will prove permanent."[6]

Accepting the permanence of the city proved easy when the city was deemed necessary to the progress of civilization. By linking the city with civilization, one could hardly reject one without also rejecting the other, or allow one to die without also undermining the very meaning of modernity. Weyl pointed out that "[t]he city is the visible epitome of a young and venturesome civilization in which the whole nation, united by railroad, telegraph, and telephone, comes together somewhat confusedly, and works together with some friction at the common task of supplying common needs."[7] His brand of civilization spoke less to culture than to the technological necessities of an industrial society. Nonetheless, it also suggested a society bound by shared concerns and a commitment to collective welfare.

If the people of the United States wanted jobs and prosperity, the modern conditions of life, and opportunities for upward mobility, they would also have to bear the chaos of big cities. As Strong pointed out, "[T]he greater part of our population must live in cities—cities much greater than the world has yet seen—cities which by their preponderance of numbers and of wealth must inevitably control civilization and destiny; and we must learn—though we have not yet learned—to live in cities with safety to our health, our morals, and our liberties."[8]

Bigness and complexity were not the chief threats to body and spirit, though urban size certainly was understood to be an important contributor to the cities' great fortunes and failures. For many commentators, the basic cause of urban ills was unmanaged and unprecedented expansion, particularly in manufactures. As a writer for the *Baltimore Herald* suggested, "[I]n the main, industrial operations are the foundation and chief stimulus to urban growth."[9] Unless a city was located advantageously along a route of commerce, manufactures were considered to be "well-nigh indispensable." The validity of this observation was evidenced by the concentration of urban growth in the industrial cities of the northeastern states. The only exception seemed to be in the South, where newly established cotton mills attracted rural population to small towns. These southern towns, however, did not blossom into large and dense centers, and thus did not garner the same attention as that devoted to the industrial cities of the northeast.

Carl Hunt, a business reporter for *The Nation's Business,* provided a more subtle analysis: Industrial development, as a broad category, was not the prime cause of urban growth. Rather, it was industrial specialization—the concentration of a city's energies on the manufacture of specific high-quality goods. It is only "through specialization that permanent and desirable city growth can be most readily assured," Hunt argued, and the flourishing of Pittsburgh, Detroit, and Milwaukee, among other places, served as a testament to his conclusion.[10] These cities had the advantages—skilled and unskilled labor, a market for raw materials, transportation facilities, capital, supplementary factories, advertising prestige, community support, and a fertile exchange of information and ideas—that made them attractive to specialization. Yet, regardless of whether a city had a specialized or diverse economy, absent massive industrial investment, urban growth seemed unlikely.

Not everyone, of course, viewed urban growth as desirable. Large size was problematic. One observer noted in 1915 that "it is a statistical fact that no large city population anywhere is physically and numerically maintaining itself." As cities became bigger, he argued, environmental conditions worsened and birth rates fell. To maintain their size, cities had to attract migrants. Commenting on the article, an anonymous editor wrote that "the big city, the city great in population and area, is not as fit to serve the only purposes that a city can serve as are smaller aggregations of units which collectively we name a city."[11] Those purposes included reducing the cost of living, increasing wealth, enhancing recreation, and improving health. Size seemingly made cities less fit for human habitation.

The more dominant criticism of the big city was a moral one. It revolved around two intersecting comparisons: that between the city and the countryside and that between industry and agriculture. Opponents of the big city and its rapid growth used these themes to express their disapproval.

The critical points of contention were the large-scale rural migration that fueled expansion of the urban population and a falling birth rate in the cities. In his 1913 *The Atlantic Monthly* article, "The Drift to the Cities," G. S. Dickerman noted that of 2,941 rural counties, 798 had lost population between 1900 and 1910, and 378 had declined in population between 1890 and 1900. At the same time, almost no cities demonstrated any loss of population in the first ten years of the century. He concluded that "[i]t all points to a widespread movement from the farm to the town and the metropolis," with detrimental consequences for agriculture as farmers and farm hands migrate to the city in search of industrial jobs thereby leading to a fall in agriculture production, a rise in farm prices, and a drop in agricultural exports.[12]

In the same year, however, Mark Jefferson, also writing in *The Atlantic Monthly,* proclaimed that "[t]he American exodus from the countryside is one of the three great myths of the nineteenth century!" Contrarily, he argued that, first, the population of the countryside had grown over the past thirty years; second, while some rural folk do move to the cities, others move to other rural areas; and, third, immigration exceeds migration from the countryside. Moreover, he claimed that the city and the countryside were organically related, such that the growth of one depended on the expansion of the other. No city can either last or grow, he concluded, "[i]f the country folk ever really take it into their heads to flock to the cities."[13] It is the surplus agricultural population, along with immigration, that creates cities. Nonetheless, Jefferson's argument did not dissuade those who viewed the city and the countryside as engaged in mortal—and moral—combat.

Dickerman and others, though, really had a different agenda, one that did not depend on how large cities were or even how they managed to expand so rapidly, with or without the resultant costs and confusion. Their agenda was righteous disapproval of city living and its detrimental effects on the long-term viability of the country's moral fiber. Cities, they contended, created "artificial appetites" for such "stimulants and narcotics" as alcohol, cigarettes, and gambling and eventually undermined commitment to hard work and family values. A professor at the University of Pennsylvania wrote that "[c]ity life—at least in its present form—saps the vitality of the population, diminishes the average span of life and reduces the percentage of survivors." Under such conditions, cities would self-destruct rather than reproduce, and their demise would have national consequences. With physical decline and decreasing birth rates—necessary correlates of city growth—"every modern nation is doomed to slow but certain extinction."[14]

Public commentators evoked dramatic images to establish moral claims. Dickerman wrote that

> [p]eople are wanted on the farms to raise corn and grow stock for the markets; but they are wanted there far more for the training of manhood and womenhood in moral worth, in religious sensibility, in all the traits of a strong, upright personality. In the future as never heretofore, our cities with their multiplying wealth and lavish luxury are likely to need the country for that steady renewal of their better life which shall keep them from relaxing into sensuality and sinking into decay.[15]

In this way, Dickerman reiterated the dependence of the city on the countryside and industry on agriculture. Ironically, he did not fully appreciate the extent to which those dependencies had been reversed.

An editor of the journal *The Independent* was even more attentive to the moral dilemmas this dependency posed, and more evocative: "The one thing certain is that unless some of the conditions of city life that prevail to-day shall be very radically changed, the 'fittest' of the year two thousand will be descending the hyperbolic curve of degeneration toward a type lower than Grecian bandits, and more nearly resembling the bloodless monsters of the ocean ooze."[16] Clearly, the God-made country was morally superior to the man-made city.

While some were castigating big cities for their immorality, others were defending them. The defense was simple: Urban life represents the further evolution of practical virtues. Busbey White, writing in *The Unpopular Review* in 1918, could find no evidence that the cities were "centers of frivolity, immorality and crime, in comparison with the primitive virtues of the rural districts."[17] Using data on church membership, divorces, homicides and suicides, and capital crimes, he pointed out the greater numerical presence of these evils in rural as compared with urban areas. Further counterattacking, he noted that whereas rural communities and agricultural interests were continually in search of protective legislation and financial assistance from the national and state governments, city dwellers complained little about the severe regulations on railroads and manufactures and taxed themselves heavily to provide needed public services. Cities were more virtuous and less dependent. Moral claims and political interests were thus intertwined, a theme that would reappear in the 1920s.

One portion of the turn-of-the-century discourse, then, reflected on the perceived threats that big cities and rapid urban growth posed to the survival of a romanticized countryside and continued agricultural dominance in the national economy. Its premise was that the moral underpinnings of the nation had been cultivated out of rural and small-town values. Urban problems were generated by the nature of the city. In contrast to the subsequent discourse, though, these problems were not considered the forerunners of decay and decline. Instead, commentators were more likely to see them as inevitable consequences of growth and opportunities for reform. Two of them were particularly bothersome: first, congestion and slums and, second, municipal corruption. Commentators looking at the former tapped directly into the workings of the capitalist economy while those considering the latter focused more on political machinations. Eventually, both became targets for civic improvement.

A SINCERE AND EARNEST EFFORT

The overcrowded tenement was a dominant image of the industrial city of the early twentieth century and a fact of daily life for the many foreign immigrants and rural migrants who took employment in large factories and innumerable sweatshops. For the commentators of the period, the issue was one of congestion—the concentration of population—and slums. City dwellers were crammed into tenements, tenements were crammed into neighborhoods, and stores and factories were wedged into the remaining spaces. As Adna Weber noted, "Our metropolitan cities have assumed such gigantic dimensions that the evils of congested population are more and more forcing themselves on public attention."[18]

The root causes were economic. On the one hand, excessive rents led to the intensification of land use and high residential densities.[19] On the other hand, blighted districts, districts in which property values were stable or falling, often turned into slums: areas of mixed land uses, overcrowded dwellings, and worsening social conditions. The slum problem, moreover, had multiple consequences. Slums bred higher mortality rates, disease, crime, drunkenness, fires, and other threats to the lives of their inhabitants and of people in surrounding neighborhoods.

The aversion to slum conditions was accentuated by the presence of municipal corruption. The absence and, later, lax enforcement of building, health, and land use regulations (rudimentary as they were) exacerbated the environmental problems created by an unfettered capitalism. The emerging middle class viewed government as a potential bearer of reform that would rationalize and improve the cities, but as long as the rascals were in charge, governments could not be counted on to fight congestion. Too much money was being made through unrestrained growth. Walter Wyckoff, who in 1901 spent two days in the slums of Chicago, came to a commonly held conclusion: "In truth we know, in our haunting new-found knowledge of social solidarity, that [slums] form a sore which denotes disease in every part of the body politic."[20]

Much credit for exposing municipal corruption goes to Lincoln Steffens, a muckraking journalist whose series of six articles in *McClure's Magazine* during 1902 and 1903 (later to be published together as *The Shame of the Cities*) probed the municipal governments of six of America's largest cities.[21] His subjects were the disenfranchisement of citizens, the graft attendant to public contracts with local businessmen, corrupt police departments, the mutuality of voting lists and tax assessments, and the passivity of citizens in the face of widespread lawlessness. Common to all of these problems was the political machine and its boss, a self-serving arrangement of government and business interests. Although not all of his cities were corrupt—"Chicago was an illustration of reform, and New York of good government"—Steffens could not help but suggest, in reflecting on Philadelphia, that "[a]ll our municipal governments are more or less bad." In fact, where municipal governments had been corrupted, he found that "[t]here is no check upon [the] machine excepting the chance of a mistake, the imminent fear of treachery, and the remote danger of revolt."[22]

The dominance of political life by business values, Steffans and others argued, had led to a moral failure of the city, both governments and citizens alike. Big cities and their big governments became linked in a discourse of illegality and immorality. Albert Shaw, writing in *The Review of Reviews* in 1895, asserted that "[o]ur city governments have been our most conspicuous failure and the most dangerous of all evils which threaten national life."[23]

The distinction between the governments of the cities and the cities themselves often became blurred. Such conflation makes sense if one understands the city as a public realm in which people exercise their civic duties. Local governments, though, tended to weaken civic involvement. This seems to be the position taken by the Progressive reformer Frederick Howe when he wrote in 1907 that "our cities are untrained to political organization. We have no traditions of what a city should be. . . . In consequence, we have no municipal experience, no social sense, to fall back on."[24] The reform of governments was synonymous with the reform of cities, a joining together that later contributed to merging the numerous and varied problems of the city into a single perception.

As the Progressive Era came to a close, a collective sense of control over corruption, and thus over the city, had emerged. *The Independent* in 1916 introduced an article by Rudolph Blankenburg, former mayor of Philadelphia—a city deemed by Lincoln Steffans "the most corrupt and the most contented"—by celebrating his accomplishments: Blankenburg "retains the distinction of having given to boss-ridden Philadelphia four years of clean and businesslike administration."[25] This was high praise, and it required minimal persistence to earn it. Corruption was so pervasive and deeply rooted that it turned glimpses of reform into shining lights.

The World's Work, a few years earlier, had featured four articles by
Henry Oyen on the awakening of cities to their municipal ills and
misrule. "Up to 1908," Oyen wrote, "the story of American city government was one of inefficiency."[26] No more. Civic consciousness had
been aroused, business methods were introduced into city hall (likely
to the chagrin of Steffans), reformers instituted civil service procedures, and the city's better citizens took hold of a new spirit of responsibility. The "progressives" did it, Oyen suggested. He concluded, a
bit cautiously, that "the epoch of the physical regeneration of American cities may be said to have got fairly under way."[27]

Howe had shifted positions by 1912. He no longer saw the city
as a political failure, but instead pointed out how municipal governments were highly efficient in certain areas: taxation, library systems,
fire departments, playground development, common schools, city
beautification and city planning. He concluded that "[t]he most
costly failures of our cities are not personal or political, as is usually
assumed; they rather relate to the physical side of the city. We have
not yet acquired the big-visioned outlook on city building."[28]

Progressive reform was not to be confined to the administrative
machinery of municipal government and the political behavior of
elected officials. Progressives broadened the responsibilities of local
governments.[29] As reformers searched for ways to eliminate corruption and graft, they also searched for opportunities to utilize municipal powers and resources in attacking congestion and slums, the
spread of disease, the lack of skilled factory workers, and the efficient movement of goods and individuals through the modern
industrial city.

The movement for civic improvement also championed city planning with its belief in the city as a realm of integrated functions and
interdependent and responsible people. The goal of city planning was
to rationalize the city. The premise was stated succinctly by the editor of *The World's Work:* "Town-life is town-life, chiefly because it
is organized—necessarily organized in every way and for every purpose. Organization is the most effective tool and weapon of modern
life."[30] Yet, that organization often broke down in the face of rapid

growth and uncoordinated competition. Reforms pushed against this disorderliness.

Reformers wanted to do more than eliminate problems, they also wanted to make the city beautiful and orderly, and this is what city planning promised. Frank Carlton asked in the *Toledo Times,* "How shall [the cities] be made healthful, clean, beautiful and well-governed? How shall they be made the centers of art and culture as well as business and trade?"[31] Such considerations, particularly when they involve the city, are only a thin veil over affairs of morality. The political commentator and pacifist Randolph Bourne made the moral dimension explicit when he wrote that "[t]o say that the American city in its design and styles represented our spiritual capacity would be almost to say that we were a nation of madmen." His argument was not without a certain mean-spiritedness: "From the chaos and ugliness of American cities flows too palpably our economic and human waste." Nevertheless, Bourne believed a solution was needed, and available: "The well-planned city pays immediately from the social point of view."[32]

It thus came to pass that city planning emerged as a focal point of Progressive reform. Civic beautification societies arose to bring art, culture, and physical improvements to the small-scale urban realm.[33] Business interests and governments joined forces to follow the precepts of the "city beautiful movement" with its call for large-scale civic centers to replace the jumble of buildings normally situated at the center of big cities. Across the land, from Harrisburg and Cleveland to St. Louis, San Francisco, and Honolulu, city governments instituted plans to transform their central business districts. Tree planting, limits on building heights, and majestic boulevards were meant to transform the industrial city. The objective, as noted by Charles Caffin, was "to make the city more adequately express the high ideals of the community and to increase for all, even the poorest of its citizens, the decencies and beauties of life."[34]

Clinton Woodruff, a frequent contributor of articles on municipal government and city planning, reviewed the civic efforts of numerous big cities around the country in 1911 and found that only recently have we "begun to appreciate the sordidness of much of our city making and the need for rebuilding along broader, more comprehensive and esthetic lines." His observations, he noted, "all tell the same story of a sincere and earnest effort to improve municipal conditions with an eye to beauty as well as utility, with an eye to the largest possible good to the greatest possible number, with an eye to the future."[35]

His words were echoed by the former president of the Commissioners of the District of Columbia. Henry Macfarland proclaimed that the idea of city planning had come to fruition in numerous cities across the United States. Many urban dwellers "suddenly opened their eyes for the first time to see that they lived in smoke, amid ugly and incongruous buildings with unattractive highways, often poor and almost always inadequate, and without suitable parks, park space, trees and other aesthetic essentials."[36] Men and women, he continued, had finally taken responsibility for their cities, learned the causes of municipal ills and discovered that most of the city's ills were curable and preventable. His prediction was that "[a]t the end of this century, cities of incomparable beauty will be found in all the states and provinces of America."[37] The flaws of the city were cause for alarm. Yet, unlike the discourse of the post–World War II years, they were neither evidence of decline nor a rationale for neglect and abandonment.

Optimism about cities was fueled not only by urban growth and the seemingly successful efforts of Progressive reformers, but also by a belief that flowed beneath the surface of all scientific analyses and reform initiatives: Men and women were developing the knowledge to gain even greater control over their affairs. Students of government, industrial scientists, sociologists of the city, economists, public welfare specialists, and a host of other emerging disciplines and professions claimed an understanding of the world that would enable them to propose and implement successful reforms.

Of specific relevance for the discourse on cities were the voices of those who would later be labeled urban sociologists. In a variety of articles and books, they expounded on the structures and functions of city development, industrial growth, and life in the big cities. The Sociological Society in 1908 established a Cities Committee to promote study of the city. Patrick Geddes, a leading British sociologist, proposed the main task of this committee: to develop orderly methods of observation and description (e.g., surveys) that would enable a scientific study of the city to be practical.[38] Empirical and objective knowledge was the goal, the only rational basis for effective action. Newly organized philanthropic foundations supported activists in their surveys and mapping of poverty, disease, and slums. Social investigation would be the basis of reform.

Of course, scientific interest in the cities was not a recent phenomenon. Almost twenty years before the Cities Committee was formed, Albert Hart had analyzed the factors involved in the siting, distribution, and size of American cities. In a reference to small New England seaports, he had even considered the potential for urban decline: "[I]n this eager current of growing population there are some eddies. Even in America, some considerable cities are stationary or moving backward."[39] Growth and its attendant problems, however, masked any sense that the desirability of cities might be waning.

In 1902, Richard Hurd, a financial advisor, provided an analytical sketch of the dynamics that created the physical structure of cities. He identified the determinants and pathways of growth and, while doing so, noted the possibility that sections of cities would decay as the outward movement of activity proceeded in line with overall expansion.[40] These and the many concerns of reformers were synthesized by Robert Park in 1915 in the now classic "The City: Suggestions for the Investigation of Human Behavior in the Urban Environment."[41] Woven throughout his essay was the city not only as a physical but also a social phenomenon. Culture, physical structure, and social and economic organization all combined to define the city. Reinforcing the premise of city planning, the city was portrayed as tending inherently to organization and thereby susceptible to control by government, courts, church, school, and the family. Although Park proposed the city as a laboratory for study, he put forth no guide for action.

Sociologists and numerous other commentators were convinced that investigation of the dynamics of cities would reveal social laws by which cities could be collectively governed. Charles Henderson of the

University of Chicago encapsulated the confidence of his peers when he wrote that "[n]one of the urban plagues which have been mentioned are in the realm of destiny or blind nature; all are products of human choice and conduct; and by human energy, guided by science, they can gradually be diminished or removed; but none will disappear without effort."[42]

Throughout the first two decades of the twentieth century, then, public opinion toward cities oscillated between condemnation and praise, aversion and commitment. Nonetheless, predictions of impending demise were exceedingly rare. The dominant tendency in the discourse was one of reform, hope, and progress. Lurking behind that tendency, though, was trepidation and dismay. In 1915, *The Forum* published a short story that reflected the complexity of the urban discourse. The protagonist, unnamed, initially sees squalor, decay, and exploitation. "Imagination" takes him on a tour of the freight yards, sweat shops, and clamorous streets where, quite contrary to expectations, he finds beauty, hope, and even happiness. He now sees the city in a different light, one that evokes a sensual pleasure: "[A]gainst the purpling skies the edges of the warehouses stood out like battlements, gilded for an instant by the last rays of the setting sun. To the west, behind the black outline of the city, the end of the day reposed a moment in orange, in scarlet, in magenta, in violet, and then slipped off into memory in an indigo mysteriousness. The waters of the river were a velvet black now, and the lights glowed more vividly."[43]

REPRISE

The discourse of the Progressive Era joined the costs of urban growth to the optimism of government reform. Not yet a discourse on urban decline—one whose pivot is the impending demise of cities—neither does it neglect big-city problems. These problems were tolerable and manageable because cities were growing, reform had taken hold, and scientific understanding was advancing. National prosperity, moreover, was increasingly dependent on the fate of the cities.

Thus, even though the discourse of these early years expresses an ambivalence about cities, that ambivalence clearly leans in their favor. Celebration of the modern city was so engrained in educated circles, and its benefits so widespread, that naysayers were quickly dismissed. Commentators were seemingly convinced of the great rewards of modernity and the opportunities available to dampen the contradictions of industrial and, later, corporate capitalism. Optimistic about reform and undaunted by the city's ills, they were inclined to praise the good.

At the same time, conditions were such that growth and prosperity seemed inevitable. Cities were the place to be if one wanted to be at the center of society. Consequently, the discourse supported the city, not solely because growth seemed to be its own cure, but also because reform promised an even better future. Those looking for guidance could easily read the signs.

With the historical closing of the Progressive Era in the third decade of the century, the pace of urban growth quickened and the effects of reform ostensibly took hold—prosperity spread even further and deeper into American life. Yet, despite the similarity in conditions, the discourse began to shift. Starting in the 1920s, the city became less and less favored.

CHAPTER 3

Not Those of Decadence

W hen the Census Bureau in 1920 declared that the United States had become an urban society, it was a statement about statistical categories and not novel social and cultural arrangements. Neither was it meant to forecast future trends. The number of people living in urban places—places of 2,500 people or more—had simply exceeded 50 percent of the national population. Almost four-fifths of the previous decade's population growth had occurred in urban places and, though immigration had diminished sharply, the great internal migration from country to city had continued unabated.

After a brief postwar recession in 1919, prosperity reemerged. The 1920s witnessed a sustained economic expansion with spectacular levels of construction activity, rising personal fortunes, and heightened urbanization. The cities grew to unprecedented size, as if to so solidify "urban" society that it could never be undermined.

For the most part, the reforms of the Progressive Era had taken hold and the problems of the cities were no longer ones of health, municipal misrule, and slums. Moral reform returned; the do-gooders of the 1920s concerned themselves with roadhouses and saloons, crime and corruption, demon rum, and mob behavior. Commentators reflected on a "lost" generation of intellectuals who had discarded society's norms, while civil liberties were threatened by the Ku Klux Klan and various tests for un-Americanism. Such concerns were part of the alarm at the massive size of contemporary cities, though none rose to prominence in the discourse.

Large size was a mixed blessing. It exacerbated problems of congestion and posed new challenges to the city's management. It also was a measure of progress. Out of this tension emerged a sense that urban growth would eventually slacken, not because cities themselves were inherently flawed, but because their great size compelled new forms of human settlement. Paradoxically, population loss emerged not as a problem but as a solution to seemingly excessive growth, with decentralization as the likely precipitant.

The city of the 1920s thus seemed to be the height of modernity and the deliverance on the promise of the Progressive Era. One could be ambivalent about the city, but one could not ignore its accomplishments and attractions. Though one had to guard against its sinful temptations, the city was where fame and fortunes could be made. The real worry was whether any room was left.

Large size, though, had its own contradictions, and they would eventually provide the seeds for a fully developed discourse on urban decline.—In the 1930s and 1940s, however, people had few choices; their energies were directed first to survival during the Depression and then to victory in the war. Afterward, they would return to the reform and renewal of the cities. They would do so against the backdrop of the first signs of mass suburbanization, the decentralization that would not only relieve population pressure but also ignite decades of decline.

BLIND AND HEEDLESS GROWTH

In 1926, the economist George Soule asked whether the cities would ever stop growing. "Mere momentum," he offered, "is carrying the cities beyond the point of diminishing returns." Soule, undoubtedly, was responding to the 1925 population estimates published by the

Census Bureau. In the two and one-half decades since 1900, the eighteen cities with populations in excess of 400,000 had grown by an average of 71 percent, with Los Angeles having had a population increase of 609 percent and Detroit one of 331 percent. Even Cincinnati, the city with the lowest percentage increase, grew by 25 percent.[1]

Driving this intense urbanization was migration from the countryside to the city. The editors of *The Literary Digest* commented in 1925 that "the great American trek to the cities continues and gains in speed and power."[2] The cities' economic vitality and their jazz-and-flapper image lured those whose quiet rural existence portended only a marginal and dull future.

Reflecting on the dynamic growth of cities, one commentator focused on a book by Edward Pratt about the problem of congestion in New York City. He observed, "It seems to be universally true that, to quote his [Pratt's] words, the greater the city becomes the greater the attractive force it will exercise."[3] Size seemed to be feeding on itself. Factories attracted more workers, workers attracted more stores and factories, and more employment opportunities attracted more people.

The process was neither lawlike and immutable nor a natural phenomenon. Civic boosters were active in the pursuit of bigness. Cities within the same region competed for dominance, and progress was "measured by the growth of a city's population, the number of its skyscrapers and the length of its transit lines."[4] Growth generated wealth, and real estate investors, industrialists and elected officials were uncritical supporters. The architect Frederick Ackerman noted that modern man "has woven himself into a complicated web of inflated values and capitalizations *which involve the necessity of growth and concentration.*" In fact, he wrote, a "community with a stable population is now referred to as a 'dead one'," a criterion that would be particularly troublesome in the decades to follow.[5]

Nevertheless, it was becoming obvious to many observers that the growth of cities amplified the problems associated with congestion and increased the potential for breakdown. Countervailing forces emerged as growth undermined the efficiency of production and circulation and hindered the wealth-generating capacity of cities. As Soule pointed out, with rapid growth comes rising land values and "[h]igh land value leads to multi-family construction and overcrowding. . . . Up go risks of sickness, death, fire, crime, accident. Up go costs of sanitation, institutions, police, courts, hospitals, fire protection."[6]

Not clear at the time was what specific forces would stop this incessant expansion. One observer proposed that "[w]hen a town has acquired the habit of growing it goes on growing until some great external change compels it to stop and perhaps to decay."[7] His counterbalancing forces were both internal and external: the greater cost of living in the city under uncomfortable conditions, a mother's desire that her children should have fresh air and room to play, the expense of transporting raw materials from the countryside, the loss of light, and the dirtiness of air. Still, this observer could not imagine what would stem the tide of migration. Cities would continue to grow as long as the population continued to grow.

Other commentators highlighted different countervailing factors, one of which was the speculation attendant to rapid growth. Ackerman wrote, "We are not likely to avoid the collapse that will follow the deflation of values when our cities reach the saturation point and stability succeeds the fever of expansion."[8] Property speculation laid the groundwork for its own collapse—another one of those contradictions of capitalism. Ackerman's perspective—cities being too attractive to investors—seems ironic. Rapid growth, though, is always two-sided, and one reads in the discourse of this period an increasing appreciation of this fact. Growth could well breed decline, an observation compatible with cultural pessimists and their belief that civilization is its own enemy.

Raymond Unwin, the foremost British authority on city planning, chose to focus on the human side of growth rather than on its financial consequences: "We have been so proud of the increase in the size of the crowd, that we have forgotten to care for the individual citizens who compose it."[9] Because of this, people will simply stop going to the cities, or leave. Once again, congestion, be it of investment or of people, moved to the top of the urban agenda.

Large size produced a host of urban ills. Capitalism was a major part of the problem, and city governments could not adequately cope. In an oft-cited article titled "Dinosaur Cities," Clarence Stein, the well-known architect and planner, specified the breakdowns that would likely occur or be exacerbated by increasing size and density: housing shortages and slums, water systems and sewers forced to operate above capacity, street congestion, and transportation breakdown. Overgrown cities were, by definition, inefficient. Stein commented, "For the city of our dreams is lost in another city which could occur to a sane mind only in a nightmare. It is in this second city that the great mass of people who swell the census statistics live and work and marry and die."[10] Something was being lost. Was it civilization, the dream of modernity?

The editors of the Grand Rapids *Herald* disagreed. They reversed the equation set out by Stein, Soule, and Unwin: Cities were not exceeding their organizational capacities. Instead, "[m]odern civilization is outgrowing cities."[11] Cities would soon be discarded, or drastically transformed, as a new society made novel demands on its environment. Civilization meant progress, and certain practices had to be abandoned if innovation were to flourish.

By this point, commentators were developing an averse reaction to big cities. Soule talked about emerging protests against big cities: agricultural interests complaining about the imbalance between cultivated land and factories; city-dwellers protesting the noise, dust, crowding, and high cost of living of cities; and sociologists, regionalists, and city planners pointing out the big city's disadvantages.[12] With the exception of the first, these factors are internal to the cities. Thus, whereas Cox deflected condemnation of the cities, Soule's perspective attracted it. Moreover, if cities were responsible for their own problems, then their defense would be difficult, particularly if reforms were ineffective.

Lewis Mumford, probably the country's foremost commentator on cities in the twentieth century, was outspoken in his opposition to the big city's "blind and heedless growth." He cast its internal breakdown in graphic and personal terms in 1926 when he described the consequences of one middle-income worker's move to the city: "By adding to its population, he raises the capitalized value of its real estate; and so he increases rents; and so he makes parks and playgrounds and decent homes more difficult to obtain; and so he increases his own difficulties and burdens; and his flat gets smaller, his streets bleaker, and his annual tribute to the deities who build roads and subways and bridges and tunnels becomes more immense." Mumford went on to point out the paradox: "As the city increases in 'population and wealth' it becomes less able to afford the things that make life generous, interesting, and amusing."[13]

Stuart Chase, writing in *Harper's Magazine* three years later, personalized the impending breakdown of the big city to an even greater extent. For him, it was a matter of the calculus of pleasure and pain. The sensual costs of the huge American city outweighed its sensual benefits. One could find pleasure in the play of light on architectural masses, arresting and amusing adventures, and in the arts; but greater "[p]ain is found in noise, dust, smell, crowding, the pressure of the clock, in negotiating traffic, in great stretches of bleak and dour ugliness, in looking always up instead of out, in a continually battering sense of human inferiority." A "gracious and civilized life" was no longer possible in the city. Users of it were not simply battered: "The nerves of the megalopolis are jumpy."[14] The big city was in a delirious state of perpetual nervous breakdown and functional collapse.

Mumford might have found Chase's anthropomorphizing unacceptable and his diagnosis faulty, but he nonetheless joined him in assailing the big city's ostensible collapse. Mumford was clear about the culprits, centering the debate on the relation of size to social organization. Real estate speculators and planners were responsible. The latter adopted the values of the former and foisted on cities a rectangular plan of too many streets, overregulated zoning, and monotonous blocks. Speculators, planners, and engineers were building cities with little sensitivity to the nature and function of the community as a whole. Traffic and commerce had become the "presiding deities" of "the sacred city."[15] The "continuous building up, tearing down, and rebuilding, with their steady process of congestion" was motivated by the need to provide opportunities for new investment and additional profits. The breakdown of the city, for Mumford, could be traced to "the one function that all American cities have traditionally looked upon as the main end of human activity, namely, gambling in real estate."[16]

Despite prognostications of impending decline, many commentators found the great size and growth of American cities to be unmistakable signs of the city's prominence in national life. In 1928, Charles Beard, the great Progressive historian, addressed a convention in Cincinnati where he bemoaned the antagonism between city and countryside and the displacement of the finer aspects of civilization by industrial development. He viewed industrial cities as a disgrace to humanity, but also recognized that the city was not, as Thomas Jefferson believed, a menace to civilization. "On the contrary," he said, "it is from the urban centers that the national economy of the future will be controlled, whether we like it or not, and it is the culture of urbanism that promises to dominate the future."[17]

Other commentators took similar positions. Gerald Johnson, writing in *Harper's Magazine* in July of that same year, lamented the increasing political dominance of the city as it continued to grow in population, a dominance that subsequently threatened the interests of country folk. Urban control over the countryside, he observed, would be every bit as stupid and tyrannical as rural control over cities had been. Resigned and pessimistic, he concluded that "[t]he city is going to be king. We may as well face the fact, since we can do no better."[18] Here was a discourse on urban decline that both lamented the city and, often reluctantly, embraced it.

THE FOURTH MIGRATION

Many commentators recognized the forces underway that would diminish the size of big cities. Only a few believed, though, that diminished size meant eventual decline. Although aware of the trends, commentators in general did not perceive them as threatening to the cities' economic, political, and cultural dominance.

Contradictions internal to the cities and the congestion brought about by rapid growth encouraged a migratory movement that began to counterbalance the flow of households from the country-side to large urban centers. As early as 1923, the centers of a number of great cities were declining in population. An article in *Current Opinion* observed that city officials in London, Paris, and New York were delighted that their populations were shrinking: "[T]he people are migrating to the country in all three great capitals as rapidly as transit facilities permit, and . . . this movement is considered a subject for congratulation." Despite the expansion of New York City, for example, the population of its central area, Manhattan, fell from 2,284,103 in 1920 to 2,271,892 in 1922 "and is still going down as land for office buildings becomes more valuable and transit facilities improve, and make it feasible for more workers to live in the fresh air and sunshine of the country and commute to their work amid the sky-scrapers of the metropolis." The editors of that journal then went on to suggest that bigger was not better. A city, at some point, would need to reverse its growth and discard surplus population.[19]

Mumford labeled this trend "the fourth migration."[20] The first migration had led to the clearing of the continent, the second to the rise of the factory towns, and the third, in the twentieth century, to the establishment of cities as financial centers. The fourth migration was away from the cities. New forms of communication such as the telephone, the popularization of the radio and parcel post, as well as new means of transportation (notably the automobile and the truck) were freeing people and businesses from central locations. The only question for Mumford, a severe critic of "dinosaur cities," was whether we would allow this fourth migration to produce human settlements as destructive and inhumane as previous tidal movements of population had done.

City centers were experiencing a decrease in population growth. A quota system on immigration, internal breakdowns, and a movement to the suburbs were contributing factors. The editors of the Philadelphia *Record* in 1928 commented that "in some communities, notably Philadelphia and New York, there has been a great exodus from city to suburbs in the last few years—a tendency that is much more in evidence than it was in the decade from 1910 to 1920."[21] People were using their feet to vote against the big city, and their behavior suggested to some commentators that the urban society proclaimed by the Census Bureau in 1920 would be short-lived. A professor of sociology from Northwestern University wrote that "American life to-day is largely and increasingly *suburban.* The twentieth century city which would be up-to-date in its outlook and projects cannot ignore these suburban developments."[22]

Henry Ford, the great industrialist, did not need to be convinced. In a 1924 article of Drew Pearson's in *Automotive Industries,* Ford announced the demise of great cities and the rise of small towns clustered around individual factories and inhabited by people who worked their farms and also labored in manufactures. His rationale considered the large size and internal disorganization of the city of the 1920s: "The overhead expenses of living in . . . [big cities] . . . is becoming intolerable. The cost of maintaining interest on debts, of keeping up water supply, sewerage and sanitation systems, the cost of traffic control and of policing great masses of people is so great as to offset the benefits of the city. The cities are getting top-heavy and are about doomed."[23] (Modestly, Ford did not mention his own contribution to decentralization.)

The decade of the twenties thus witnessed the first faint signs of a deeply pessimistic discourse on the cities. That discourse would be further elaborated in the years preceding World War II and fully developed in the decades thereafter. Still, striking differences exist. Up until 1929, the city had not yet begun to suffer major losses of population and economic activity. In fact, cities prospered. Yet, their prosperity made them vulnerable to breakdown. The Depression of the 1930s and war mobilization in the 1940s deepened that vulnerability and raised the probability of urban decay. In assessing the Jeffersonian claim that the city would destroy civilization, Charles Beard, in an otherwise critical speech, proclaimed that "it is from the urban centers that the national economy of the future will be controlled, whether we like it or not, and it is the culture of urbanism that promises to dominate the future."[24]

POSSIBLE DISINTEGRATION

As the 1920s drew to a close and economic trauma washed over the nation, population growth slowed and the fixation on big cities and their numerous inefficiencies began to wane. Certainly, as one commentator noted, we "heard much less bragging about volume of business and increasing population."[25] Still, because the large cities of the previous decade had developed a multitude of disadvantages that hardly disappeared with the onset of the Great Depression in 1929, the internal contradictions of urbanization did not wholly retreat from public scrutiny.

Warren Thompson, the director of the Scripps Foundation for Research in Population Problems, published two articles in H. L. Mencken's *The American Mercury* in 1930 that crystallized the sense that big cities were inherently unstable. Thompson argued, albeit equivocally, that "the large city is being found wanting as the most efficient type of economic organization for certain purposes."[26] High wages and high rents were causing factories to leave, the spatial reaches of the city were a terrible drain on the energy and time of people going to and from factories, and congested streets were discouraging commerce. Moreover, new forms of communication and transportation were opening up areas outside of cities for business and residence. Electrical power, Thompson suggested, would allow factories to decentralize and become smaller, the telegraph and the telephone would decentralize the office end of business, and trucks would supplant railroads, thus further abetting dispersal. Because people go where the jobs are, this geographic rearrangement of industry and commerce had the potential to build a new social and economic order.

Thompson also prophesized a "rapid decline in our rate of population growth and the prospect of a stationary population within the next three to five decades." Still, he stopped short of "predicting an immediate or even ultimate loss of population for particular cities . . . [though] . . . [t]he latter may very well happen."[27]

If all this were to occur, city dwellers would have to overcome their addiction to growth: "Our worship of size as such is, then, an extremely important factor in keeping the large American cities growing."[28] In addition, sounding quite like Mumford, Thompson noted that society would also have to confront those groups that profit from the continued growth of cities: real estate interests, downtown store owners, newspapers, hotel men, jobbers and wholesalers, and professional boosters. The very desirable outcome of such a confrontation would be cities with less crowding and more privacy, cities "so livable that people residing there will be willing to reproduce."[29]

Harold Ward, writing in *The Nation,* agreed with Thompson's overall criticism of large cities, but was less concerned with the urban birth rate, and more bothered by the puppet-like behavior of the "third migration." His evaluation was difficult to misinterpret: "An internal migration movement of nearly 700,000 people a year, most of them merely shuffling along in obedience to forces of which they have no understanding, following the line of least resistance toward the nearest job opportunity, piling up an enormous backlog of housing problems, health and hygiene deficiencies, crime, delinquency, suicide, and destitution—this is the seamy side of the great outward show of American cities on the march."[30]

Still, not everyone was convinced that large size was undesirable or would lead to shrinkage. The editors of one national magazine, *Collier's,* took a contrary view: "The competition of our American cities to grow in numbers is not so silly as it seems. Behind the noisy boasting about size and population is a very sure instinct." Growing cities, they continued, were an indication of "great stories of achievement" and "an inspiring picture of the power of the new economic forces which are so swiftly rearranging our world." Reminiscent of an earlier concern with industrial specialization, they cited the automotive industry in Detroit, motion pictures in Los Angeles, petroleum in Tulsa, and aviation in Wichita as prime examples of this dynamism. All were "proof that men have been thinking and working and that our civilization is surging with life."[31]

Census Bureau data on population change indicated continued but slackening growth, some signs of decline, and variations in where people were living; but did not point to a sharp shift away from bigger and bigger cities. By 1930, and by definition of the Census

Bureau, 56.2 percent of the total population in the United States was urban, an increase over 1920.[32] The pronounced drift of population to the cities had not fully abated, and the political consequences of this unrelenting even though diminished trend were obvious. In response, the editors of *The Literary Digest* noted that "[t]he city's grip on the control of the nation is tightening, and the rural political grip is slipping."[33]

At the same time that people persisted in migrating from farm to factory, urban growth began to shift to different parts of the country, with a corresponding shrinkage of older cites. The Associated Press reported in 1930 that "[c]ities showing 50 per cent. or more increase in the ten years are mostly in the South and West." This growth, though, had a less desirable counterpart: "Half a dozen cities have shown decreases from ten years ago. Three of these are in the East, including Fall River, Massachusetts, which showed a decline of 5.3 per cent., and now has 114,348 people; three are in the Southwest."[34] In addition to anomalies and regional differences, and particularly in the ninety-five metropolitan regions of the North, "the percentage increase of the outside population during the last ten years has been considerably larger than that of the central city itself."[35]

As *Business Week* reported, "With the end of the boom of the Twenties the cities slowed their rates of growth, even lost population in 1933 and again in 1938—temporary losses, but unprecedented in all the years since the continent was colonized."[36] Rural migration, regional population shifts, and urban population decline all existed simultaneously—quite a change from what had been reported previously.

The Depression, later joined by the war, repositioned the great growth and large size of cities on the public agenda. In addition, the stagnation of the economy exacerbated slums and brought to the forefront another problem—decentralization—that would become a nemesis of the postwar city. The discourse of the late 1930s to the mid-1940s focused almost exclusively on these two indicators of decline. Initially, their threat to the city was not viewed as fatal, but as postwar prosperity failed to alleviate—and even exacerbated—urban decay, the optimism of the early 1940s began to fade.

SLUMS AND BLIGHTED AREAS

In the 1930s, slums and blight returned to form the core of an emerging discourse on urban decline. The economist Mabel Walker, in her 1938 study *Urban Blight and Slums,* viewed slums, residential areas characterized by extreme conditions of blight, as the essence of urban decay. Others focused more on the economic obsolescence of buildings and areas, and further distinguished blighted areas of mainly commercial structures from slums of mainly residential structures. In practice, though, the two problems were inseparable.

The Urbanism Committee in 1937 called slums "the most glaring symptom of urban disintegration."[37] Shabby and obsolete structures, high disease and crime rates, and overcrowding were the indicators. Slums and blight characterized extensive portions of many older, industrial cities. Approximately 9 percent of all residential areas in Buffalo was slum in 1930, and it was occupied by 17.5 percent of the population. In Birmingham, Alabama, the blighted area of the city, almost 9 percent of the total built-up area, contained 22 percent of the city's overall population and 51 percent of the city's African-American population. The largest slum was in Cincinnati—4 square miles. Louis Pink, formerly of the New York State Housing Board, claimed that nearly one-third of the built-up area of Brooklyn was blighted.[38]

In retrospect, the presence of slums was not surprising; they had existed at the turn of the century and had continued in place through the 1920s. The prosperity of that decade had not reached all parts of the city or all of its people. Although slums were not seen as spreading during that time, neither did they disappear.

The Depression greatly curtailed investment in plant and equipment as well as buildings, and the general economic condition of cities worsened slums and blight. In sixty-four cities surveyed by the Department of Commerce in 1934, one-sixth of the 1.5 million dwelling units were substandard, and a large proportion in a state of disrepair. Unemployment was at unprecedented heights, construction at unprecedented depths. Twenty percent of all employable persons in the ten largest cities were on relief.[39] Clarence Dykstra, a former city manager, commented before the New York *Herald Tribune* Forum in 1939 that "[f]undamental among our problems is the fact that millions who make up these teeming populations have such low incomes, and because of the technological development of our industries, live in such precarious insecurity in so far as their jobs are concerned so, in fact, that life is a long drawn-out nightmare."[40]

New housing was virtually unavailable. The lingering remnants of turn-of-the century slums became magnets for further blight and deterioration. City governments approached bankruptcy, and public services and infrastructure were neglected. Central business districts were also in disrepair and faced the onset of economic obsolescence. *Business Week,* in a special report to executives, remarked that "[d]uring the past decade central business districts have lost as much as 25% of their gross volume of retail sales, which have been redistributed to neighborhood centers. Downtown merchants have had to boost their expenses by establishing outlying branches to follow the migration of their customers. Skyscrapers have 20% of their space vacant, while businesses in search of lower rent move away from the center of activity."[41]

Nonetheless, the discourse of the 1930s and 1940s did not as much refer directly to a prior period, pointing out an earlier failure to eradicate these problems, as it turned to a stage theory of city development. This was an important variation in the discourse. In speaking to executives across the country, *Business Week,* in its 1940 special report on cities, stated the theory concisely and with implicit condemnation: "The urban land policy of American cities has been defined as consisting of three successive stages: speculative exploitation, gradual neglect, and eventual abandonment."[42] Here was the first of a subsequent torrent of pessimistic diagnoses that crept closer and closer to a belief in the inevitability of urban decline.

The magazine *Survey Graphic* offered a more complex assessment. In a pictorial essay of eight images titled "The Life and Death Curve of an American City," the editors presented a sequence that commenced with "beginnings" and "growth," and ended with "ultimate decay and vacant land" in the center of the city while development spread to the suburbs. Suburban development was an intermediate stage in the generation of urban slum conditions. When gas stations and taverns spread along suburban roads, blight was soon to follow. What began as a landscape of Victorian houses on large plots of land ends with a run-down church surrounded by ramshackled housing and fronted by an empty lot.[43]

A less impressionistic perspective was provided by George H. Herrold in *The Planner's Journal*. His concern was the obsolescence that takes hold in those areas—zones of transition—that divide central business districts from residential districts. More specifically, he wished to explain the declining utility and market value of residential districts resulting from the expansion of the adjacent central business district and its fringe areas as well as the changeover within residential districts as lower income households increasingly occupied slum properties. He is explicit about two stages in this process and then implies a third. The first stage occurs when rental units appear in a district of single-family, owner-occupied homes. This causes different types of people to enter the district, owners to move out, and values to recede. In the second stage, less desirable families continue to replace desirable ones "until the district becomes a slum." Such districts then become targets for unattractive industrial and commercial uses. The third stage is spiritual—people lose confidence and faith in the district, and obsolescence deepens.[44]

Like residential areas, central business districts were not immune from blighting influences. In 1940, Henry Propper, one of the charter members of the Citizen's Housing Council of New York, commented that "[t]he real problem is the decay of the city at its core. Its cure demands the eradication, not alone of residential slums, but the business and industrial slums as well."[45] Business slums had been created by the depression-induced collapse of real estate values and investments, high interest rates, low municipal revenues, and weak profits. Exacerbating these problems was that growth at the urban periphery was occurring at the expense of the center. As a result, there was no motive to invest or reinvest in these central districts. One report gave to this argument an exaggerated sense of scale: "Every American city of 6,000,000 or 6,000 population shows symptoms of identical dry rot at its core."[46]

The Urban Land Institute, a real estate research organization, offered an analysis that defined blight as an economic condition in which the market value of property, a value dependent on adjacent land uses, was somehow lost. As illustration, it noted that "[h]igh buildings are believed by many to be a cause of blight. They have a depressing effect on nearby property. Too intensive use of one plot of land necessarily reduces the utility of others."[47]

An economist at the University of Pennsylvania wrote of two types of blight: absolute and relative.[48] Absolute blight was characterized by nuisance land uses, overcrowding, the destruction of neighborhood amenities, the encroachment of incompatible and nonconforming uses, poor accessibility, and undesirable neighbors. Relative blight occurred when other areas of the city or region improved substantially more than the soon-to-be blighted area. As a result, investments switched to more desirable locations. Such a viewpoint additionally allowed for the blight of commercial and industrial districts to be influenced by the slums of nearby residential areas. Growth itself could be a blighting influence, particularly when investment in central business districts caused adjacent property owners to disinvest in hopes of speculative prices for their properties. This perspective also hinted at the relation between growth on the fringes of the city and decay at its core. This latter notion echoed Lewis Mumford—the excessive expansion of cities causes them to decay at the core and to overextend themselves in a ragged fashion.[49]

Boyden Sparkes alluded to this when he wrote in *The Saturday Evening Post* (in a less economistic mode) that "(b)light is the consequence of an anemia which follows the steady loss of a city's residents."[50] In this, Sparkes and Mabel Walker agreed: Population decline was central to the emergence of blight. As the entire district took on a "down-at-the-heels appearance," Walker wrote, "the exodus of more prosperous groups [was] accelerated."[51] For Sparkes, outmigration was the cause and blight the consequence. Walker reversed the relationship. Regardless, as residential and business districts deteriorated, they became slums. Falling land values, failure to maintain or improve buildings, and substandard housing were consequence and cause.

The regional planner Henry Wright, reflecting on "sinking slums," agreed with Mumford about the effects of overexpansion and also pointed out, as Mumford did in other writings, that the unprecedented spread of the city, combined with the slowing down of the growth of commercial and light-industrial areas, was abetted by real estate speculation.[52] The fall in the value of land and property brought about slums, and the persistence of slums was a result of speculation, "the discrepancy between the value which the owner places upon the land (and to some extent upon the obsolete improvements thereon) and the uses to which the property can appropriately and economically be put."[53] High prices interfered with the changeover in ownership and use essential to a well-functioning land market. Owners held to their land and to its perceived value in a way that caused deterioration. "Excessively high land values are cited as a cause of blight in central districts," the Urban Land Institute claimed.[54]

Earlier, commentators had believed that speculation was both the disease and its cure. After a while, speculative investments would so out-distance real market values that speculative profits would disappear, investors would go bankrupt, and prices would fall once again. The lack of demand for property, in part depressed by speculative values, was seen as transitory. To that extent, prices could remain high in anticipation of the renewed interest that would be expressed after the Depression or the war had ended. The architect and planner Catherine Bauer took a more aggressive stance. For cities to become prosperous, she wrote, "Every drop of purely speculative hope must be wrung out: property values must be reduced to actual use-values in a stable modern community."[55] Her statement implied intervention, but by whom was left unstated.

For Bauer, in a muted reference to stage theory, blight and slums were inevitable, part of the "crisis of maturity" that all cities eventually had to face.[56] A crisis of maturity, of course, is quite different than a crisis of inaction, and many commentators who agreed with Bauer went on to point out the potential for reversing these trends. Robert

Moses, the (in)famous "builder" of New York City in the twentieth century, offered his opinion: "It is safe to say that almost no city needs to tolerate slums. There are plenty of ways of getting rid of them. The only exceptions are in cities so decayed, so associated with temporary booms or natural resources, so lacking in morale and pride, so badly located as to trade, or so controlled by dirty politics, that the situation is hopeless. There are few such places in the United States."[57]

Bauer and Moses accepted the existence but not the persistence of slums and blight. As cities aged and grew, areas would lose their social and economic value before taking on new uses. This process, as the postwar discourse pointed out more emphatically, could be managed. Propper stated the situation in a more colloquial manner: "[O]ld buildings and entire sections of our great cities cannot be sold for junk or towed out to sea and dumped. The city must face its obsolete districts as long as they exist."[58]

The solution was redevelopment, programs of slum clearance and rebuilding using governmental powers and financial subsidies, and involving the private sector, specifically developers, in the process. Slums and blight could be removed, but they would not be removed if the task was left solely to households and private investors. As Herrold noted, "The tendency for cities to decay cannot be successfully combatted except through organized and wisely directed community or governmental action."[59]

As important for the story of urban decline as the recognition that parts of the city had decayed was the general awareness that rapid urban growth had ceased. Internal decay and aggregate stagnation together constituted a formidable challenge. Wright called for a "reorganization of the purpose of our city development, adjusted to a stabilized population rather than anticipated growth."[60]

Although city governments were burdened by slums and blight, and were experiencing fiscal difficulties, these problems were also isolated within certain sections of the city. The entire city was not in the throes of decay and, with the exception of roadside blight, the countryside was untouched. Although slums and blight were formidable obstacles and clearly contributors to urban deterioration, the decline of the city *as a whole* was barely conceivable.

UNCONTROLLED DECENTRALIZATION

Even during the depths of the Depression, the city planner Thomas Adams was moved to claim, "I see no evidence of possible disintegration of the great industrial city."[61] Overcrowding and congestion persisted as evils, but Adams predicted rapid growth in the future. The federal government's Natural Resources Committee agreed: "The city expands but does not often disintegrate."[62]

It was precisely this expansion that threatened the long-term growth and vitality of cities, an expansion that took the form of decentralization—the fourth migration. "The whole financial structure of cities, as well as the investments of countless individuals and business firms, is in jeopardy because of what is called decentralization," the city planner Harland Bartholomew observed in a 1940 speech before the Mortgage Bankers Association of America.[63] Population and industry were moving beyond the political boundaries of the cities and into adjacent municipalities, and although such movements were not unique, they were cast more ominously than they had been in the past. The editors of *Business Week,* in reference to the importance of public perception, stated this clearly: "Until perhaps five years ago the problems of decentralization were undetected by all but specialists in urban planning. Since then the number of individuals and organizations aware of the danger has multiplied."[64]

With this awareness came a return of both the conflict between the city and the countryside—this time with the suburbs taking the place of rural areas—and confusion over the actual meaning of that place called the city. With the once-central city in decline and the suburbs robust, many commentators rethought the relation of the city to its surrounding area and proclaimed the larger metropolis as the "real city." Not just "real," it was also growing, despite the weaknesses of its core.

In 1940, decentralization, the scattering of communities "with explosive force over larger and larger areas," came under intense scrutiny by the Urban Land Institute.[65] Based on a survey of 512 reports by expert appraisers and brokers from 221 cities, the Institute identified sixteen causes of decentralization. They ranged from automobile congestion in the central business district to premature suburban expansion. Ribbon development of business was a primary cause, even though automobile congestion in the central commercial area headed the list.

Also included in the Urban Land Institute litany were rigid local tax systems, bad zoning and planning, poor schools, the insecurity of urban home ownership, the destruction of neighborhood life, the lack of zoning protection for industry, "(t)he jumble of indescribably bad architecture," and the smoke, dirt, noise, and general unsightliness of cities. The consequences were bad: the loss of retail businesses in the central business districts and the flight of middle-class residents. Cities had deteriorated to the point where the "large part of urban dwellers do not like . . . [them] . . . and seek to escape from them if their work permits and if they can afford to do so."[66] The prognosis was financial ruin—if decentralization continued. As the editors of *Business Week* argued, "Decentralization hits not only a city's treasury but also every other urban activity."[67]

Earl Draper, in paraphrased comments from the 1942 Harvard University Conference on Urbanism, inverted the analysis of the Urban Land Institute and looked not at the factors internal to the city that were repelling population and businesses but at what was not happening in the cities in relation to what was happening elsewhere: "the cessation of immigration, the lowered birth rate and the fact that city services are now available in the country."[68]

On Draper's first point, the National Resources Planning Board agreed: "City populations do not reproduce themselves."[69] Birth rates tend to be lower in the cities than elsewhere, and lower than the replacement rate; that is, the rate sufficient to maintain the initial size of the population. Consequently, cities need to attract migrants—both from outside the city and outside the country itself—if they are to grow.

The second point is closely related to the first: Census data indicated that the birth rate had declined. For some commentators this was cause for serious alarm; it could not be explained away simply by reference to the dismal prospects that had faced families during the Depression. Warren Thompson, writing in the *Journal of the Ameri-*

can Institute of Architects, took an extreme position: The "dominance of the urban classes is being eroded . . . [because the] . . . values developed by city living . . . have led to city dweller belief that children are not worthwhile."[70]

The third point fits more comfortably into the decentralization perspective: What had once been available only in the city was now also available outside of it. This included not only schools and water filtration plants but also retail stores and factory employment.

A few years earlier, however, the National Resources Committee had developed a much different picture. Concentration and centralization were the themes of its analysis of urban decline. Cities and their hinterlands were integrated, but it was still clear where problems began and where they ended. "Urban" problems were endemic to an industrial society faced with massive technological change. The core of these problems was the inability of cities to respond to the over-centralization of business enterprises. In 1929, 5 percent of the three thousand counties contained 74 percent of all industrial wage earners, 81 percent of salaried employees, 79 percent of wages paid, 83 percent of salaries paid, 65 percent of industrial establishments, and 80 percent of value added to manufactures. The counties with the eleven largest cities accounted for over one-half of all wholesale trade, and the ninety-three cities with populations in excess of 100,000 had over three-fourths of the wholesale trade total. Overall, the Committee concluded that "[t]he faults of our cities are not those of decadence and impending decline, but of exuberant vitality crowding its way forward under tremendous pressure—the flood rather than the drought."[71] The Census data from 1940, however, would swing the discourse from centralization to decentralization, no matter how nimbly urban advocates constructed their analyses.

Of course, Census data are only the indicators once- and twice-removed from the numerous decisions, events, and trends that contributed to decentralization. One of the most important of these events was World War II. The massive mobilization of investment during the war, along with the concomitant deficit spending meant new factories along with new homes for soldiers and war industry workers. Unemployment fell precipitously, and poverty drifted from public view. For some cities, the war was a great boon. For others, even those with expanding defense plants, the wartime economy only increased pressure on infrastructure and on a weak housing stock.

Rapid wartime industrial expansion was achieved in part through the construction of factories and adjacent homes in the countryside. National policy located new plants for war production and housing for their workers away from vulnerable coastlines. As a result, small towns in the interior, many of which were agricultural communities, received large capital expenditures and sizable infusions of population in a short period of time. In Milan, Tennessee, "Where only dirt roads, strawberries and humpshouldered barns had been before, there were now eighty-five miles of railroad, 497 separate new buildings, 207 miles of roads and highways, a vast complex of electric, sewer and telephone lines." Ironically, such new development created innumerable problems during the war and also portended even more serious problems for these communities after it.[72]

In comments at the Harvard urbanism conference in 1942, Dal Hitchcock of the Bureau of Labor Statistics indicated that the great surge in industrial development brought on by war mobilization had occurred in regions and metropolitan areas already experiencing industrial growth, though airplane factories and plants for explosives constituted the principal exceptions. He concluded optimistically that war production would not "cause any substantial permanent change in the size and relative importance of the larger urban communities . . . [and that] . . . the distortions caused by the war may be expected to tend to disappear shortly after the end of the emergency."[73]

Catherine Bauer, a mere two years later, was not so sanguine. For her, the consequences of the war were threefold: increased urbanization; the movement of industry and industrial population to the West and South, with an impending national stabilization of population; and decentralization, leading to vacant structures, tax delinquency, and blight and decay in the central cities. With improvement of functions that must remain centralized, progress in transportation, and planning for population and employment growth, the end result would be "Better instead of Bigger; stabilization rather than expansion; the evolution of cities from simple agglomerations to regional organisms."[74]

The impact of decentralization on central cities did not reach its peak until after hostilities had ended. While the war was underway, the large cities gained population. Arthur D. Little, Inc., a major consulting firm, noted that "[s]hipbuilding and airplane industries have been the magnets in most of the most notable cases of population increases, but powder and shell loading plants, often in rural areas, and the construction of army camps caused much smaller but intense concentrations." Only after the war did wartime investment outside the cities cause problems. By then, decentralization was deeply entrenched and seemingly immune to reversal. The words of the consultants are prescient: "Since most migration is irreversible, it would appear that, as the people march, the markets, the industrial areas and the population problems of post-war America are being decided."[75]

Rexford Tugwell, drawing on his vast experience as an administrator of federal resettlement programs, put it bluntly: Practically every city in the United States is "decaying at the center and growing at the peripheries."[76] Decentralization, however, had yet to become suburbanization and had not overwhelmed urban prosperity. Now, though, in a confession that the balance of city and hinterland was undergoing a profound transformation, commentators began to refer to the city as the "central city."[77]

As early as 1933, the editor of *The Nation* suggested that the city in 1929 had reached its highest point of development. One piece of evidence was visual: "Ten thousand empty offices high above the street are lighted at night only by the reflection from some passing airplane, and even at street level chasms yawn where once the latest fashions or a solvent bank flourished."[78] (Of course, this was during the depths of the Depression.)

By 1940, *Business Week,* reporting on preliminary results from the recent Census of Population, claimed that the data demonstrated conclusively "that our cities are 'flattening out,' and are at or near the peak of their population."[79] Of the twenty-five largest cities, seventeen had gained population while eight had lost. Houston, a newcomer to this elite group, had the most spectacular gain—

32.1 percent—but many of the largest cities (e.g., New York, Baltimore, and Washington) also experienced increases. One preliminary Census report listed sixty-two of the largest 274 cities with population losses, and data released in September of 1940 showed that of the fifty-eight most populous cities, fifteen had population declines.[80]

In 1943, Homer Hoyt, known for his path-breaking work during the 1930s on the economics of urban development, looked back on the effects of the Depression and the war and saw cities increasingly unable to either attract migration from rural areas or expand employment opportunities. As a result, cities were losing population: "In fact, 27 of the 93 cities in our nation that have a population of over 100,000 lost population from 1930 to 1940." He went on to point out that this "waning power" was also reflected in building activity. The depression had stopped all urban building for several years: "When new construction began in sizable volume again in the period of 1934–1941, there was a change in the urban pattern."[81] The large industrial (and central) cities were at a turning point.

The Director of the Census Bureau, William Austin, attributed the population shifts to the "tremendous migration of city residents to suburban areas."[82] Moreover, the movement of population from the countryside to the city was no longer a pressing issue. Within all of the top-ten metropolitan areas, population growth was faster outside than within the nucleus city. In fact, four of the ten nucleus cities—Philadelphia, Boston, St. Louis, and Cleveland—had an absolute population decline.[83] Rural in-migration was about to be replaced in the discourse by suburban out-migration.

Harland Bartholomew, influenced by these data, wrote in 1940 that the "decentralization of American cities has now reached the point where the main central city, at least, is in great jeopardy."[84] Prior to the 1940s, decentralization had not threatened the viability of cities; few had experienced population decline. With the simultaneous shrinkage of central cities and the amplification of decentralizing tendencies, the central city seemed poised on the edge of a foreboding precipice.

In its boosterish fashion, the Urban Land Institute voiced its support of central cities. Despite the depth and multiplicity of urban problems, cities were still sites of intense capital investment. Numerous investors, workers, and residents had made long-term commitments. The Institute noted additionally that "we cannot afford to let our cities destroy themselves through uncontrolled decentralization. The city is itself a nexus."[85]

Despite gloomy evidence of present and future conditions, the Institute's response was still the most typical view, and the general tone of the discussion remained optimistic. Commentators were not yet willing to abandon the city to the forces of decentralization. As World War II drew to a close, Boyden Sparkes wrote that "New York's planners are persuaded that a tendency for people to move back to cities which has been revealed in wartime is not a temporary one, simply due to no cars and no gas. They believe that there is an underlying dissatisfaction with the inconveniences of commuting to work. . . . They believe, too, that when there are enough modern neighborhoods in all cities, decentralization will cease to be a foremost problem anywhere."[86]

Such optimism came wrapped in a belief that "Americans are incorrigible city dwellers" and that governments and their citizens had to respond assertively to the urban problems generated by decentralization.[87] As early as 1932, the housing reformer and city and regional planner Carol Aronovic had called for metropolitan planning that would bring about a complete revaluing of the physical structure and equipment of cities in line with new social trends. He challenged his readers: "Let the cities perish so that we may have great and beautiful cities."[88]

Quite surprisingly from our present perspective, Aronovic and others believed that the development of suburban areas, particularly if controlled, could be the first step in rebuilding the cities. The next Census would show a movement back to the land, the editors of *The Nation* surmised, "[b]ut we shall not look upon the news as final or expect the cities to fall into decay."[89] A newspaper reporter specializing in business and economic research wrote in the early 1930s that "[i]ncreasing numbers are leaving the cities for year-round living in nearby suburbs and country towns . . . ; [t]he larger the city that dominates the region, the greater the exodus toward country freedom."[90]

People wanted to be near the jobs, which were disproportionately in the cities, but they also wanted to be close to nature.

These population movements represented a trade-off between a need to be close to the investments that created employment and a desire to distance oneself from the congestion, pollution, and high housing costs that those investments engendered. American ambivalence about cities was being expressed geographically, and urban sociologists began to write of a novel variation from previous approaches to urban life. Louis Wirth suggested that we were witnessing the "rapid growth of a new type of urban community—the supercity, or metropolitan region."[91]

The architect Eliel Saarinen, called by *Time* magazine in 1942 "the greatest living authority on city planning," argued for an adaptation to the forces of decentralization. In Saarinen's scheme, that adaptation was called organic decentralization—satellite towns scattered outside but adjacent to the central cities. This configuration would produce a more efficient arrangement of land uses.[92]

Saarinen believed additionally that one of the central problems facing the cities—slum conditions—could be eradicated through decentralization, but this would mean abandoning the city. He suggested that decentralization and slums were signs of a diseased city, and that the cure had to be drastic: "[D]ecentralization is a logical derivative from and through the principles of flexibility and protection, if the aim is to free the city from the contagious danger of slums." Continuing his organismic analogy between the city and the human body, Saarinen's solution was to "open adequate arteries so that both the city and the population can spread themselves to the country—toward air, light, and nature."[93] There, they would reconcentrate in satellite towns, and the central city would be rejuvenated.

URBANISM WILL DOMINATE

Underlying the discourse of this period was a strong belief in the importance of cities to national life, a theme that had pervaded the urban discourse of the Progressive Era. In recognition of this, Columbia University established its Institute of Urbanism in 1934 to explore the evolution, administration, social organization, economic problems, and construction and expansion of cities, particularly New York.[94] The rationale for such an institute was offered by Freeman Tilden earlier in the decade. *The World's Work* had hired him to write a series of articles celebrating cities. In his initial piece he established his belief that every great city has a soul that cannot be killed: "Once a city, always a city." More importantly, he viewed cities as sources of innovation and meaning for the country as a whole. As he put it, "The voice of the United States is increasingly the voice of its cities."[95] National prosperity and urban vitality were inextricably linked.

Three years later, in an address before the American Transit Association, the city manager of Cincinnati, C. A. Dykstra, concurred. Even though "[i]ts citizens are in large numbers unemployed, its finances are in chaos, its services and its structures are deteriorating, and both public and private hopes are sagging," the large city is a product of the machine age, and the machine age is here to stay. Thus, "[u]rbanism will dominate the future."[96] Or, as he put it three years later, "Nor can the nation flourish without its urban industrial centers or without the countryside; or without an organic balance between them. As never before the fact of the city must be reckoned with."[97]

The political commentator Walter Lippman also believed that it was necessary to strike a balance between the city and the country if the nation as a whole were to prosper. His prejudice, however, was decidedly for the city. He expressed this in an article in the *Woman's Home Companion* in 1931: "[W]e shall have to stop thinking that cities are social diseases. We shall have to learn to regard them as genuine centers of our civilization." Cities cannot, he continued, be separated from the nation, for it is in the cities that "the activities of the whole nation come to a head."[98]

Civilization and nationhood, of course, are strongly identified with forms of popular governance that allow ideas to flow freely and human potentials to be realized. For commentators writing in the United States, such ruminations turned the discourse back to the Jeffersonian concern with the relation between cities and democracy.

Charles Merriam, a political science professor, reflected on these relationships: "Urban standards, urban practices, urban leaders, and urban ideals will determine the position and policy of the United States twenty-five years from now. And if these fail, America fails, and if America fails, democracy fails."[99] The obvious implication for Merriam was that local–national relations had to take precedence over local–state relations. His position drew on not only the federal government's active involvement in urban affairs during the Depression, but also on the weak powers of city governments. More interestingly, it foreshadowed the federal government's postwar commitment to redeveloping the cities and the importance of that commitment to the discourse on urban decline.

As World War II drew to a close, then, commentators began to think about how the cities would fare without the burdens of an economy in disarray and without the constraints of war mobilization. Phillip Hauser of the Census Bureau, for example, investigated the potential for postwar metropolitan population growth.[100] Of the 137 metropolitan areas that he studied, thirty-three were classified as having very doubtful prospects for postwar growth, fifteen fair prospects, and eleven prospects that depended strongly on their ability to convert to peacetime pursuits. Just over 40 percent of the metropolises studied were not sure bets to recover from the previous decade and one-half. They included such places as Philadelphia and Pittsburgh, Cleveland and Chicago, and Akron and Wichita. Another 18 metropolises (places like Minneapolis, Fresno, and Binghamton, New York) had lost population during the war but were given excellent chances for a "comeback."[101]

Louis Wirth told the International City Managers' Association in 1944 that cities were in a state of crisis. The "seemingly limitless growth" had come to an end, decentralization of industry was deepening the decay of the central cities, and the flight to the suburbs was unlikely to stop. Wirth wrote that "the post-war period has already arrived for many cities, and that the foundation for a wholesome life for these cities must either be laid now or they will not exist." Lest one take this for resignation, he offered his solution: "Only large-scale rebuilding of our cities, especially at or near their centers, will halt the catastrophic downward spiral."[102]

While Wirth was motivated by crisis, others were motivated by opportunity. No less an authority than the director of the Urban Development Division of the National Housing Agency asserted that "[t]he building of cities will be one of the great world tasks of the next two decades." Charles Ascher believed that nearly every city in the country had vacant, usable land on which to accommodate its population and that we could not afford to abandon the freedom, the sense of civic solidarity, and the "participation on a great stage" that city life provided. Ascher proposed, "Rather we must with faith and imagination rethink our cities from the ground up in light of a true understanding of what cities are for."[103]

Others optimistically anticipated a postwar building boom. Despite the disintegration of large cities and the long-standing housing shortage, these commentators relied on an immutable American commitment to urban living that would lead to the eradication of decay and to robust new construction. The administrator of the National Housing Agency, John Blanchard, stated in a 1945 symposium in *The American City* that "[w]e have estimated that 12½ million new homes will be necessary in the first ten years of peace to take care of our returning veterans, new families, families now living 'doubled-up,' and to make substantial progress toward replacing our clearly substandard housing."[104] Postwar prospects involved not just new investment in housing, but also investment in productive activity. Hoyt warned that future growth depended on peacetime industries being attracted to cities by economic advantage or government allocation, the development of quality housing, and the interaction among new housing, industry, and commerce.[105]

The discourse on cities that occurred prior to World War II, then, had none of the pervasive pessimism to which people in the postwar period would become accustomed. Few commentators in the interwar discourse doubted the potential for subsequent reinvigoration. Many had been fearful of the effects of decentralization and the twin problems of slums and blight in the city's central areas, but they also believed—as had those in the earlier decades of the twentieth century— in the powers of human intervention to resist such decay. Urban growth had been interrupted, not deflected, and during the late 1940s commentators were generally confident that a return to economic prosperity would preserve the city, even if the city had to be transformed in the face of new social and economic realities. As Charles Ascher commented, "[T]he communities of the future must be nobler embodiments of the democratic respect for the worth of the individual, if our war effort is to be justified."[106]

Some commentators reflected on the possibility of long-term decline of cities, and the Census data of the 1930s and early 1940s also portended deeper problems. Still, they were in the minority, and the more objective statistical criteria could easily be explained away as the consequence of a profound and enduring Depression coupled with the diversion of investment into the protection of the country from its German and Japanese enemies. Long blessed with robust cities, commentators found it difficult to imagine their demise; the problems facing the cities seemed to be only temporary discontinuities in the evolution of the United States as an urban society. The discourse that had accumulated before 1945 thus traveled into the postwar period with sustained but wavering optimism, initial and tentative calls for collective intervention, and a strong belief in the continual importance of the central city.[107] After the war, and with support from government programs, the country would return to an earlier and urban way of life.

Escalating Downward

"I want you to design me some old-law tenements; I think I can sell them to the slum-clearance commission at a profit."

CHAPTER 4

The Unhappy Process of Changing

E ven before Japan had surrendered and World War II had been
declared officially over, commentators on the urban scene
began to think ahead to peacetime. The cities had experienced
fifteen years of depression and war, and many observers expressed the
need to respond swiftly and forcefully to the resultant deterioration.
Cities would have to inventory their assets, embark on numerous
schemes to fight blight and slums, and generally refocus the attention
of the nation on the big cities—the driving forces, prior to the 1930s,
behind prosperity and growth.

During the mid-1940s, *The Saturday Evening Post* published a
series on "America's most colorful cities." The articles depicted the
postwar problems and prospects for large urban areas. Cincinnati's
story was indicative. Its problems could be found in every large,
industrial city in America: staggering traffic congestion, polluted
waterways, rudimentary airport facilities, inadequate sewage disposal, smoke-filled air, blight, a "passive" city government, slums,
and a weakened tax base. Nonetheless, the mood was hopeful; turnabout seemed possible. As the article stated, "With increasing fre-
quency these days, Cincinnatians raise troubled voices in public and
ask if their city is not sick. They ask whether, as a result of declining vitality or indecision in meeting civic problems, the city has not

lost much of whatever it is that makes a city magnetic and compelling—the thing that enables it either to acquire or create the new enterprise essential to continued regeneration."[1] For the most part, the public response was encouraging; cities had not lost their compelling attraction.

That the depression was clearly brought on by speculative fever made a return to the unrestrained boosterism of the twenties unattractive. Cities had to study their needs and resources carefully and plan their economic futures by replacing lost industries, building new facilities, and broadening their economic bases. Governments had to become more directly involved. The City of Pittsburgh undertook a massive survey of its industrial assets. The study revealed extensive decay; Pittsburgh was physically run down, and the local economy (because of the dominance of heavy industry) subject to violent economic fluctuations. Nonetheless, the report's conclusion was optimistic: "Pittsburgh will remain a great center of steel and heavy industry."[2] Such confidence was shared almost universally throughout the United States. The executive director of the Providence Redevelopment Agency along with a local reporter summed up the situation around the country: "The job of rebuilding American cities has begun in earnest, but it is only in the tooling-up stage."[3]

Rebuilding the cities was going to be a formidable task, but it was far from impossible. Cities were in disrepair, but with a bit of demolition here, a little reconstruction there, and a final fine-tuning, they would capture their earlier glory. Such a strategy, though, was hardly compatible with the ascendance of outlying communities that lured population and economic activities from the central cities and challenged them for regional supremacy. Now labeled *suburbanization*, decentralization turned more ominous and pushed aside most other concerns about the city. The terminology changed accordingly and new images were fashioned: urban sprawl, metropolitan explosion, strip cities, megalopolis.

Rebuilding would also require a complementary defensive strategy (such as annexation) in order to retain investment and households. The emergence of the metropolis made a pure, city-based strategy a poor choice. The ambivalence of Americans to urban living was about to be expressed in a landscape of prosperous suburbs and declining central cities. The modern city of the late nineteenth and early twentieth centuries was about to disappear.

At the same time, a migration counter to suburbanization was in progress, and it had the potential to testify to the enduring attractiveness of the city and contribute to bolstering its fortunes. The migrants, however, posed a problem for both commentators and the larger public. They were mainly African Americans from the South, and even though rural minorities had traveled to cities in previous decades, their expanding presence (made visible by continued segregation and the shrinking number of white households) was cause for alarm. Decay and race would be thrown together in a discursive unity, and this flow of people to the cities, despite the glaring need to replace the loss of the white population, was not cause for celebration on the part of civic boosters.

Regardless, the rebuilding of the cities would go forward. The target was slums and blight, now more extensive and more entrenched than they had been earlier. Postwar urban commentators further distinguished the two phenomena. Slums were now strictly residential and social as well as racial in character; demolition and public housing were the responses. In fact, the slums came to be fused in the discourse with minorities and poverty, not just physical deterioration. Blight became wholly economic and a trait of central business districts where expensive land needed to be repossessed through a combination of site clearance and the construction of new office buildings, luxury residential enclaves, and retail complexes. Moreover, the two were linked. Slums would have to be cleared so the commercial district could expand and downtown housing built for the middle class.

Even while cities were tooling up for redevelopment, the discourse shifted character. From being reluctantly inclined toward the cities, commentators in the early postwar years began to debate stark choices: rebuild existing cities, construct new suburban cities and allow existing cities to pass naturally into a less central role, *or* abandon big cities altogether. Listening and reading this discourse, it became more difficult for the average household or investor to decide how to act. As the discourse changed its basic attitude toward cities, its practical advice turned murky. With the flourishing of the suburbs, however, those choices took on a new clarity.

NO QUICK ANSWER

The enhanced complexity of choices and the spreading awareness of the depth of urban problems triggered a fresh addition to the emerging discourse on urban decline. An idiosyncratic optimism surfaced in the discourse. Whether "new" cities would emerge, the old ones be refashioned, or big cities abandoned, became an explicit function of how one felt about the future possibilities for significant reform and the depths of present realities.

In 1948, *The Nation* published a twenty-four-page compilation of expert opinion on a hypothetical housing program that would be implemented over the next ten years. One of the contributors was Lewis Mumford. His response to fifteen years of urban neglect turned away from the city and, in predictable Mumford fashion, addressed the need for new types of urban places. He suggested that "[o]ur great metropolises are overcrowded, financially topheavy, environmentally lopsided; and the excessive costs of congestion they promote are rivaled only by the costs of remedies for alleviating it." This was not a simple call for rebuilding Cincinnati, Pittsburgh, and other "colorful cities." Rather, it was a plea for large-scale planning and the building of new, self-contained communities of lower densities surrounded by parks and greenbelts. Neither was it an abandonment of industrial cities. Rather, Mumford expressed less an ambivalence triggered by incipient suburbanization than a strategic embrace of decentralization. As Mumford wrote, "We must plan and build new communities on a large scale, before we can adequately replan and rebuild our old centers."[4]

Mumford's rejection of cities "as they were" and prescience in calling for the control of nascent suburbanization were a minority perspective. In fact, his measured balance of city and countryside was lost in the subsequent debate between the "rebuilders" and those who viewed the large, central city as no longer viable. One of the more candid proponents of this latter position was the economist Mabel Walker, then the executive director of an organization called the Tax Institute. In a speech before the Municipal Finance Officers Association in 1947, Walker claimed that the city was obsolete because it was functionally outmoded. She built her argument on two observations:

first, that "people did not come to the city in the first place because they liked living in the city, but because the city offered them the means of livelihood" and, second, that "[t]he process of urbanization has reversed itself."[5] Industries were decentralizing and new forms of transportation enabled people to reside outside the cities. Moreover, the cities were shrinking in population. What she termed *the war-induced congestion* was being naturally dispersed. Attempts to reverse these trends, Walker strongly suggested, would be "largely futile."

Whereas Walker argued that these problems were inevitable, other commentators viewed them as susceptible to control. The former mayor of Philadelphia and in 1959 senior U.S. Senator from Pennsylvania, Joseph Clark, called for the federal government to stop acting as if it were still a rural nation and to create a cabinet-level Department of Urban Affairs. Urban problems were to be seen as national problems. As a political scientist from Williams College admonished, "A politics that fails to make [cities] its focal points cannot attract the imagination of the citizen." Nonetheless, the task was daunting, with one commentator suggesting that "there is no quick answer to the problem of the American city."[6]

Any long-term solution would require more than the imagination of a different type of city. It would also compel hard and detailed thinking about how to produce that other city. Luther Gulick, the president of the Institute for Public Administration, and others were asked by *The American City* in 1949 to reflect on this and predict the progress that would likely be made in the 1950s. Gulick offered more of everything: more population, more suburbs, more automobile and traffic congestion, more public housing and slum clearance, more wealth per capita, and a continually rising standard of demand. For him, the future was simply a better present. The executive directors of the U.S. Conference of Mayors (Paul Betters) and the National Association of Housing Officials (John Ducey) predicted an expansion of governmental programs to remove slums and blight, eventually producing a different city by the 1960s. Respecting the possibility of an even more drastically altered present, Betters cautiously prefaced his remarks with the phrase, "If we don't have WW III."[7]

Guy Greer, a city planning consultant, countered Betters's touch of pessimism with a strong dose of cautious optimism: "Cities and towns that are truly good places in which to live and work and play need not to be essentially different tomorrow in the Age of Atomic Power from what they ought to be today, in an age of the automobile and the flying machine."[8] Many observers could not imagine the late twentieth century city except as an early twentieth-century city without slums and blight, wealthier, and possibly bigger.

Mabel Walker, ever the pragmatist, reiterated her position in favor of decentralization, a process abetted by central city traffic congestion, industrial dispersal, the threat of atomic warfare, inadequate water supplies, a rising standard of living, and the rationalization of the house-building industry. She saw "every reason to believe that the reversal of the century-old population trend to central cities which first began to get underway in 1910, and which developed along new and stronger lines in the '30s and '40s, will be vastly accelerated in the '50s." The forces disrupting the cities would not dissipate until after the 1950s had ended. On their demise, a "considerable residue of those who prefer the urban way of life or cannot readily move away" would remain in the cities. Her conclusion: "The city gives no sign of disappearing, but it is in the unhappy process of changing its forms and functions."[9]

Not surprisingly, the actual future was not as Walker and others had envisioned. After a brief postwar recession, the economy sustained a trajectory of growth that, except for business cycles, remained unabated until the mid-1970s. Organized labor consolidated its position as numerous industries, producing durable goods—from washing machines and televisions to automobiles and airplanes—thrived. White collar employment also swelled, fueled by the growth of insurance companies, headquarters of manufacturing firms, and increased demand for legal and other business support services. For the average American, the standard of living rose appreciably; by the early 1960s, ownership of an automobile, a television, and even a detached single-family suburban home was no longer merely a middle-class dream.

Across the United States, consumer spending exploded during the first two decades after World War II. The increased pace of suburbanization instituted a buying frenzy of the many accessories required by and associated with the suburban home: A private automobile, home appliances, patio furniture, lawnmowers, encyclopedias, and commuting tickets were only a few of the items on the list. The teenager appeared: pampered in the suburbs, delinquent in the cities. An idealized American family also took form: father, mother (as homemaker), and children all living under the same roof. Neither many men nor women—though more of the former than the latter—had gone to college, but this would change dramatically; in the new suburbs dad was likely to have been a veteran who matriculated on the benefits of the GI Bill. The 1950s were a decade in which people believed in education, the mechanism that drove the escalator of upward mobility—from working class to middle class, from city to suburb, from blue-collar to white-collar. At the same time, it was a decade of conformity. The "man in the grey-flannel suit" rode the train to work in the big city, where he fit into a large and bureaucratized organization. Even on the weekends, conformity was key; one had to "keep up with the Joneses."

The putative leveling of cultural inclinations was reflected in the centrism and moderation of national politics. President Dwight Eisenhower, throughout most of the fifties, led the country quietly and with little rancor. The United States slowly and patiently established its economic and political hegemony across the globe. It spoke for the "free world" against communism, provided economic aid to war-ravaged countries, and served as home to the United Nations. International humanitarian beneficence, however, had its darker side. Fueled by the Cold War, a national sense of righteousness led to a virulent anticommunism within the United States and constant pressure for shows of military might. Though often viewed as a quiet decade, the fifties were also years of activism. The civil rights movement gained momentum and achieved successes over these years. The federal government established strong ties to the cities in order to help with rebuilding. Many local governments underwent reform as liberals and municipal experts fought political machines of an earlier era.

A number of key events in the 1950s and early 1960s had direct and important geographic consequences. The country experienced little immigration, but rather a massive internal rearrangement of population. White middle-class families left the cities for the suburbs, and minority families—African Americans and Puerto Ricans mainly—along with poor whites from Appalachia took their place in the inner neighborhoods of older, industrial cities. Inner-city industries and downtown department stores reduced operations, closed, or moved to the metropolitan periphery, their relocation eased by a just-built system of interstate highways and the emergence of new forms and types of development: suburban tract housing, shopping malls, retail strips, and industrial parks. The metropolis eventually became increasingly polarized as the white middle class established a firm and defensive posture in the suburbs, while the minority working and lower classes were trapped in the central cities. By the sixties, central cities had become places of massive investment in urban renewal and public housing projects. Notwithstanding, their prosperity paled in comparison to the scale of the capital, industry, and housing being positioned in adjacent communities.

For the next twenty years, the discourse on urban decline would slowly incorporate what, in retrospect, were sea-changes. Until race riots radically transformed the discourse in the mid-1960s, however, commentators continued to rehearse issues that had plagued cities since the turn of the century. Then, the discourse shifted dramatically. It turned away from the physical condition of large cities (blight and slums), regional forces (suburbanization, urban sprawl, metropolitanization), and the plight of city governments. The racial crisis, with its multiple and dispiriting social correlates, was overwhelming.

As the nature of urban decline changed and its pace quickened, the optimism of former years weakened. Fred Vigman, in one of the earliest appearances of the phrase—it was 1955—believed that cities were "in throes of urban crisis."[10] The city was increasingly viewed as incapable of overcoming the endemic problems of blight, slums, and urban sprawl. No longer a temporary aberration brought about by nearly fifteen years of depression and war, urban decline had become a chronic national condition.

SYMBOLIC OF PROGRESS

Throughout the twentieth century, the Census Bureau played a pivotal role in affirming impressions and documenting the conditions and prospects of American cities. The Census of 1950 was no different: "As predicted, the great trend of 1950 has been toward small gains for cities, large gains for suburbs."[11] Yet, the reality, or at least its representation, was neither so simple nor so unequivocal. As the population burst beyond city boundaries in large numbers, a simple distinction between the countryside and the city could no longer be maintained.

Depending on how one interpreted the meaning of urban, the data could yield quite diverse meanings. For example, Donald Bogue, the associate director of the Scripps Foundation for Research in Population Problems, saw no diminution in urbanization from 1940 to 1950. "During the decade just finished," he wrote, "which ushered in the atomic bomb, there is no evidence of a suspension of growth in the large centers and a major transferral of growth to the smaller ones."[12] Twenty-two metropolitan areas were created during the decade, and this could hardly be viewed as a deviation from the path of urbanization.

Mabel Walker, once again playing an important critical role, contested such statements. She was outspoken in her criticism of the Census Bureau's definition of urban; Walker found the statistical city to be highly elusive. In commenting on the controversy surrounding decentralization, she wrote that it "amounts to little more than ruffling the sound waves, since each speaker feels free to follow the Alice-in-Wonderland technique of making the word mean what he wants it to mean. The use of such colorful terms as exploding serves further to emotionalize and obscure the subject."[13] In her estimation, Census boundary lines and terminology were fabrications that distorted the reality of population shifts. To the contrary, "the evidence appears to indicate clearly a pushing away from the congested centers of populated places, both large and small."[14]

Rather than a continuation of predicted trends, *Newsweek* reported that the "[p]reliminary results of the nation's 1950 census showed the greatest population growth—and upheaval—in America's history."[15] The population of the nation exceeded 150 million, and over 64 percent of it resided in urban areas. Close to seventy million people lived in the 157 metropolitan areas, and almost fifty million lived in central cities.[16] In fact, twelve of the largest metropolitan areas with 28 percent of the total population accounted for 35 percent of the overall gain. Moreover, a huge spurt in births occurred in what came to be called the baby boom. Between 1940 and 1950, thirty-two million babies were born in the United States.[17] In addition, a tremendous amount of internal migration was taking place. Not only did people continue to move to the suburbs and to migrate from the North and Midwest to the South and West, but 1,597,000 blacks moved from the South to the North in the 1940s and another 1,457,000 in the 1950s.[18]

The movement of white households from the cities to the suburbs became a defining theme of the discourse. From 1950 to 1956, 84 percent of the nation's population growth occurred in the 168 metropolitan areas, but less than 20 percent occurred in their central cities and nearly 10 percent was in nonmetropolitan urban areas. Pointedly, the growth rates of the suburban rings not only exceeded that of the central cities between 1950 and 1955, but also had done so from 1940 to 1950.[19]

A study by the Metropolitan Life Insurance Company in the late 1950s noted that suburbs and rural communities adjacent to the large cities are "bursting at the seams with population increase," while "the rate of growth for the cities themselves is below the average for the country as a whole."[20] For example, the Boston region grew by 16 percent between 1950 and 1954, while the central city grew by 1 percent. The central city of Baltimore registered no gain, but the surrounding areas grew by 30 percent. Los Angeles and Houston had population losses in their central areas while experiencing growth rates of 7 and 16 percent, respectively, in adjacent communities. All of this led *Business Week* to conclude that "[t]he big city is still the magnet that pulls into its orbit people from the farmlands and the small towns. But this magnet's pull is stronger in the outlying areas than in the heart of the city."[21]

As early as 1947, Walker had summarized these trends: Statistical evidence indicates "that rural areas, or the open countryside, if you prefer, are now at long last holding their own, as compared with villages and cities; that small cities are growing at the expense of large ones; and that the peripheral, or sparsely settled areas of cities, are growing at the expense of more congested central areas."[22] Current statistical evidence was helpful in understanding present trends, she argued, but one also had to acknowledge the significance of decentralization during the war and the depression. The trends established then were not likely to be suddenly redirected. As she claimed in 1952, "[t]he decentralization forces are too great to be reversed and they hold within themselves too great promise for human welfare for the attempt to be made to reverse them."[23]

Decentralization did not have to result in a loss of population for the central cities, even though it did. The 1920s were evidence of this. Between 1950 and 1960, however, with decentralization accelerating, nine of the ten largest cities in 1950 lost population, the only exception being Los Angeles.[24] Although such population losses in the large cities had been virtually unheard-of before 1930, cities throughout the United States had had population declines since then. Between 1930 and 1940, for example, Philadelphia, Cleveland, St. Louis, and Boston all shrunk in population size, while Pittsburgh barely held its own. "From 1910–20 none of the ninety-two largest cities declined in population. Only four declined from 1920–30, but twenty-eight of these ninety-two cities actually lost population from 1930–1940, despite any annexation that may have been made." Among the 412 cities over 25,000 population, "13 lost in each of the decades 1910–20 and 1920–30, while 104 lost from 1930 to 1940."[25] Urban decline as population loss was no longer an anomaly.

Not all large cities shrunk between the end of the war and 1960. A number of them, many in the West and the South, had major growth spurts. Tampa, El Paso, and Phoenix more than doubled in size, and, for the first time, moved onto the list of the top fifty cities. Los Angeles took over third position; ahead of Philadelphia, while Houston went from fourteenth to sixth, Dallas from twenty-second to fourteenth, San Antonio from twenty-fifth to seventeenth, and Atlanta from thirty-third to twenty-fourth.[26]

Displaying an industrial and northern bias, the editors of *The American City* reinterpreted the population figures by debunking "the great track meet" of cities through the urban hierarchy. Their argument was two-pronged: First, population density was a more important measure than overall population for assessing urban conditions. Second, "when urban areas reach these high concentrations of people . . . a leveling of the population figures is a good, constructive action, symbolic of progress rather than an indication of decay."[27] A loss of population could help relieve overcrowding and improve land use, thus enabling the older, industrial cities to be rebuilt. New York and Chicago, first and second in density at 24,000 and 11,000 people per square mile, respectively, were losing population, while Los Angeles, which was growing, was not even ranked in the top 20 densest cities.

One consequence of these population shifts and the discussions about them was the widespread adoption of a term that had appeared only a few years earlier. While once commentators had talked easily about *the city,* they now felt compelled to qualify their comments with the term *central city,* the core area of a larger urban configuration often termed the *metropolitan area.* This distinction simultaneously separated the problems and peoples of the core from those of the periphery, yet tied together their fates within a common geographic unit. Eventually, the central city and its surrounding suburbs became antagonists.

BABIES ARE WONDERFUL DECENTRALIZERS

From the mid-1800s through to the early 1940s, the cities had been the prime sites of population growth and investment. Decentralization had always existed, but the dominant population movement had been toward the now "central" cities rather than surrounding municipalities or rural areas. When major development took place outside the larger cities, annexation was often the response. As the suburbs gained in political influence, however, this option disappeared; decentralization became suburbanization, and the shift in terminology expressed a political realignment as well. Urban areas were redefined as central cities and suburban rings, and the central cities experienced both relative and absolute decline.

The editors of *Time* magazine noted in 1955 that decentralization had progressively plagued the central cities since the end of the war: "While suburbs have boomed, the business and residential hearts of cities have choked and decayed."[28] Ultimately, suburban growth and urban decline became locked in a discursive opposition that framed the postwar discourse on cities. That discourse's primary subject was the central city's loss of population and investment. Secondary themes considered the fiscal problems facing central city governments, the lack of urban leadership, and the segregation of minorities into slum neighborhoods. All of the themes were understood in relation to this dominant dichotomy. In simple language, as *The American City* presented it, "While the suburbs are growing spectacularly, the centers of many cities are quietly rotting."[29]

What seemed clear throughout the fifties was that the perilous conditions of the cities could be effectively resolved if the central cities were allowed to annex and incorporate fringe areas where growth was occurring. Two self-proclaimed "suburbanitis" experts, Thomas and Doris Reed, wrote that "while the problems may vary, all of our cities have this in common: they must be permitted to grow. If they don't, they will die."[30] Yet, by 1930, the option of annexation had been virtually closed to the older cities of the Northeast and Midwest. As the problems of the city multiplied, and the resources and people in suburban communities expanded, fringe areas were less and less desirous of becoming part of the city and more and more politically able to resist it.

Regardless, city governments continued to attempt annexation as a solution to the loss of households and investment. During the early 1950s, annexations increased from one year to the next, peaking in 1955 when 526 cities of over five thousand population engaged in some form of consolidation. Unlike earlier decades, the annexations were small in scale. While one out of every five cities annexed some fringe area in 1955, the individual annexations averaged 0.7 square miles each. A combination of antiquated laws and the political resistance of the formative suburbs prevented large-scale annexations, at least for the older, industrial cities.[31]

One commentator noted that "Everywhere administrators are trapped between embattled fringe dwellers fighting 'encroachment' of growing towns and beleaguered cities asked to render more service for less tax."[32] Decentralization and years of neglect had left the cities financially weak yet having to undertake massive investments to eliminate blight and slums and upgrade infrastructure and public services in order to stem out-migration. Simultaneously, boundaries were being irrevocably fixed as new growth occurred beyond them. When decentralization had paralleled city growth, it had been tolerable. When that simultaneity disappeared and cities approached the precipitous edge of long-term decline, decentralization—now suburbanization—ceased to be a mark of urban vitality. It threatened the cities and contributed to a sense of urban breakdown. The Reeds put the relationship in graphic and organismic terms: Suburbanitis "kills cities by choking them off from further growth; by selectively thinning out the city's population—its lifeblood; and by bringing on a host of parasitical communities to feed on the already weakened city."[33]

By 1940, hard evidence was available to document the faster growth of suburban communities. Even though metropolitan areas continued to absorb the greatest share of population growth—81 percent between 1940 and 1950, and 97 percent between 1950 and 1955—growth in the metropolitan rings accelerated past that of the central cities. Between 1940 and 1950, the expansion of the rings was 1.3 times that of the cities that they encompassed. By 1955, the ratio had reached 7.0. *Time* noted in 1954 that "since 1940, almost half of the 28 million population increase has taken place in residential suburban areas, anywhere from ten to 40 miles away from traditional big-city shopping centers."[34]

Suburbanization during this period was not simply a migration of urban households to the surrounding countryside, a reversal of earlier movements from the country to the city, but was fueled by natural increase. Postwar growth in the urban periphery was spurred by an unprecedented expansion in the number of births, with the residential choices of new-formed families the link between suburbanization and the baby boom. One business journal captured this well: "Babies, as everyone knows, are wonderful decentralizers. Parents want outdoor play space, good schools, and pleasant surroundings for their families."[35] Suburbanization thus took on a moral dimension; one fled the city in order to provide a nurturing environment for personal and family development.

Nevertheless, between the end of the war and the mid-1950s, cities were gaining population, and significantly. They were rebounding from the Depression and the war. Yet, few optimists were to be found. Read carefully the phrasing of urban growth by one commentator: "During the 1940–50 decade, our 168 biggest cities gained only 6,000,000 new population, while the suburbs increased by 9,000,000, in some cases growing 150 per cent."[36] Take another example. Fred Vigman claimed that data from the U.S. Bureau of Labor Statistics showed that in the first seven months of 1947, 6,983 new dwelling units were started in the Philadelphia–Camden area, but only 36 percent of those units were being built within the municipal boundaries of the two cities.[37] The use of *only* in these observations is telling. Commentators had turned to *relative* growth as an indicator of the city's problems. Now, it was not enough to grow— the city had to grow faster than the suburbs. The city was losing its metropolitan dominance.

As suburbanization accelerated in the 1960s, however, relative growth became less of an issue. The central cities began to experience *absolute* population loss, not simply rates of growth slower than those of the suburbs. Writing in 1960, the editors of *Business Week* noted that "[p]revious censuses have shown spotty declines for mill and mining towns, and a couple of big cities lost population during the Depression. But never has the roster of losers been so imposing: New York, Philadelphia, Detroit, Pittsburgh, St. Louis, Cleveland, Washington." Unlike earlier sightings of city population loss, commentators reacted less by pointing to the isolated ills of the city than they did by noting the looming presence of the suburbs. *Business Week*'s editors made this clear: "No one can doubt that a fundamental change has come over the U.S. Once a rural country, it turned urban in the 1910s; now it has turned suburban."[38]

One of the chief culprits was the automobile. A special correspondent for *The Economist* wrote that "the automobile has crippled the city by carrying off the cream of the taxpayers to live in the suburbs."[39] Whereas decentralization had been abetted by the streetcar in the early 1900s and by the streetcar and scattered automobile ownership in the 1920s, the suburbanization of the postwar period was made possible, in part, by the widespread purchase of private automobiles. Such an individualized means of transportation both exacerbated metropolitan dispersal and made it manageable. Moreover, it allowed suburban and mainly white-collar workers to commute to new downtown offices for employment. The automobile struck a double blow against the city: first, by crowding downtown streets and encouraging the proliferation of parking lots and garages, and second, by providing the mechanism for the mass occupation of fringe areas. Congestion and dispersal thus became intertwined.

The sociologist Phillip Hauser reasoned that under the condition of fixed boundaries, the central cities had just "filled up." At the same time, they faced the "centrifugal forces of 20th century technology, as distinguished from the centripetal forces of 19th century technology."[40] Population and business dispersed via automobiles, highways, telephones, and electric power. "[S]ome degree of decentralization seems inevitable in most large cities," one commentator wrote in 1948, but "[i]f this movement is allowed to continue its present chaotic pattern it will lead to disaster."[41]

In the late 1940s, decentralization was not the only portended disaster. Often mentioned in the early postwar years was an external threat. A virulent anticommunism, directed mainly at the Soviet Union, infected popular culture. The Cold War and the development of the atomic and later the hydrogen bombs terrified many Americans. The construction of civil defense shelters, air raid drills in public schools (with students hiding under their desks for protection from atomic fallout), and the passage of legislation in the 1950s to build a national system of defense highways all attested to this anxiety.

A number of commentators extended that fear to cities. Alfred Caldwell, writing in the *Journal of the American Institute of Architects,* noted that "atomic bombs and concentrated cities cannot exist in the same world."[42] The atomic bomb became a reason, admittedly a minor one, for the deconcentration of large cities. Despite the logic of dispersing the population to minimize the scale of atomic destruction, areas continued to grow even as they also spread. In a report released in 1953, the Washington-based Population Research Bureau noted that "[n]ow, at a time when atomic-hydrogen warfare could blow our big cities to bits, we are building up ever heavier concentrations of people in urban areas."[43]

Few commentators, though, viewed the country's internal population movements as indicative of increasing concentration. The urban discourse changed its focus from population concentration in cities, the big theme of the 1920s, to the dispersal of the cities' population to adjacent communities. More specifically, the issue was sprawl—unplanned, haphazard, low-density, and rapid development of the suburban fringe. Sprawl not only meant chaotic spatial arrangements of housing, industries, stores, highways, and public facilities, but also metropolitan disintegration.

Cast in this form, most commentators understood sprawl as detrimental to the city. In Mitchell Gordon's 1963 health metaphor, sprawl was a disease that created "sick cities." As a reporter for the *Wall Street Journal,* he had long observed the symptoms: clogged streets, dying public transit, spreading blight, increasing air and water pollution, growing lawlessness, diverging educational opportunities, and neglect of park space and other community facilities such as libraries. Suburbanization was turning the nation's major metropolises into "urban dinosaurs," a reference to Clarence Stein's 1920s characterization that changed Stein's meaning from big to extinct. The urban-inclined Gordon proposed a cure: Build "new cities" beyond the present rim of sprawl and speculation.[44]

Gordon's cure, however, was flawed and likely to contribute to "the unplanned, unpredictable, to-hell-with-tomorrow haphazardness of sprawling growth,"[45] what the geographer Jean Gottman labeled *megalopolis.* Megalopolis was a new form of urban development in which cities spread continuously across hundreds of miles as one metropolis merged with another. It was "an almost continuous system of deeply interwoven urban and suburban areas." This "nebulous structure" redefined old city cores, white uptowns, suburbs, and

outer suburbia in a "new and still constantly changing web of relations."[46] As the boundaries between central city and suburbs and one
metropolis and another blurred, it became increasingly apparent that
the megalopolis was friend neither to cities, as we had known them,
nor to suburbs.

The architect Christopher Tunnard identified fifteen such
supercities throughout the United States. Leading the way was the
sprawling Atlantic Urban Region encompassing, from north to south,
Boston, Providence, New Haven, New York, Philadelphia, Baltimore, and Washington, D.C. Others included Chicago–Milwaukee,
Los Angeles–San Diego, and Seattle–Tacoma.[47] Growing suburbs
had subordinated the central cities. Now, the megalopolis was super-
seding the metropolis.

The editors of *U.S. News & World Report* were fascinated by these
new types of settlement, calling them "strip cities." "[O]ne group of
planners" had predicted that by 1975 "there will be a city 1,500 miles
long snaking its way across the face of the U.S. from Washington,
D.C. to St. Louis."[48] In 1961, these editors reported thirteen strip
cities in the country, containing almost half of the national population and accounting for almost two-thirds of national population
growth. By 1964, there were nineteen strip cities arranged along the
elaborate highway network of urban America. Outside of these concentrations of people and industry, the world seemingly remained
largely unchanged. The editors viewed all of this as a sign of vitality
and were optimistic as to its consequences: "This leaves room for people to enjoy themselves in the urbanized strips instead of being
engulfed in the kind of congestion that drove them away from the
cities in the first place."[49]

None of this was good news for the older industrial cities. Wax-
ing poetically, a writer for *The Saturday Evening Post* depicted the fate
of the central cities from the end of World War II: "Since then, the
cities have been like dying stars, sending out great coronas of flame
and energy while swiftly cooling around the central core."[50]

Growth was occurring in metropolitan areas, but for boosters of
the central cities it was misplaced. Suburbanization exacerbated the
problems of the cities and abetted decline. The departure of the

white middle class left the cities with lower property assessments and lower tax revenues, increased crime, poorer health, greater social and economic dependency, more family instability, and larger government expenditures. Julian Levi, the executive director of the South East Chicago Commission, in a speech before the Citizens League of Minneapolis, labeled these combined problems with a phrase— crisis of the cities—that would find extensive currency in the following period.[51]

The crisis had many dimensions. Residential slums and blighted business districts certainly were paramount, and the concentration of minorities in the central cities was increasingly found to be detrimental. Because they undermined the ability of the central city to reverse the onslaught of urban decay and resist the suburban out-flow of people and investment, two problems—the loss of leadership and the rise of fiscal insolvency—were particularly salient.

Most commentators viewed the flight of the middle class to the suburbs as a loss of leadership for the cities. Suburban out-migration not only deprived the city of taxpayers, workers, and consumers, but also stole its most capable individuals. One commentator pointed to "the vicious circle created as talented people desert the central city, leaving behind a leadership vacuum filled by those less skilled culturally, economically and politically."[52] This was in the early 1950s, and the costs of this loss would last for decades: "[T]he worst havoc wrought on cities by their suburbs may yet prove to be the draining off of young, alert citizens who might otherwise become the civic leaders of tomorrow."[53]

Without civic leadership it was unlikely that central cities would be able to cope with the fiscal problems posed by slums and blight, low-income minorities, and suburbanization. The editors of *Time* wrote, for example, that "[d]owntown areas, crowded with traffic, have withered and become blighted, cost more in municipal services (while returning less in taxes) and threatened cities with economic strangulation."[54] Suburbanization carried most of the blame: "[T]he outrush to the suburbs has made an unmistakable dent in the city's economy."[55] As the economy withered, it became more and more difficult for city governments to extract the revenues needed to meet growing expenditures. Thus, it is not surprising that a survey of big-city mayors by the Citizens Budget Commission of New York in 1956 found that finance and taxation ranked with transportation and traffic as the cities' worst problems.[56]

A number of variables came into play in the fiscal equation. One was the deferred maintenance and anemic investment in public facilities that had occurred during the 1930s and in the first half of the following decade. As one commentator wrote about the latter time, "The war caused a halt, not only in new construction and activities, but in all except essential repairs and replacements in pavements, buildings and equipment."[57] Second, delayed investment in existing facilities and construction of new facilities was more expensive than it would have been years earlier. Inflation was the culprit. Prices for materials and the general cost of manpower had risen sharply. Two other factors related directly to suburbanization. The loss of population and the relative shift of investment to the metropolitan periphery weakened the revenue base on which city governments could draw. And, while white middle-class and young working-class households had resettled in suburban areas, elderly and minority and other low-income households remained in the central cities. This increased the demand for basic public services (e.g., education) while leaving city governments with taxpayers having lower earnings and less property to tax.[58] Financial stringencies thus became more central to the discourse, for they too were indicative of the decay of the cities.

The problems of the city were well publicized, but few commentators identified problems in the suburbs. The discourse was sharply delineated: central city decay, suburban prosperity. Of course, the suburbs were not utopia. Cultural commentators labeled the suburbs intellectual wastelands and wellsprings of conformity, both in thought and consumption. City planners and architects deplored the chaotic nature of development and the monotony of large tracts of mass-produced housing. Furthermore, suburban governments had not yet fully responded to the host of service demands that population growth required: new schools, expanded water and sewer systems, hospitals, new roads and highways, police and fire protection, and recreational facilities. Still, such problems were insignificant compared with those facing the central cities. The suburbs, at least, could draw on growth for increased tax revenues and were hardly burdened by concentrations of slums and blight.

One solution was simply to engage in redefinition. The 1953 report of the Subcommittee on Urban Redevelopment of the President's Advisory Commission on Housing summed up this argument: "We must recognize that the real cities are entire metropolitan areas, and that metropolitan development affects very much the development potential of central cities, and their possible tax revenues."[59] In this formulation, the central city ceases to be a meaningful category; it is reduced to one element in a larger metropolitan area that itself is growing. By broadening the geographic scale, decline disappeared.

Others saw the world somewhat differently. Some commentators acknowledged the forces of decentralization and noted countervailing forces that were reinforcing the city's centrality. Robert Moses suggested in a 1952 interview that "there is as much a trend back into the cities as there is away from the cities." He went even further: "All the statistics show that the trend, basically, is still away from the country toward the city. This urban trend hasn't even been seriously interrupted."[60] Mabel Walker would have been appalled with the statement; Moses, as he had always done, was playing fast and loose with categories, statistical and otherwise.

Albert Cobo, mayor of Detroit, offered a solution that built on Moses's rejection of the problem. Cobo argued that suburban living would lose its appeal once children had grown and once expensive houses required burdensome maintenance to forestall obsolescence. The city still retained qualities that had no substitutes in the suburbs. As he put it, "People are learning that they can't do away with the downtown as a place to shop" or as a place for culture and entertainment.[61]

The well-known urbanist William Whyte also predicted that the problems of the suburbs eventually would drive people back into the cities. Rather than the burden of commuting and the allure of city living, Whyte focused on "sterile, unimaginative, unlivable" suburban housing and neighborhoods. "Suburbia is going to help the city, too," he wrote. "Within ten years there is likely to be a brutal disillusionment for thousands of new suburbanites." In fact, he already saw "definite signs of a small but significant move back from suburbia."[62] Coleman Woodbury, a professor of political science and an expert on urban issues, believed otherwise: "Some students of the urban scene think they see evidence of a backflow from the less densely to the more densely built parts of metropolitan areas. . . . No evidence I have seen so far indicates this backflow is more than minor."[63] Both Whyte and Woodbury thus signaled a lesser theme—a return to the city—that would appear later in the discourse and, in the 1980s, take a dominant position. Until then, Whyte was less prescient than aggressively optimistic.

Obvious to all was that urban decline and suburban growth were related. The urban planner Bernard Frieden observed that "growth and decline go hand in hand in the modern metropolis."[64] For the most part, the relationship was a relatively simple one. The problems of the central cities pushed new investment and population growth into the suburbs where land was inexpensive, slums and blight nonexistent, taxes lower, and home mortgages more readily available. The less affluent followed more affluent households, retail businesses chased consumers, and manufacturing firms built modern factories. All told, the direction was inside-out and the pattern seemed immutable. Still, a number of commentators put a positive face on these phenomena. Sounding like Robert Moses, Harold Martin wrote, "Decentralization and dispersion did not mean the death of cities. . . . They meant, instead, that the city was a fertile seedbed, spawning new, strong growth."[65]

However, the lack of the political power to annex and thus capture this growth led one housing expert to comment in 1953 that "it is safe to say [that] nearly all of our major cities are strangled by a circumferential band of separately organized suburbs."[66] By the early 1960s, it was more widely recognized that this powerful suburban ring was also a suburban noose. Moreover, that ring was predominantly white and the central cities increasingly African American. Full recognition of this situation, and the subsequent problems it posed, would drastically shift the discourse on urban decline.

DARK TIDES WERE RUNNING

The importance of foreign immigration and rural migrants to the growth of cities had been a major part of the urban discourse prior to the 1920s. Beginning in the 1920s, though, immigrants were no longer the main source of new city residents—rural, mainly white, migrants were. During World War II and thereafter, however, the main flow consisted primarily of African Americans from the rural South traveling to the industrial cities of the North. This was a profound shift. A reporter for *Newsweek* wrote in 1957 that "[c]ities are gaining newcomers, but most of them are low-income ruralites, Negroes, Puerto Ricans, and other minorities."[67]

In the 1940s, 1.6 million African Americans migrated along the metaphorical path of farm to factory. During the 1950s, it was 1.5 million. Added to that in the latter decade were 430,000 Puerto Ricans. For the most part, the new migrants were young and from large families. Their presence drove up demand for housing, further exacerbated overcrowding, and contributed to the intensification and expansion of inner-city slums. As rural folk, moreover, the new migrants lacked the skills and work discipline demanded by urban factories. Ironically, that did not matter so much; within these central cities, manufacturing itself was perched precariously on the edge of decline. With such knowledge in mind, Frieden called this migration "one of the most striking population shifts of our time and perhaps the greatest challenge to the contemporary American city."[68]

For these migrants, housing and employment opportunities in the urban centers were either of low quality or inaccessible. Racial segregation was the norm, and African Americans and Puerto Ricans were denied access to many neighborhoods. As a result, housing left by white out-migrants was not necessarily occupied by non-whites.[69] Physical decay was exacerbated, and the problems of poor housing, unemployment, poverty, and crime became increasingly associated with inner-city minorities.

Segregated into specific neighborhoods, minorities also found themselves relatively alone in worsening public schools. William Whyte felt compelled to write that "[f]or most city parents, of course, the school problem is the 'public school problem,' a euphemism for the 'Negro problem'."[70] Not only the schools were affected. Low-income and rural minorities required a host of governmental services. The contrast between their needs and the ostensible burden that white, middle-class families placed on city governments was a central element in the discourse. As one commentator observed: "Many of the difficulties which plague cities today stem from the exodus of the middle class with its resources of money and leadership and the influx of low-income families and minority groups with their expensive problems of social welfare."[71]

Not only were minorities segregated within the cities, but the suburbs were virtually closed to them. In fact, the two processes—segregation within the cities and exclusion from the suburbs—were linked by a racial discrimination that precipitated another population flow: as African Americans and Puerto Ricans moved into the cities, whites moved out. One magazine writer juxtaposed these two migratory flows: "Great human tides, made up of middle-income Americans, were flowing out of the cities into the rural hinterlands. Into the cities, to take their place, dark tides were running—of Puerto Ricans and Negroes from the South."[72] The biases of Martin's observation are readily apparent: Americans versus minorities, and human tides versus tides of a not-so-human quality.

Miles Colean was led to comment as early as 1953 that "[w]ith new construction limited mainly to downtown commercial building and to luxury residential accommodations, the central city under present circumstances tends to become a locale of the rich and the poor, with the middle group—particularly the families with small children—finding its way to suburbia."[73] This early evidence of an emerging geographic division based on class would become even more pronounced when reinforced by a similar division by race. Together, class and race contributed doubly to the problems faced by the cities. *Business Week*'s editors referred to this elliptically when they stated that "[t]he young married couples with children who are moving away are good spenders; often the young people who come into the city to make their fortunes are not. Chicago, in particular, notes a stepped-up increase in its Negro population."[74]

The injurious influences of poor minorities on urban neighborhoods, schools, public services, retail activity, and local tax revenues mixed with racial antagonisms to fuel the flight of many of the cities' middle-income and white households to the suburbs. Though decentralization had its roots in a period before the mass exodus of rural minorities to the industrial cities, minority presence coincided with an acceleration of suburbanization, even if it did not function as a sole motivating force. In the last chapter of his highly popular book *Inside U.S.A.,* John Gunther in 1947 made a number of bold generalizations about the country. One had to do with America's minority problem. "The most gravid, cancerous, and pressing of all American problems is that of the Negro, insoluble under present political and social conditions though capable of great amelioration."[75] His mix of reality and optimism would soon be tested.

In the years just after the cessation of World War II, then, it became obvious to observers of the city that although prosperity would grip the country, older industrial cities would not fully benefit. The expected rebound of the cities from fifteen years of disinvestment did not materialize. People continued to leave and at an accelerating pace. Investors began to explore opportunities beyond the city limits and numerous social problems reemerged, many linked to the expanding presence of black families in inner-city neighborhoods once occupied by white families.

The postwar discourse on urban decline was underway. One of its dominant themes was population decline, no longer a growth rate slower than expanding suburbs but now an absolute loss. People were literally rejecting the city by packing their belongings and taking up residence elsewhere. Adding insult to injury, commentators began to recognize a new urban form—the metropolis—and to use its blurring of territorial distinctions as a metaphorical refuge from urban decline. The city became the central city just in time for the title to become honorific.

Some people found the large cities attractive, but they were either non-white and driven to poverty or, if white, too few in number to counterbalance the loss of middle-income households to suburbia. Race emerged as a theme, although its full discursive development awaited its joining to the twin evils of the urban environment—slums and blight—and later to the myriad social problems, labeled *poverty* and *crime,* that had haunted industrial societies.

CHAPTER 5

On the Verge of Catastrophe

If cities were to avoid further decline, their supporters would not only have to minimize the loss of households and businesses to surrounding suburbs but also overcome the forces within the city that were fueling out-migration. In these early postwar years, the two most prominent urban problems to be solved were slums and blight. Although these were recurring themes in the discourse, they became even more alarming when the predicted resurgence of the cities stalled. In fact, their intransigence was more and more apparent and came to be associated with a variety of other urban ills. Slums were fused with race and juvenile delinquency while blight was linked to traffic congestion and fiscal insolvency, among other interlocking themes. Consequently, balanced and cautiously hopeful assessments of the fate of cities became scarce.

The persistence of slums and blight as prime subjects led to an important shift in the discourse—a stronger discursive link between the fate of the city and the viability of the central business district. Without its dominance in the metropolitan area, the city would lose its centrality and its distinctiveness. The visual and symbolic as well as the financial, retail, and cultural importance of the central business district became more and more worrisome as white households relocated to the suburbs. Neighborhood advocates recommitted themselves to the eradication of slums and the construction of public housing. Urban redevelopers persisted in their attacks on blight. Suburban growth, though, undermined their efforts.

Increasingly prominent in these years were arguments for why the city was no longer desirable, either as a place to live or a place to invest. The urban challenges were becoming insurmountable, or so it seemed. With the United States changing from an urban to a suburban society, these challenges seemed less worth meeting.

Despite deepening ambivalence, commentators were not at a loss for practical advice for those who still found the city desirable, or hoped that it would once again be so. To stop decline's momentum, national and local leaders in both government and business would have to rededicate themselves to civic reform. However, it was becoming less rather than more likely that elected officials, retailers, factory owners, middle-income households, and white-collar employers would agree and act accordingly.

WE HAVE NOT ADAPTED

The market for land in the inner city did not, as speculators during World War II had hoped, rebound with the onset of peace. Deteriorated and out-moded buildings were everywhere, and blight remained a significant problem. The distinction between blight and slums, however, had become more pronounced. The prime factor distancing one from the other was the policy debate over the appropriate forms of governmental intervention to deal with the postwar stagnation of cities.[1] Property interests, elected officials, and civic boosters were dismayed by falling land values in the central city and the financial viability of real estate investments there, the lack of new construction, and the precarious condition of downtown businesses. They advocated attacking blight through redevelopment. Public housers and other social reformers lobbied for greater attention to the insufficiency and inadequacy of housing for low-income families. Their concern was the struggling working and lower classes, urban categories increasingly populated by minorities. The solution they proposed was slum clearance and government-built, subsidized (public) housing.

Analysts, moreover, situated blight and slums in different parts of the city. Blight was confined to central business districts, slums to residential neighborhoods. An administrator for the Redevelopment Authority in New Haven, Connecticut, Edward Logue, captured the three-part division of urban decay when he wrote,

> Perhaps we need fewer statistics and instead a few good old-
> fashioned walking tours: walks through the slums, up the
> stinking stairways into the overcrowded shabby rooms; walks
> through the run-down commercial areas, taking care to glance
> above the first floor at the dusty windows of the deserted upper
> floors; walks through the oil-soaked, dreary factory lofts built
> before the assembly line was even heard of. The filth, the
> misery and the danger are all there—easy to see and, once seen,
> impossible to forget.[2]

In his 1953 book, *Renewing Our Cities,* the housing expert Miles Colean argued that the city was faced with two nonidentical but related problems: renewal and slums. Blight had its origins in the tendency of new development to "leap over and build on new land rather than to replace buildings which have become obsolete." In effect, it was created by developers and speculators and required renewal. Slums, on the other hand, existed when numerous properties became overcrowded and posed a threat to the health and safety of the occupants. The "attitudes and behavior of people and of the indifference of the community to the neglect and victimization of the underprivileged" caused slums. Landlords and government callousness were the culprits. For Colean, although "areas that are worn-out and ripe for renewal may be, and frequently are, also slum areas . . . it does not necessarily follow that a city inevitably has slums because its obsolete buildings have not been replaced."[3]

Colean echoed in part the argument favored by the economist Mabel Walker and others, such as Lewis Mumford. It placed speculation—another recurring theme—at the center of the analysis of slums and blight. An American correspondent to *The Economist,* for example, wrote that "[s]peculators and landlords have kept the values of city properties artificially high, thus forcing up the density of population in slum areas, making it difficult to do business profitably in decaying commercial districts and increasing the cost of slum clearance programmes."[4]

Speculation, though, was not the only issue contributing to slums and blight. Also important was how cities responded to problems in their midst, a theme not heretofore developed in any great detail. Colean emphasized the stifling of the self-regulatory qualities of an economic market. Speculators were obstacles to the workings of the market, but blight persisted because of obstacles to the market's inherent renewal process. Normally the market would allocate land and property to its highest and best use, thereby negating any tendency toward disinvestment or the speculative holding of properties. The obstacles to a well-functioning land market were numerous and diverse; the city's poor physical environment, street and traffic congestion, dispersed ownership patterns, false land values, government props to real estate, neighborhood resistance to change, racial prejudice, legal impediments, and fiscal imbalances were only part of the litany. All functioned as deterrents to investment.

In the business districts of older central cities, property values were falling, economic activity was depressed, the streets were congested, and buildings were deteriorating. Making renewal even more difficult, these conditions fed on each other. Falling property values undermined the incentive to maintain and reinvest in property. Traffic congestion impeded commerce. Physical deterioration eroded the "image" of the central business district and discouraged new investment.[5]

Elected officials in the large cities were convinced that downtown blight was a significant problem. In a survey of the mayors of nine hundred cities conducted in 1955 by Richard Wood & Company, 47 percent ranked "preservation of downtown commercial property values" as one of their most urgent problems.[6]

Downtown blight, of course, had been recognized and condemned almost a decade previously. Guy Greer, a consultant on city planning, told the readers of *The American Magazine* in 1948, "[I]f [your town] is typical, its central business district is likely to be surrounded by a zone of blight, characterized by grimy business shacks, congestion of people, dilapidated buildings, junk yards, vacant lots covered with cinders, disease, once-impressive mansions that have been converted into funeral parlors or tenements or cheap rooming houses."[7] Greer noted that Chicago had 23 square miles of blighted area but was hardly atypical. The centers of hundreds of U.S. cities were infested with blight and, once infested, blight took root in adjacent areas of mixed land uses as well.

One of the most discussed contributors to blight, and a theme new to the discourse, was traffic congestion—too many vehicles crowded into too little space, thereby slowing down the movement of people and goods. When stationary, automobiles and trucks also occupied valuable urban real estate. Downtown districts were being paralyzed by congestion and this stifled both investment and the much desired growth that would follow.

"The era of the auto has become an era of problems for the city," *U.S. News & World Report* claimed.[8] In innumerable central business districts where the arrangement of streets and buildings had adapted easily to the streetcar, cars simply caused traffic congestion. Traffic tie-ups were common, parking spaces scarce, and travel times exceedingly long. Congestion, in turn, discouraged business activity and drove down property values. Retail trade subsequently suffered. All of these conditions exacerbated decentralization.

One commentator called parking the gravest downtown problem. "As of 1952," he wrote, "a summary of traffic surveys estimated that 175,000 new parking spaces were needed to fill the demand in the seventy-nine largest cities."[9] On a typical business day in New York City in 1956, for example, 519,000 automobiles entered the lower half of Manhattan, 137,000 more than on a similar day in 1948. By contrast, the number of people who entered was 10 percent less. The same was reported for Chicago. In 1926, 880,000 people daily went into the central business district, 166,000 by automobile. Although that number had changed only slightly by 1958—870,000—the number of automobiles had increased by just over 100,000.[10]

The planner Constantinos Doxiadis believed that the major cities were dying because of an inability to cope with the automobile, combined with a tremendous increase in population in the metropolitan area.[11] In highly evocative and organismic language he commented that "traffic clots main arteries . . . and then the . . . 'heart' slowly withers and dies." Victor Gruen, architect and city planner, went further and implicated the automobile in a two-prong attack on the city. The cities' troubles, he said, were caused by "the misapplied usage of . . . [the automobile] . . . for mass transportation in heavily built-up areas. The automobile is also responsible for urban sprawl and suburban scatterization."[12] With the construction of limited-access highways, the automobile made commuting from and living in the suburbs that much easier. In a profound way, it linked the city and the suburbs, not only providing a means to commute back and forth and "creat[ing] frustrating traffic jams but . . . produc[ing] a way for the well-to-do to escape to the suburbs, indifferent to the slums they left behind."[13]

Attachment to the automobile was spreading rapidly and few people were willing, despite its costs, to give up the new-found freedom of mobility. Simultaneously, mass transit began to deteriorate, further constricting the options for moving about the city.

While many commentators focused on the incompatibility between the automobile and the physical form of the industrial city, one prescient observer discovered that the city was undergoing a more subtle and deeper type of transformation, a transformation of its economic base. In 1959, Raymond Vernon published *The Changing Economic Function of the Central City,* a seminal study of thirteen large cities. While he recognized the population shift to the suburbs as an important contributor to the lack of growth in central cities, his attention was directed primarily at the city's structural obsolescence or, to use Colean's term, blight. To explain this, Vernon compared central cities with their suburbs. Labor costs were not drastically different, but tax levels were higher and traffic congestion greater in the central cities. The main agent of obsolescence was land values. Office and industrial spaces were much more expensive in the urban core. The discrepancy was significant for industrial development. The costs of buying and clearing land for new industrial use virtually barred redevelopment in the cities. Particularly affected were wholesalers and manufacturing firms and the proportionately large employment that they represented.

Nonetheless, Vernon argued that the cost discrepancy was not a problem for central city office and retail development. The out-migration of offices was mainly a function of the migration of consumers and young women to the suburbs and the evolution of data processing and computer technology, while retail shifts were more sensitive to the location of consumers and the preference for automobile transportation over mass transit. On the whole, he proclaimed a "new phase in the development of large central cities of the nation," one in which central cities would become increasingly differentiated and specialized and thus more sharply distinguished from their suburbs.[14]

From this perspective, structural obsolescence was not necessarily demise. But others were less optimistic. They saw a settlement pattern on its way to extinction. Luther Gulick, then president of the Institute of Public Administration, believed that the "old" city was being challenged by a completely new pattern of urban settlement—the metropolitan community—and the city center was seriously outmoded. Even major efforts on the part of city governments to combat blight with renewal projects were unlikely to change this. For Gulick, "[e]very large American city is now physically obsolete."[15]

Business Week used Vernon's study to argue that the "gray belt" surrounding the city's core, the area of blight and slums, could not be rescued from continued decay despite the vitality of central business districts. A number of insurmountable forces were abetting the overall decline of cities. One was the increase in commuting distances as metropolitan areas spread. Combined with shrinking mass transit, both forces would eventually "discourage white females from coming in to form the pool of clerical labor." A third counterforce to the reconsolidation of the central business district was the introduction of data-processing equipment that would reduce office staffing needs and change skill requirements. In addition, the editors agreed with Vernon's comment that "[t]o expect middle-income families to return to the city in larger numbers would fly in the face of deep-seated historical trends." Overall, *Business Week* suggested to its readers that "the prognosis for the central city is relative—if not absolute—decline in comparison with the whole metropolitan area."[16] The central city would have to rely on office activity for its economic survival, an activity that would redefine its business core but do little for the remainder of the city.

As had occurred previously in the twentieth century, such prognostications and warnings became the bases for reform. The rationales linking diagnosis to cure were numerous. Hal Burton reminded his readers of accomplishments in the face of adversity. He believed that "the problems are appalling" but that no city was doomed. He used a city in western Pennsylvania as an example: "That no city needs to lie down and die is best established by a visit to Pittsburgh, beset in its time by every known form of municipal illness." The link could also be forged by pointing to the continued viability of cities even as they experienced disruptive change. Boyd Barnard, chairman of the Central Business District Council for the Urban Land Institute, was quoted at the same time as stating, "On the contrary, our studies prove that the city is a growing, basically healthy organism which will continue in the future, as in the past, to form the cornerstone of our industrial civilization."[17] Mayor Albert Cobo of Detroit concurred but offered a third rationale: "There's more confidence now that cities can become the real core of the metropolitan area—a center of shopping, entertainment, the professions."[18] For Cobo, attitude was at least as important as evidence.

City governments funded planning studies and investors committed resources to downtown redevelopment projects. Governments subsidized and developers and corporations built new office buildings and hotels. Retail stores enjoyed an increase in sales, and, as a result, many commentators were optimistic that urban prosperity would reappear.

Their efforts were guided and supported by Title I of the federal government's 1949 and 1954 housing acts. Title I enabled local gov-

ernments to establish local redevelopment authorities that could purchase and clear blighted land and slums and contract with developers
to build office towers, sports stadiums, apartment houses, and other
downtown projects.[19] Backed by real estate and downtown interests
and elected officials, such projects became ubiquitous within the
larger cities. The federal commitment would enable local governments to eradicate decay and implant new growth. This was the plan,
at least.

The executive director of the U.S. Conference of Mayors declared
that "[h]istory will certainly record that 1949 was just the beginning
of a long-range attack on our slums and blighted areas," while *Newsweek* proclaimed in 1954 that "[c]ities all over America are busy getting their shapes changed, their faces lifted, and their downtown
hearts replaced."[20] In article after article, commentators called forth
specific cities as examples: Philadelphia with its Penn Center office
development, Chicago's rebuilding of the Loop, the redevelopment
of the southwest section of Washington, D.C., and Detroit's river-
front development of offices and a convention hall. *Time* magazine
asserted that "[a]cross the nation, the sound of jackhammers and
heavy earth movers told of similar large-scale building projects under
way in the hearts of scores of other U.S. cities. Whole blocks of
old buildings, acres of overcrowded downtown areas, were being
ripped out. In the gaps, new buildings were beginning to rise, units
of planned medical, residential and civic centers, set among broad
avenues and spacious parks."[21] Business district blight, reformers predicted, would soon be eliminated.

Public housers resisted the move by real estate interests and
others to center the discourse solely on blight and the anemic land
values of central business districts. Slums and the housing that comprised them could not be overlooked. The sociologist Phillip Hauser
declared that "[o]ur slums [have] become a matter of national and
international disgrace and also a matter of national politics."[22]

In 1948, Mayor Hubert Humphrey of Minneapolis noted in a
radio address that "[s]lums, rotten broken-down areas, are the ulcers
which may develop into the cancer that will consume the physical and
economic structure of the industrial city. Slum areas are extravagances

that eat up our revenues and destroy our strength." And he warned, "Either we lick the slums or the slums will destroy the city."[23] Indicative of the lack of progress that would ensue, Edward Logue expressed a similar view ten years later: "Locally, cities must take slums seriously and recognize them for the cancer they are."[24]

The housing expert Charles Abrams claimed that more than one-third of the population was occupying substandard housing. He pointed to the 1940 Census with its finding that 38 percent of non-farm housing was unsatisfactory and noted that "[t]he slums continue simply because their inhabitants cannot afford good housing and private enterprise will not supply it at prices they can afford."[25] Many people simply did not earn enough income to live well. Investors could not provide decent housing at an acceptable profit to those whose incomes were low. Moreover, while these problems were not strictly confined to cities, slums were almost wholly viewed as urban. The editors of Newsweek provided a graphic depiction of a typical slum: "The southwest part of Washington has a huge slum without enough heat, light, or toilets, a place where tenants put pop bottles in holes to keep out rats. A favorite Communist propaganda picture shows some dirty Negro kids playing in a yard of garbage against a backdrop of the sharply focused Capitol dome."[26]

Even though housing demand had remained high from 1929 to 1945, a shortage of capital had led to a deterioration of the housing stock and a dearth of new construction. Vacancy rates were low, but the costs of removal and replacement were too high. In 1947, Junius Wood stated the problem bluntly: "Populations in the already overcrowded cities are still increasing. The overseas army has become an army of home-hunters. Marriage bureaus are busy. The nation faces peace with a 1945 population and a 1931 supply of homes."[27] New construction after the war did not keep pace with population growth and the formation of new households. Few housing units were vacant, thus indicating strong demand, but that demand was not great enough to spur a concomitant housing supply.

The housing shortage persisted throughout the 1950s despite out-migration from the cities. A combination of substandard inner-city housing and the slum clearance—and thus housing demolition—

undertaken by urban renewal agencies diminished the housing stock even further. The increased number of households in the central cities (even as overall population declined) helped to maintain demand at or above earlier levels. Slums expanded as low-income black households were channeled into segregated neighborhoods by real estate agents and discriminatory lending practices.

The private market did not respond to the housing shortage, so local governments took up the challenge. The federal government helped by passing Title II of the 1949 Housing Act. That title provided the legal mechanisms and financial backing for clearing slums and replacing them with public housing.

In its rush to act quickly, the government constructed large-scale public housing projects that became, though not in all instances, the slums that they were meant to replace. *U.S. News & World Report* in 1957 reported 142 slum-clearance projects underway around the nation costing $42 million in public funds and $2 billion in private monies. In addition, three hundred more projects were planned.[28] Eugene Raskin, a professor in Columbia University's School of Architecture, condemned the new housing projects: "This is a machine-for-living with a vengeance." The projects, he believed, were neither human nor urban, and undermined the variety, contrast, and freedom that characterized good city life. He warned his readers: "[B]y this time even the most die-hard reactionary is willing to admit that getting rid of our slums is a good idea. . . . Now we must take care that in carrying it out we do not also get rid of our cities."[29]

Racial minorities increased their presence in the cities and found themselves crowded into substandard housing and deteriorating neighborhoods. Bernard Frieden bemoaned the concentration of poor, elderly, and minority households and called the migration of non-whites from the South to northern cities "one of the most striking population shifts of our time and perhaps the greatest challenge to the contemporary American city."[30]

The expanding presence of minorities and the diminishing proportion of young, white, and affluent households was not the only social problem facing the city. The discourse expanded to subsume more and more concerns. The commentators discovered a criminal element in the form of unruly teenagers. Juvenile delinquency teamed with slums to create an image of the city as a "social jungle." The sociologists William Form and Joel Smith undertook one of the first studies of youth gangs in the postwar city. They found social disorganization but also concluded that such conditions were not pervasive or inherently urban. "There are tenement districts and skid rows in large cities," they noted, "but even there people manage to make a go of it and have many social contacts."[31]

Still, minorities could not be overlooked or simply tamed by the scientific jargon of social disorganization. A small number of commentators began to explore the problems posed by the clustering of African Americans in the slums and the forces that brought about this segregation. In an article written with a local reporter, the executive director of the Providence Redevelopment Authority highlighted the dilemma: "In most cities, the clearance of slums is complicated by the fact that the worst housing is usually occupied by Negroes. Displacement of these families is not a housing problem alone but runs straight into the problem of segregation."[32]

Additionally, commentators recognized the limits of governmental involvement in the eradication of slums and blight. Through urban renewal and public housing, the federal government had committed itself to eliminating slums, but that commitment paled in comparison to the scale of the problem, and was hindered by more immediate concerns facing local governments. Not only did the cities have serious fiscal problems, their capacity to respond was itself problematic.

Fred Vigman's historical study of municipal government and politics—*Crisis of the City*—listed slums and blight as one of the three principal elements of urban decline. The first element was municipal insolvency caused by the disappearance of tax revenue sources, inflationary pressures on local finances, and local citizen resistance to higher taxes. Civic indifference and negativism was the second element. It led to the capturing of local governments by political machines. Both of these factors made it difficult for city administrations to cope with the third element: urban deterioration and exodus. Housing and the municipal plant had fallen into disrepair. City governments had failed "to provide and enforce measures to counteract the worsening of sanitary conditions following on greater congestion and the spread of blighted areas and slums."[33] Blight and slums were rooted as much in political deficiencies as economic perversities.

NOT SO MUCH A DISHONOR

Although slums resisted eradication and the renewal of blighted business districts posed formidable obstacles, the general mood was optimistic. Solutions were at hand, and the early results looked promising. The conventional wisdom suggested that a strong dose of redevelopment would return cities to prosperity. As redevelopment stalled, however, the initial optimism began to fade.

Notions of urban decline that had been developed before the end of World War II had excluded the potential for a significant transformation of the central city. The large city had problems, but a return to growth, many believed, would likely lead to their elimination with no significant change to the city's essential qualities. In the 1950s, however, commentators came increasingly to accept that an economically robust, socially attractive, politically influential central city dominating its hinterland was less and less likely. Instead, the urban core was on a path to become geographically encased by suburbs that were themselves economically, socially, and politically independent.

The discourse entered a new stage of ambivalence in which commentators began to explore the possibility of long-term decline of the central cities even with successful redevelopment. Optimism and pessimism became more sharply defined and began to frame the discourse in new ways. Those with little hope began to believe that suburbanization would bleed from the cities all of their assets, leaving empty hulks with no purpose or value. Was not the out-migration of families and investors the beginning of the end?

Of course, suburbanization did not require, nor could it tolerate, the demise of the city. The American Institute of Planners recognized "on the one hand, that powerful forces of change are already remaking our cities; and on the other, that [the] tremendous capital investment and strategic locations of our cities make abandonment impossible."[34] William Zeckendorf, president of the real estate firm of Webb & Knapp, agreed—too much had been invested in the cities to abandon them. He posed the situation rhetorically in his 1951 lecture at the Harvard School of Design: "How can we keep cities that represent the toil and sweat and invested labor and capital of generations from becoming ghost towns?" To ward off any likelihood that the audience missed his point, he closed by stating: "I don't believe that cities are lost unless we are prepared to abandon them."[35]

Other commentators harkened back to an earlier theme. Their commitment was based on the relation of the city to civilization. Not just sunk costs, but the symbolic importance of cities was at stake. One commentator from Chicago and another from Philadelphia provided useful insights. Julian Levi, the executive director of the South East Chicago Commission, concluded his speech before the Citizens League of Minneapolis by announcing, "What is really at stake in the problems which confront us are the fundamentals of American civilization and democracy."[36] Joseph Clark, the Democratic senator from Pennsylvania, proposed a simple equation. He wrote that "in many ways, the city is civilization. It is more than form; it is substance, life, spirit. . . . And the desire to live in cities, the desire for urban culture—these will continue as long as civilization lasts."[37]

The American people were faced with a challenge: deal with the problems of the cities or stand by as civilization decays. Elected officials—at least those with urban constituencies—did not shy away from championing the city. Mayor Robert Wagner of New York City told the National Municipal League that "[t]he biggest challenge of the 1960s, I suggest, is to awaken fully to the fact that we are an urban nation." That same year, U.S. Senator John Kennedy expressed a similar sentiment: "This is the great unspoken, overlooked, underplayed problem of our time."[38]

Before taking up the challenge, the more analytically inclined needed a better sense of what the future might bring. Predictions were in order. In the midst of the baby boom and rapid metropolitan growth, however, it was difficult to forecast anything but further expansion. Kenneth Hoover, director of a Washington, D.C., mass transportation survey, noted that earlier estimates had calculated a national population of 149 million people for 1957, whereas the actual number was 170 million. By 1975, he predicted, 225 million people would inhabit the country, and most of the additional 55 million would reside in urban areas.[39] Such predictions helped to stimulate debate and inform opinion. They also shaped a commitment to action.

That action involved not only rebuilding the aging cores of the large industrial cities, but also providing for the new population. Based on a predicted large-scale population growth between 1957 and 1975, Edward Chase suggested that "[i]t will be necessary between now and then to have built something equivalent to fifty cities the size of San Francisco to accommodate us. This is a growth that is inevitable, plans or no plans, like it or not."[40] A similar prognostication, one that factored in the inevitability of urban decay, was offered by Donald Bogue of the University of Chicago: "In the next half century the urbanized areas of the United States will double or even treble in size. At least one half of the cities as they now exist will be torn down and replaced by 2050."[41] Bogue's belief in the powers of redevelopment were astonishing.

The editors of *The American City* went beyond mere population predictions. They were concerned with what the cities would be like in the near future. They foresaw persistent urban renewal, the improvement of mass transit, the cleaning up of cities, a return to apartment living, and greater interurban cooperation in metropolitan areas. In addition, the cities would have a sounder financial base: "Economically, this nation's urban areas can expect the 1960s and beyond to continue increasing the real income of people. Economists seem so universally agreed on this point as members of this profession can be."[42] Whatever the future—or the prognostication—many commentators concurred with the housing expert Coleman Woodbury— the form of the city was likely to change in response to the implosion of central cities and the explosion of the suburbs. Cities did not just become bigger or smaller, they also mutated. As Woodbury wrote, "In the lifetime of most of us, not only the face but the physique of urban America is going to be changed—radically changed."[43]

Pessimism and optimism toward the central city existed in almost equal degrees during this period. The differences between them, however, were becoming clearer. Eventually, fewer commentators would occupy a middle ground.

One pessimistic view was voiced by Mitchell Gordon in his 1962 article "Doomed Cities": "It remains to be seen whether . . . the cities will be able to save themselves." Gordon's pessimism was cautious. It left open the possibility that urban renewal might be effective. Although less equivocal than Gordon, the mayor of Detroit, James Cavanaugh, and Edward Logue, urban renewal administrator for New Haven, Connecticut, used their pessimism as prelude to a strategic reaction. Cavanaugh warned that "the decay is spreading faster than we can clean it up. You can work one part of town and look up years later to see other areas that have started to go."[44] Logue took a different tack but arrived at the same destination: "It is up to everyone to face the hard truth that the American dream is tarnishing, the American way of life becoming a mirage, for tens of millions of our fellow citizens who live in cities."[45]

The use of feigned pessimism and the prediction of dire consequences constituted a rhetorical strategy for leveraging commitment and action. Such a device, it became quickly obvious, could easily overwhelm the good intentions that motivated it, however. In 1961, Paul Ylvisaker, while praising "the miraculous city," commented that "the approved way to talk about cities these days is to speak solemnly, sadly, ominously and fearfully about their problems. You don't really rate as an urban expert unless you foresee its doom; the city must, of course, always be in crisis and on the verge of catastrophe."[46] Doom, crisis, and catastrophe were words that could just as easily justify withdrawal.

Prompting that doom were the expanding suburbs. Their growth not only hemmed the central city within fixed boundaries, but also drew off middle-class taxpayers and leaders as well as capital investment. *U.S. News & World Report* suggested that the central cities were faced with "a desperate fight for survival against the threat of 'strangulation'."[47] Donald Campion, in a review of Vigman's book *Crisis of the Cities,* went even further and predicted the outcome of that struggle: cities as "great industrial plantation[s] where employees must perforce live and from which all strata of population will seek to escape."[48] This future was grim. Shifting the problem from slums and blight—both treatable with urban renewal—to suburbanization seemed to deepen the pessimism. *Business Week* offered a "realist" equivocation: "Whether all this spells the slow demise of the big city is a hotly debated question."[49]

For some commentators, this pessimism was a logical extrapolation from the belief that the city was simply obsolete. "[I]ts competitive alternatives have become so much more available," Herbert Dorau commented in 1949. Alluding to the rise of suburban towns and the expansion of small cities, he claimed that "the city has lost its bargaining power."[50] About the same time, the Committee on Land Policy of the American Institute of Planners arrived at a similar conclusion, but one that turned inward to the city itself. It stated, "[T]he physical 'plant' of the cities has become increasingly obsolete."[51]

Obsolescence might have been caused by "the natural decay resulting from the aging of the city itself," as Carl Feiss suggested in 1953. Yet, there was also technology to consider. The automobile and the computer had enabled the decentralization of workers and economic activities.[52] To think of cities as aging was to allow their obsolescence to be stemmed only by major transplants or the redevelopment counterpart of the Fountain of Youth. On the other hand, technological obsolescence could be reversed by newer and more benign technology.

In reality, the large cities were overwhelmed by the automobile, the pressures of population, the loss of business and industry, municipal budget burdens, and even the threat of the atom bomb. Paul Windels, three years earlier than Feiss, wrote that "[i]n all of our older central cities we find the requirements of modern life have outstripped their antiquated designs. They fall short of being effective instrumentalities of a civilized social order."[53] Functional obsolescence seemed to be irreversible.

The implications of Henry Churchill's comments back in 1945 were now becoming hauntingly obvious to many. In considering the question "What shall we do with our cities?", Churchill had reasoned that the "industrial and mechanical technology of the last fifty years has rendered our city pattern obsolete. A city exists for two things only: it is a place in which people earn a living, and it is a place in which people live and play."[54] If neither were possible, cities would disappear. For these commentators, the city was due to be replaced; it could no longer serve the tasks for which it was designed.

Just as growth breeds decline and familiarity contempt, the pessimism engendered by urban decline had its optimistic counterpart. Even Churchill perceived the evolution of a novel city pattern "suited to the new technological requirements of our world of electronics, jet propulsion and super-power."[55] One city would decline and another would neatly take its place. Rather than hope that suburbanization would somehow culminate in new types of cities, the architect Victor Gruen opted for a nascent rejection of suburbia coupled with the eradication of slums and blight. He claimed that "some counterforces have arisen and a trend back to the city has become apparent."[56] He offered no empirical confirmation for his assertion. Instead, Gruen pointed to isolated examples of business leadership of renewal processes in such cities as Boston, Paterson (New Jersey), Cincinnati, and Rochester (New York). The logic was rudimentary: Successful renewal, by definition, meant a return to the city.

Renewal activities were a pivotal source of the optimism that pervaded the discourse. Mayor Cobo of Detroit told *U.S. News & World Report* that urban renewal was the key: "I don't think that big cities can die if they do the things they should, and do it soon."[57] During the late 1950s, the "things" to do were to demolish slums and blighted properties and clear the land for new investment. Once renewed, modern downtowns would once again attract shoppers, shoppers would attract businesses, and workers would live nearby. In 1959, *Newsweek* proclaimed a bright future: "Across the nation, the cities are rebuilding, refurbishing, marching ahead."[58]

Still, commentators found it difficult to isolate the positive qualities of central cities from their problems. During these times, even optimists were equivocal at best. *Business Week* noted that "[t]he central city has its problems, to be sure. But it already has a huge capital investment in bricks and mortar, steel and pavement. It has a broad tax base, well diversified among housing, commercial and industrial property. This base isn't declining with population."[59] William Whyte agreed, though he did not contrast weaknesses with strengths as much as he found strength in the city's supposed deficiencies. "Their problems are appallingly difficult," he wrote, "not because the cities are 'decayed' or 'obsolete' but because they have vitality. Their streets are packed because there is business to be done, their slums are jammed because there are jobs to be had. Nor are the cities old and tired."[60]

By the early 1960s, with few signs of the political and cultural turmoil that would soon be unleashed, commentators oscillated easily between optimism and pessimism. The divide between them, though, was hardly an unbridgable chasm. The optimists saw a future for the central city that reinstilled its regional, now metropolitan, dominance. The pessimists saw a future in which the central city became just another community in a vibrant metropolitan area. In addition, challenges were still there to be met. Two urban experts captured this well. One was Martin Meyerson of Harvard University and the other Barbara Terrett of ACTION, the American Council to Improve Our Neighborhoods. They wrote, "[J]ust as the citizens of this country have repeatedly succeeded together in spite of many a stupidity or speculation along the way, so they will see their own interest in meeting a challenge of Metropolis in Ferment, too, and will devise a hundred ways of meeting it for every form it takes."[61]

UNHAPPY PROCESS OF CHANGING

The discourse of the first fifteen years of the postwar period laid the rhetorical foundation for the claim of urban decline. Because that foundation had frequently been countered by commentators more optimistic in outlook and by evidence not easily interpretable one way or the other, however, the discourse was never wholly consistent. Cities continued to play a major role in national life and wield influence within their metropolitan areas. The bleakness of urban decline was still overwhelmed by the brightness of the city's future. Slums might have invaded neighborhoods and blight spread throughout central business districts, but these afflictions, many commentators thought, would soon be eradicated by urban renewal. Population growth would not diminish, and, even in the face of suburbanization, cities would be reconfigured to adapt to new metropolitan realities.

As Meyerson and Terrett wrote, "Urban communities by their very diversity seem to encourage adaptation, birth, growth, transfer, or demise of activities as their importance rises or declines."[62] Households were leaving but not abandoning the cities. The editors of *Senior Scholastic* phrased this perspective for their juvenile audience: "In other words, although many people are deserting the cities proper, they are not severing their ties with them or their reliance on them."[63] The only flaw in this Polyannaish argument was the growing presence of minorities, a point that cannot be overemphasized. Until the early 1960s, however, that presence was a bothersome condition attracting concern rather than alarm.

Later, the problems of the city came to be seen as endemic to its existence, and thus as contradictions that would not disappear with national growth or self-renewal. But in the 1940s and 1950s, such attitudes were rare. Nevertheless, the flight of affluent and middle-income households, industrial investors, and retailers along with the difficulties of attracting developers to urban renewal projects all portended an overall dissatisfaction with the city.

If one had to move or invest, equal consideration had to be given to the soon-to-be prosperous central city and the growing suburbs. Either way, the advice was to stay within the metropolitan area; it was not threatened. Commentator ambivalence was finely tuned; passionate embrace and outright rejection were rarely mentioned possibilities.

Only a few commentators appreciated the moral implications of what was happening. One senses a hint of this in the comments by

Phillip Hauser. In 1958, he reflected on the pace of urban decline. "When the time came to grow obsolete and decay," Hauser wrote, "we did this in the American way, too. We did not decay structure by structure, we decayed by whole sub-division, by community and by a neighborhood at a time."[64]

Suburbanization, as we now know, became the physical manifestation of a moral rejection of the city and its social problems. Those locating in the central city were poor and minority households, slumlords, and firms in declining industrial sectors. Physical deterioration became rampant, the city's political influence was eroded, the economic future looked bleak, and social disintegration lurked on the horizon. Urban decline in the mid-sixties would become irrefutable and seemingly irreversible.

From One Crisis to the Next

CHAPTER 6

Every Problem a Racial Dimension

Although urban decline was arguably one of the most prominent
domestic problems of the 1950s, along with civil rights, subsequent historical events threatened to displace it from public
consciousness. Political unrest and cultural turmoil, the traumatic loss
of young men and women in Southeast Asia, and the deaths of the
nation's charismatic leaders maneuvered for center stage in a wrenching drama that exploded the myth of an American nation anchored
in contentment, common aspirations, and shared prosperity. America seemed to be unraveling from within, while its international prestige and position became increasingly tenuous. The problems of the
city receded in comparison.

Ultimately, urban problems were redefined rather than displaced.
Momentous events shook the cities. Protest and violence resonated
with racial tensions, and race eventually became the defining characteristic of the urban crisis. From the early 1960s through to the mid-
1970s, its haunting specter pulled together the multiple strands of the
discourse on urban decline.

In 1968, Richard M. Nixon, a man who ironically would make
his own contribution to the traumas and doubts besetting the United
States, concluded his presidential acceptance speech to the Republi-

can National Convention in the following way: "As we look at America, we see cities enveloped in smoke and flame. We hear sirens in the night. We see Americans hating each other; killing each other at home. And as we see and hear these things millions of Americans cry out in anger: Did we come all this way for this?"[1] Of course, the unsettling dilemmas facing the country involved more than urban decline and extended well beyond the consequences of growth and prosperity.

More than ever before, Americans were acting collectively and outside normal political channels to establish their identities, gain control over their lives, and protect themselves from oppression and harm. As they did, the temporarily-hidden fissures within society emerged into fuller view. The Civil Rights Movement, with its sit-ins, Freedom rides, voter registration drives, and later calls for Black Power, grabbed national attention and confronted decades of institutionally-embedded discrimination. Women's Liberation unsettled the relations between men and women in the home, at the workplace, and in public life. A movement much more diffused than these two, often termed "the counterculture," challenged prevailing beliefs about free speech, marriage, upward mobility, and the underpinnings of American democracy; "hippies" dropped out and "turned on," radicals joined organizations such as Students for a Democratic Society to confront The System. Others dedicated themselves to an environmental movement that called for alternative energy sources, environmental protections, and ecological awareness. Many young people joined VISTA and set out as volunteers to help the residents of poverty-stricken rural communities and distressed urban neighborhoods.

The Anti-War Movement eventually displaced Civil Rights in the public consciousness and on the nightly news of national television networks. Though centered on the campuses of colleges and universities, it also reached outward to the streets, construction sites, churches, and government agencies. Protesting against the American presence in Vietnam, as well as military excursions in Cambodia and Laos, antiwar activists incessantly challenged the policies of Presidents Richard Nixon and Lyndon Johnson, marched on the Pentagon, and confronted institutions that they labeled complicit in the American war machine. The police riots at the Chicago Democratic Convention in 1968 and the National Guard killings at Kent State in 1970 were the most infamous incidents in an unprecedented democratic uprising against an unpopular foreign policy.

The Vietnam War was only one of the many military conflicts that threatened to tear apart the social fabric that had kept the nation whole for nearly a century. President John Kennedy in 1962 virtually orchestrated the Cuban Missile Crisis, risking war with the Soviet Union over the deployment of missiles on that island nation. The Cold War was fought out in Berlin as that city became more permanently divided and its western half ever more isolated. Of course, we never ceased our interventions in Latin America, Chile being the most prominent example of the early 1970s. Vietnam, though, dominated foreign policy, leading eventually to President Johnson's decision not to seek reelection, an event counted as a victory by antiwar activists.

Further contributing to the shattering of a mythical American cohesion and the erosion of American confidence was the heightened vulnerability of national leadership to removal and assassination. Lyndon Johnson withdrew from the Presidency and, seven years later, Richard Nixon became the first U.S. president to resign under threat of impeachment. Assassins killed Martin Luther King, Jr. (1968), Malcolm X (1965), and both President Kennedy and his brother Robert.

From a perspective that privileged consensus and "the nation," America had little of which to be proud. It seemed a violent society, one rotting from within and without legitimate leadership. The country's leaders offered prosperity, space exploration, and winning the Cold War as national goals, but they failed to achieve consensus as people from a variety of backgrounds relentlessly questioned the discrepancies between claims to democracy, humanitarianism, and freedom, and the actual conditions under which many Americans lived.

Because the cities were the sites of numerous protests by antiwar and civil rights activists, and of the less confrontational (but still disconcerting) "be-ins" and "happenings" of hippies, and also because their plight deepened and future dimmed as resources shifted into military coffers, public commentators recast the discourse on urban decline and extended rather than pushed it aside. The fact that the cities were the communication centers from which national traumas were broadcast and the places where many commentators lived made these debatably "urban" events newsworthy. The city, though, was not privileged: The counterculture favored both organic gardening and urban communes (Haight–Ashbury in San Francisco becoming its model of city living), the antiwar movement had difficulty extending its organizational skills to urban constituencies, the women's movement transcended place, and fervent environmentalists were more concerned with a yet-unspoiled countryside. On the other hand, the Civil Rights Movement reached out to housing activists and called for increased minority employment on construction sites and in local governments, thereby making contact with the cities.

During the first few years of the sixties, the discourse on urban decline maintained a relatively loose, though transitional, character, deploying many different themes. Slums and inadequate housing, blight, sprawl, suburbanization, minority migration, and economic decentralization alternated as major symptoms and causes of the deterioration of the central city, while traffic congestion played a minor role and governmental fiscal instability, although acknowledged, only slowly emerged into public consciousness. Commentators seemed to be searching for the discursive element that would fuse the discourse and give it moral weight and broad symbolic meaning.

In 1963, racial disorders in Birmingham, Savannah, Cambridge (Maryland), Chicago, and Philadelphia began to reshape the representation of urban decline. By the summer of 1967, the discourse had been crystallized by a single issue around which all the other symptoms and causes could be arranged. The sociologist Nathan Glazer in 1967 called "The Negro Problem" the "most decisive of the social problems that we think of when we consider the urban crisis."[2]

The ills of the central city in the 1960s, and through the early years of the subsequent decade, became almost exclusively attached to urban blacks. As Glazer wrote in 1970, "Almost every urban problem in the United States has a racial dimension, and the racial dimension in almost every problem is a key factor."[3] African Americans were situated at the core of physical deterioration, white flight, anemic capital investment, crime, poverty, poor schools, and unemployment. Binding these core themes together was fear, fear that centuries of racism and inequality would finally culminate in insurrection. With race as the dominant discursive thread, the various fragments of urban decline became whole cloth.

The discourse shifted abruptly from the physical state of the city to the characteristics of one of its fastest growing components, and the geographic focal point moved from the metropolis to the ghetto. The slum problem was transformed into the ghetto problem, sprawl and suburbanization were overwhelmed by racial polarization within the metropolis, and urban governance became a matter of Black Power. The city's function as a nurturer of immigrant upward mobility did not seem to apply to African Americans from the South. Blight was isolated under the rubric of urban renewal, a program that quickly earned the epithet "Negro removal." Even the nascent fiscal problems of city governments were bound to the presence of the nonwhite minority. Their tax contributions were minimal and their public service needs extensive.

With the African American population expanding, the suburbs closed to it, and racial discrimination and poverty seemingly insoluble, the future of the central city looked bleaker than had yet been imagined. Whereas in 1963 William Foster, the editor of *The American City,* wrote of "the brightening morning of the golden urban age" being brought about by hundreds of renewal projects across the land, by 1969 *Newsweek* had titled its March 17 issue "The Sick, Sick Cities" and quoted with little skepticism political scientist Edward Banfield's opinion that "[t]he serious problems of the cities are largely insoluble and will be for the foreseeable future."[4] Little changed in the next five years. Mayor Coleman Young of Detroit told the editors of *Ebony* that "[i]n the mid-1970s, the continuing disintegration of large American cities is precipitating a national urban crisis threatening the very existence of the nation."[5]

That crisis, as this and the following chapter demonstrate, quickly extinguished whatever ambivalence had lingered from an earlier period. Then, urban renewal seemed poised to eliminate slums and blight and to stanch the flow of white middle-class families to the sub-urbs. Urban decline was no longer a list of curable ills but a problem both embarrassing and insoluble. African Americans became the scapegoat for urban decline. Linked to race, urban decline could not be overcome simply by adding capital and households to the city. Institutions and social behaviors transcending the geographic bound-aries of the city had to change, and change in ways that redressed decades of prejudice, discrimination, and oppression.

The discourse thus turned to the social responsibility and civic obligations of those outside the cities and of those within but insu-lated from the poverty and physical decay experienced by ghetto dwellers. By admitting, even if obliquely, to racism, white society became reluctantly complicit in urban decline. If urban decline was (now) inseparable from the concentration of minority poor in cities and insoluble in the absence of the cessation of racial discrimination, and, if racism was a dynamic whose roots grew from white society's most fertile soil; then the return of the cities to prosperity and desir-ability would occur only when white society recognized its moral obligations and took responsibility for its contribution to the geo-graphic embeddedness of socioeconomic and political inequalities.

Framed in this way, the conditions of cities in decline became overwhelming. Urban renewal was not going to be effective and, fur-thermore, was being stalled by investors who feared racial unrest and subsequent abandonment of cities by the white population. Indeed, the common response was to flee. The white middle class had already begun its out-migration, and now the white working class followed. Businesses redirected their investments to the suburbs. Even middle-income minorities tried to leave, only to find their path blocked by discrimination. Whatever the practical advice listeners and readers took away from the discourse, the clear recommendation was to avoid living or investing in these cities. For now, if not for a long time to come, the suburbs were the safe bets. Such advice distanced sub-urbanites physically from the cities and insulated them from their social obligations.

In the early 1960s, a number of commentators flirted briefly with a slowing of suburbanization and a return to the city. Their optimism was unfounded and quickly pushed aside by the eruption of race riots. Subsequently, commentators explored the changing economic functions of the central city, considered the "suburban noose," and assessed the potential for even greater federal assistance. With race looming ominously over every debate and solutions particularly elusive, the discourse by the early 1970s reached a high point of despair—the "urban crisis" was officially announced.

NOT TO BECOME BIGGER AND BETTER

Despite continued population loss from the central cities during the 1960s and early 1970s, a loss accelerated by riots, references to a return to the city by suburbanites and related hopes for an urban resurgence appeared both at the period's start and at its end. Fueled by an awareness of the many-sidedness of urban decline, a number of commentators engaged in what might be cynically viewed as denial. It was, however, a minority position and difficult to sustain against the weight of contrary evidence. Eventually, demographic despair became dominant and denial untenable.

In 1962, the editors of *U.S. News & World Report* asked whether a flight from suburban communities was underway. They pointed to a slowdown in the "headlong rush to the suburb" and an increasing disenchantment with suburban life: costly and time-consuming commuting, skyrocketing real estate taxes, and burdensome home maintenance. Households were turning instead to apartment living, a form of housing associated with the cities. Between 1955 and 1962, apartments had jumped from 8 percent to 28 percent of total new housing units.[6]

Little more was heard about this trend until the early 1970s. In reference to rural–urban rather than urban–suburban migration, *U.S. News & World Report* pointed out that whereas metropolitan population growth had occurred at a rate of 1.6 percent each year in the 1960s, between 1970 and 1972 it had fallen to 1.2 percent.[7] The suburban growth rate between 1950 and 1960 had been four times that of the central cities, whereas between 1960 and 1963 the suburban growth rate was only two and a half times greater. Comparing central city growth to suburban county growth, William Foster was optimistic: "Expressed another way, during the past three years an average of 77,500 people moved into each of the central city counties. In that same period, an average of only 28,200 moved into one of the suburban counties. These are scarcely symptoms of a death-bed rattle."[8] Such a pro-city viewpoint, though, was based on a disingenuous substitution of counties for suburbs.

Nonetheless, municipal planners also claimed a "small but definite trickle of middle-class whites into cities after years of suburban exile." A combination of factors operated to make suburban living ostensibly less desirable: a sudden and dramatic rise in energy costs, no-growth policies in the suburbs, a considerable fall-off in rural–urban migration, a desire for smaller families, a rebellion against suburban conformity, and the turn to apartment living. The editors of one magazine concluded that "[o]ver the long haul, urban specialists see conditions favoring a return to health for cities."[9]

Robert Moses, New York's "city builder," consistently maintained that the cities were vibrant and desirable despite evidence of counterurbanization. As early as 1968 he proclaimed that "[t]here are quite a few people moving back into the city. These are people who never were really happy in the suburbs, away from the sights, sounds and smells of the city streets. The minute their children grow up, they want to get back into town, where they feel at home."[10] Moses's faith was not shared by other urban experts. His implicit equating of suburbia with a family's child-rearing years was unacceptable to Robert Wood, the former undersecretary of the Department of Housing and Urban Development. Wood noted wryly that "[p]eople are not going to turn around and abandon their barbecue pits and crabgrass." Neither did George Sternlieb, the director of the Center for Urban Policy Research at Rutgers University, envision a rush back to the cities. He offered a different reason than Wood, though: "People want to live where the jobs are. The jobs are mainly in the suburbs."[11]

The purported trek back to the city was overwhelmed by a continuation of the earlier decade's leakage of central city population.

The evidence seemed indisputable. James Cunningham, director of a neighborhood alliance in Pittsburgh, pointed out that between 1950 and 1960 "[o]f the twenty largest cities, twelve lost population during the last ten years. Of the ten largest, nine lost population." He went on to note that "eight families move to the suburbs for every family that moves back to the city."[12] Overall, the suburbs grew by eleven million people between 1960 and 1966, whereas the cities gained about one and a half million people by 1963, "then stopped cold."[13] The counterurban trend drowned out any migration from the suburbs to the central cities.

Suburban growth and urban decline did not occur evenly across the country. Estimates by the Census Bureau in 1969 suggested that while major cities such as New York, Chicago, and Philadelphia—centers of finance and commerce—might be attracting more people than they lost, most other cities, particularly manufacturing centers such as Pittsburgh, Detroit, Cleveland, and St. Louis, would continue to have fewer in-migrants than out-migrants. Only Washington, D.C., and Los Angeles were expected to have above-average growth.[14] In the aggregate, the population of the fifty largest cities increased by 4.8 million, or 4.5 percent, between 1960 and 1970, indicating that some central cities were growing. Most of this growth, though, was in cities in the South and West, particularly in California.[15]

The slowing of metropolitan growth in the 1970s suggested that rapid suburbanization and the further expansion of megalopolis might be over. Nevertheless, metropolitan areas did not lose their appeal. Subsequent analyses discovered that between 1970 and 1975 the population of the largest cities and suburbs grew by 4.2 percent.[16]

Rural population, moreover, continued to shrink, and experts were concerned that continued rural decline would require federal assistance to the countryside and exacerbate problems in the cities. In fact, during the late 1960s federal officials and elected representatives debated the need to balance economic and population growth between urban and rural areas.[17]

Other commentators rehearsed now-familiar themes related to suburban sprawl. In 1966 the editors of *U.S. News & World Report* wrote that "[f]or many decades, city growth had been characterized by a steady oozing out from the edges—a suburban 'sprawl' that has destroyed green areas in its relentless and planless spread."[18] Fewer commentators than previously, though, expressed wonderment and alarm at megalopolis. *Changing Times* voiced a perspective frequently heard during this period, one that equated population growth with an increase in the number of full-size cities: "Every month we add to our population a city the size of Toledo. Every year we add a new Philadelphia." Its conclusion was even less restrained: "Cities grow, not to become bigger and better but to become grotesque, misshapen, unmanageable, and unlivable."[19]

AGITATORS NAMED DISEASE AND DESPAIR

What made the years between 1960 and the recession of 1973–1975 unique in the discourse on urban decline was the emergence of a single theme—race—that unified the discourse's various fragments and converted urban decline into a societywide problem. The problem was the concentration, misery, and rebellion of African Americans in central cities. The reaction was one of fear and eventually panic. Commentators now had to recognize the impact of racial prejudice and institutional discrimination on the cities.

Max Ways of *Fortune* magazine, a business monthly, wrote in 1966 that " 'The Negro Problem' represents a crisis within a crisis, a specific and acute syndrome in a body already ill from more general disorders." Continuing, he offered specifics: "The double crisis in the U.S. can be seen as a rear-end collision in which accelerating Negro expectations have rammed into a sluggish tendency of American whites to demand too little of the quality of life in the city and to appraise too humbly the quality of citizenship that the city of the future should demand of them."[20] As the editor of *Life* had noted three years earlier, "The city is . . . replacing the South as the arena of our No. 1 domestic problem, that of Negro rights."[21]

Census data for 1960 indicated that, on the basis of their 1950 boundaries, all of the fifty largest cities had experienced an increase in the non-white proportion of their populations.[22] Only cities that had annexed predominantly white suburbs experienced a shrinkage, suggesting a statistical concealment—reminiscent of earlier observations by Mabel Walker—rather than an actual countertrend. Overall, the rate of growth of the African American minority in nearly every one of the fifty cities was greater than that of the white majority. And it was hardly surprising that the number of minority households did not increase proportionately in the suburbs.

In fact, African Americans were concentrated in a small number of cities and within specific neighborhoods. Charles Silberman, a frequent commentator on racial issues, reported that "[m]ost of the Negroes moving North have crowded into the slums of the twelve largest cities, which today hold 60 percent of the Negroes living outside the Deep South."[23] Negroes leaving the South in the immediate postwar period had traveled disproportionately to the North and the Midwest. The heaviest out-flows were from Mississippi, Alabama, North Carolina, South Carolina, Georgia, Arkansas, and Louisiana, and the heaviest in-flows to New York, Illinois, Michigan, Ohio, and New Jersey.

At the same time that Negroes were moving into the central cities of these five states, whites were moving out. Chicago and Philadelphia were typical. Between 1950 and 1960, 678,000 whites left the Windy City, while an additional 153,000 Negroes took up residence. The comparable figures for Philadelphia were 344,000 and 63,000, respectively. As a result, the percentages of Negroes in these cities jumped from 13.6 to 22.9 percent and from 18.1 to 26.4 percent, respectively.[24]

The stark discrepancies between the out-flows and the in-flows meant that cities were also experiencing overall population decline. Between 1960 and 1968, the white population shrank in absolute terms in all of the central cities, whereas the minority population swelled. These numbers, moreover, included prosperous cities in the South and West.[25] William Shannon in 1965 wrote in *Commonweal* that "[i]n the past fifteen years, nearly a million whites have moved out of New York City and nearly a million Negroes and Puerto Ricans have taken their place. There can be no effective solution to this flight by the whites until the Negroes cease to be associated in white minds with crime, drug addiction, juvenile delinquency and slums."[26]

An article in *U.S. News & World Report* in 1966 could barely conceal its alarm at the prospects: "If present trends continue, Negroes will outnumber whites in 8 out of the 10 biggest cities in the U.S.— or come close to it—by the year 2000, a date that is now just 34 years away." Pointing out that such a numerical majority could be translated into political influence, the editors suggested that "[u]nless something occurs to check the current trends, some of the most important cities of this country are going to wind up under Negro control."[27]

This expanding urban population was hardly unique in its rural origins, but this was certainly a detriment, given the incompatibility of rural job skills and postwar employment opportunities. *Senior Scholastic* claimed that "many of the blacks who have moved to the cities came from rural regions, lacking the education and training necessary to crack the increasingly specialized urban job market."[28] Educational levels were low, and once in the city these migrants often were underemployed or unemployed or ended up on public welfare. Negro unemployment throughout the postwar period remained double that of whites, and from 1954 through to 1968 had stayed above the recession level of 6 percent that economists considered acceptable. Moreover, black men were disproportionately concentrated in the least desirable jobs paying relatively low wages, and were more than twice as likely as white men to have unskilled or service jobs: "In 1950 five out of every six Negroes who migrated to Northern cities found jobs. By 1960 the figure was down to four out of six."[29] As a result, minority neighborhoods in central cities were places of high unemployment and often developed irregular economies that operated on the margins of mainstream economic activity.

The employment problem contributed directly to the poverty experienced by black families. Non-whites living in central cities were almost twice as likely to be poor as whites, and 81 percent of the non-white families headed by women lived below the poverty line.[30] Mayor Sam Massell of Atlanta, speaking at an interracial luncheon forum in that city in 1971, claimed that "[i]n the past ten years, Atlanta lost nearly 60,000 whites and gained approximately 70,000 blacks. Reports indicate that our average white-homeowner family of medium size has an annual income of $13,400. Our average black-homeowner family of medium size has an annual income of $8,900." The average black home-renter earned $5,600 per year.[31] Thus, whereas the net flow of population favored growth in Atlanta, quite an anomaly when compared to most declining cities, the net balance of income was highly unfavorable and typical. Daniel Patrick Moynihan—then an advisor to President Johnson on Urban Affairs—commented in 1967 that "[p]overty in the United States is now largely an urban phenomenon" . . . [and] . . . "[u]rban poverty is concentrated among Negroes and other ethnic minorities."[32]

For the poor, one haven was public assistance. During the late 1960s and early 1970s, the rapid expansion of welfare rolls became another dimension of the urban crisis. By 1963, the City of Chicago provided nearly 90 percent of its Aid to Dependent Children, its major public assistance program, to African American families. Nationwide, 56 percent of Negro children had received public assistance at some time during their lives, while the comparable figure for white children was 8 percent. The welfare problem was exacerbated by broken homes, high rates of illegitimacy, and crime.[33]

Adding to the alarm experienced by the white majority was that non-white women were giving birth at a rate nearly half again as great as that for white women. Although urbanization had previously been associated with low birth rates—that is, with rural migrants eventually abandoning their desire for large families—black families, particularly those on welfare, came to be viewed as unmindful of the logic that linked small families to city life. Theodore White, in his book *The Making of the President 1964,* provided a particularly alarmist response: "Both Negro and white families are haunted by the biological potential of the despairing Negro for upsetting the entire course of American urban civilization."[34]

Urban decline eventually became inseparable from the African American ghetto in the discourse. Most southern blacks had migrated to northern industrial cities. There, they were concentrated in deteriorating neighborhoods plagued by abandoned housing. Often, they ended up living in large, dehumanizing public housing projects. The editors of *Life* magazine commented in 1965 that "[t]he Negro ghetto is no place for a good life. It is *the* shame of the modern American city."[35]

Two economists wrote that the "decline of central cities has been hastened by a conviction in the white community, both individual and corporate, that the ghetto would continue its rapid expansion, carrying along its associated problems of concentrated poverty and social disorganization."[36] Possibly inadvertently, they attributed decline to a white-held belief rather than to the decisions and actions of powerful corporations, governments, and households with the means to flee the city or isolate themselves within it. They also captured the fear that the white community felt toward the ghetto rather than any compassion for its victims. The fear was that the ghetto would migrate to the suburbs.

Within the ghettos, the schools were woefully inadequate, crime rates were high, police and fire services insufficient, and retail, personal care, and medical services likely to be of poor quality and overpriced. The expanding presence of minority students in city school systems was particularly worrisome because it often coincided with falling test scores and rising dropout rates. It became another reason for whites to avoid the city. Edmund Faltermayer reported in *Fortune* that "Philadelphia's population, for example, is about 30 percent nonwhite, but in the public schools the proportion is 59 percent."[37] White families were avoiding the public schools, either placing their children in private schools or leaving the city altogether. The decisions made by these families were validated by a "tired Harlem teacher" in *Look:* "You don't worry about teaching kids here. You just keep them from killing each other and from killing you."[38]

Just as race fused the disparate strands of the discourse, the ghetto served as the symbolic reference for the many social ills that early urban sociologists had associated with social disorganization and the city. As the National Advisory Commission on Civil Disorders wrote, "The ghetto too often means men and women without jobs, families without men, and schools where children are processed instead of educated, until they return to the street—to crime, to narcotics, to dependency on welfare, and to bitterness and resentment against society in general and white society in particular."[39]

Isolated from the larger city, the ghetto provided few opportunities for economic or social mobility. There, segregation and poverty intersected "to destroy opportunity and hope and to enforce failure."[40] Unlike past ethnic enclaves in American cities, the black ghetto lacked the resources to be viable or to provide the wherewithal for its inhabitants to combine social with residential mobility.

The social psychologist Kenneth Clark assigned blame: "The dark ghetto's invisible walls have been erected by white society, by those who have power, both to confine those who have no power, and to perpetuate their powerlessness. The dark ghettos are social, political, educational and—above all—economic colonies."[41] African Americans faced a structure of institutional discrimination that denied them access to quality education, job training, legal justice, good-paying jobs, decent housing, adequate health care, and numerous other services that might create the opportunity for them to escape from the conditions in which they found themselves mired. One commentator attributed blame outside the ghettos: "The difficulties are a consequence of two centuries of slavery and a century of segregation, economic deprivation, inadequate education, and political inequality."[42]

The intractability of The Negro Problem led eventually to understandings that suggested that its roots were so deep-seated as to constitute a culture of poverty. Drawing on the work of the anthropologist Oscar Lewis, Nathan Glazer and others put forth the notion that poverty itself could become self-perpetuating as the poor passed on self-defeating attitudes and behaviors and failed to create or reproduce attitudes and behaviors that allowed for social advancement.[43] Daniel Moynihan, in a famous 1965 report prepared at the U.S. Department of Labor, claimed that "[a]t the heart of the deterioration of the fabric of Negro society is the deterioration of the Negro family." He went on to assert that "the family structure of lower class Negroes is highly unstable, and in many urban centers is approaching complete breakdown."[44] In response, the political scientist Edward Banfield suggested that one possible solution to such a dilemma involved removing children from their parents so that they would have an opportunity to grow up outside, and thus away from, the influence of this debilitating culture.[45]

The problems of the ghetto thus seemed insurmountable; either they were so complex as to defy any but the most radical solution or they were so embedded in the values and behaviors of ghetto inhabitants that the ghetto would have to be destroyed in order for its people to be saved. Those on the outside were fearful. Many were also indignant that such conditions existed in the world's richest nation. Nevertheless, they did not know how to change the situation in any significant way. Those on the inside were, by necessity, less fatalistic.

Ghetto residents were frustrated. Beginning in the mid-1960s and extending to the early 1970s, this frustration led to summer after summer of racial disorders. In black, Puerto Rican, and Chicano neighborhoods in inner cities across the country, grievances accumulated so that some single, seemingly isolated incident was enough to unleash anger and send hundreds and thousands onto the streets to chant demands, confront police, loot and burn stores, and articulate in raw terms an ideology of Black Power that more radical leaders were advocating. Rioters, police, and innocent bystanders were killed and injured; property damage in the ghettos was extensive. Ironically, the material consequences fell primarily on African Americans, the homes they rented and owned, and the stores they frequented.

"From Providence, R.I., to Portland, Ore.," *Time* magazine reported in 1967, "communities large and small heard the snipers staccato song, smelled the fire bomber's success, watched menacing crowds on the brink of becoming mindless mobs." The riots had begun in a few cities in 1963; in 1967, riots seemed to be ubiquitous and contagious, spreading from one city to the next. By early August of that year, thirty-one cities had experienced the frustration of the black ghetto. The death toll had reached eighty-six individuals, another 2,056 had been injured, and 11,094 arrested.[46] The worst riot, a week-long affair, had been in the Watts district of Los Angeles. There, thirty-four people had been killed, 1,032 injured, 3,952 individuals arrested, six hundred buildings wholly or partially destroyed, and approximately $50 million in property damaged. Nearly every building along the community's main avenue was either ruined, fire-bombed, or looted.[47]

Watts' dubious distinction was taken over in 1967 by Detroit. The precipitating act was a Detroit Police Department raid on a private social club in which illegal drinking and gambling activity were known to take place. On a warm and humid Saturday night, July 22, the club was host to a good-size party. Arrests among the eighty-two patrons attracted a large crowd, and rumors circulated that excessive force had been used in the raid. Incited by that, and by an earlier incident in which a black serviceman had been killed by a gang of white youths, the crowd grew in number and hostility. By early morning, an estimated three thousand residents had gathered, and a police sweep was unsuccessful in sending them home. Looting began, fires were set, and soon a riot had erupted that would not end for five days.

Forty-three people were killed—33 Negro and 10 white—more than 7,200 persons were arrested, and nearly 2,000 injured. An estimated 1,400 fires were reported, and 1,700 stores looted. Property damage was estimated at $22 million, excluding the loss of business stocks and private furnishings as well as damages to churches and charitable institutions. Seventy percent of the over three hundred structures damaged by fire had to be demolished. To contain the riot, 4,700 U.S. Army troops had been used, 7,100 National Guardsmen, over 2,000 city police, and 350 state troopers.[48]

Whites and non-whites alike were victims, and those who lived in these cities were in a state of shock bordering on panic. White suburbanites were increasingly fearful, and urban commentators were quick to deploy alarmist imagery. A few weeks after the Detroit riot, *U.S. News & World Report* proclaimed that "anarchy has become a threat to all of America's cities, including the nation's capital."[49] Words and phrases such as *anarchy, guerrilla war, snipers, looting, race war, mob,* and *riot* focused attention on the lack of self-control and community restraint within the ghetto and the inability of the larger society to contain or rectify the ghetto's problems. Without such controls, the riots' causes were unleashed, and the combination of anger, frustration, and unpredictability was truly frightening.

The editors of *U.S. News & World Report* attempted to allay such fears by following up their article on urban anarchy with one meant to dispell thoughts of national chaos. In the same issue, they included a piece on the pleasant and safe towns and small cities of America, places inhabited by law-abiding citizens who were astonished by the riots. These citizens lived in communities such as Concord, Massachusetts, and Middlebury, Vermont, or in the small towns in the Shenandoah Valley of Virginia or Bighorn Basin in Wyoming. So as to assure that the point would not be lost, the article concluded with a moralizing optimism: "But the fact that so many Americans do live apart from the crime-ridden and riot-plagued central cities in an atmosphere of law, order and stability is seen as a reservoir of strength for the U.S."[50]

The next year, black America would lose its spiritual and political leader to an assassin's bullet. On April 4, 1968, at 6:05 P.M., Martin Luther King, Jr., was gunned down at a motel in Memphis, Tennessee. He died an hour later. African Americans once again took to the streets. Between April 4 and April 11, riots erupted in 125 cities. The litany of consequences was familiar: 39 people killed, more than 3,500 injured, over 20,000 arrested, approximately 2,600 cases of arson, and property damage exceeding $45 million. Almost 7,000 U.S. Army and National Guard troops were called out to support the police and quell the riots.[51]

The rhetoric became overheated. Stokely Carmichael, chairman of the Student Non-Violent Coordinating Committee (SNCC) and one of the more radical black leaders, told a gathering in Washington, D.C., the day after Dr. King's death that "[w]hen white America killed Dr. King last night, she declared war on us." White America had incurred debts to the black community and "[t]he execution of those debts," Carmichael continued, "will not be in the courtrooms. They are going to be in the streets. . . . There no longer needs to be intellectual discussions."[52]

For the following few years, each summer brought a fear that blistering temperatures, ghetto joblessness, and the conditions under which African Americans were forced to live would bring forth additional rounds of unrest. In May of 1971, *Time* magazine presented its summer forecast with this sentence: "It is the season for that glum annual speculation: Will the nation's cities erupt in racial violence?" There seemed to be no doubt because "the frustration of the ghettos is as deep or deeper now than it was at the height of the riot season several years ago. Some explosions seem almost certain."[53] Some people must have read this as unduly pessimistic, others as simply realistic.

In July of 1967, President Lyndon Johnson appointed the National Advisory Commission on Civil Disorders—also known as the Kerner Commission after its Chairman, Governor Otto Kerner of Illinois—to determine what had happened and why. Most importantly, Johnson wanted to know what could be done to prevent future occurrences. The Commission's basic conclusion, subsequently one of the most famous and oft-quoted sentences in the discourse, summed up the general mood of the time: "Our nation is moving toward two societies, one black, one white—separate and unequal."

The Commission report paid particular attention to the "most bitter fruits" of white racism: pervasive discrimination and segregation, black in-migration and white exodus, and black ghettos. These three ingredients catalyzed frustrated hopes, legitimated violence, and articulated the powerlessness felt by the African American minority. To this "explosive mixture" was added police brutality. Black frustrations were thereby directed at just those authorities whose task was to maintain order in the ghetto. In sum, the Commission maintained that the disorders were "symptoms of social ills that have become endemic in our society and now affect every American."[54]

The Kerner Commission thus laid the blame squarely on white society: "White racism is essentially responsible for the explosive mixture which has been accumulating in our cities since the end of World War II."[55] Conspiracy theories, unlike their appeal in the Kennedy assassination, failed to find adherents, except for ultraconservatives like Senator Strom Thurmond of South Carolina. He blamed the disturbances on "Communism, false compassion, civil disobedience, court decisions and criminal instinct."[56] The only conspiracy pointed out by the Kerner Commission, though, was that organized against blacks by a white society infected with institutional racism.

Attorney General Nicholas Katzenbach, in statements before a Senate subcommittee in 1966, was more precise and colorful in his interpretation of who was responsible: The riots, he claimed "were indeed fomented by agitators, agitators named disease and despair, joblessness and hopelessness, rat-infested housing and long-impacted cynicism."[57] The head of the mayor's human rights office in Boston was even more direct: "When the black kids find that they can't get a piece of the pie, they're going to get a piece of the action."[58] Commentators did not excuse the criminality associated with the riots. Rather, more important issues were being recognized: the frustration and anger of African Americans in an oppressive white society.

CLIMBING UP OVER THE WALLS

The historical persistence of "The Negro Problem" and the fact that rioters were mainly concentrated in urban ghettos led the discourse fairly directly to the notion that the problems of the cities—now collected under the rubric of the urban crisis—were endemic. Without dispersal of the ghetto, The Urban Crisis and "The Negro Problem" were simply inseparable: The inscrutable essence of the latter made the former virtually insoluble. The presence of African Americans — particularly those who were poor, jobless, uneducated, and frustrated—discouraged city living by the white middle-class, threatened downtown renewal by repulsing investors, burdened local governments, turned away tourism and conventions, and tarnished the city's image.

No longer a physical attribute of the city, as it had been in an earlier period of the discourse, urban decline became equated with a group whose presence was geographically and morally threatening, one whose image now dominated perceptions of the city. Black presence ostensibly repelled those who were considered essential to reversing decline: white, educated, skilled, and relatively affluent individuals with good jobs, able to contribute more to the tax base than they take away, alien to crime and violence, and likely to create strong neighborhoods and support a vibrant central business district. Without this group, the city itself was doomed. Kenneth Clark made it patently clear that the Negro ghetto was a profound threat: "The

poor are always alienated from normal society, and when the poor are
Negro, as they increasingly are in the cities, a double trauma exists—
rejection on the basis of class and race is a danger to the stability of
society as a whole."[59]

Despite anecdotal evidence and wishful thinking that the middle
class would cease their suburban migration or even return to the city,
the discourse on decline was dominated by the possibility that the city
had to be abandoned to African Americans, Puerto Ricans, and other
minorities, all of whom comprised the ranks of the dangerous lower
class. Alex Poinsett, writing after the riots in the magazine *Ebony*,
expressed the view from the black community. His perspective evoked
opportunity. "[I]f the 1960s was the decade of direct action and street
rebellions against white racism," he wrote, "the 1970s can be the
decade of massive black political empowerment." Black control of
city governments could be a boon, but it was also fraught with difficulties. Poinsett continued: "Since the cities are getting poorer as they
get blacker, since they are plagued with shrinking tax resources, rising demands for public services and a chronic potential for explosion,
it appears—at first glance—that blacks can merely gain control of
white-abandoned urban misery. But the control of city government
brings a significant degree of political and economic leverage."[60]

Poinsett's bittersweet opportunity was indicative of a broad
recognition that the urban crisis was insurmountable. Mary McGrory
suggested in the Jesuit publication *America* that "nobody knows
exactly where to begin to halt the appalling disturbances in the
cities."[61] Whereas other immigrants had been able to use the city to
advance along the path of upward mobility, that path seemed closed
to African Americans. "The Negro is unlike the European immigrant
in one crucial respect," Charles Silberman noted, "he is colored. And
that makes all the difference."[62]

Many viewed the contemporary city as one of the gravest social
dilemmas the nation had ever faced, but could only offer platitudes
as solution: "The slums are too large and too numerous, the plight of
the Negro too desperate, for the U.S. to pin its hopes for racial calm
on police action or hasty economic palliatives. What is needed in
addition is proof positive to the Negro that he can find justice and

hope in America, and that he can find it soon."[63] The solution was to be found in a compassionate society that guaranteed equal opportunity for all its citizens.[64]

Generally, commentators were resigned to an urban crisis without end. All that could be hoped for was an accommodation to periodic rebellions and the isolation of the ghetto from "civilized" society. The political scientist Norton Long proposed a startling and unforgettable response along these lines. He argued in 1971 that the only way that the city would survive would be through the development of a new specialty. "[P]erhaps the most noteworthy . . .", Long suggested, ". . . is a role as an Indian reservation for the poor, the deviant, the unwanted, and for those who make a business or career of managing them for the rest of society."[65]

George Sternlieb agreed with Long but also took a position quite at odds with the great majority of commentators. Sternlieb claimed that "the crisis of the city is not a crisis of race." Rather, "[t]he crisis of the city is a crisis of function. The major problem of the core areas of our cities is simply their lack of economic value." He asked, "What is left to the city that it does better than someplace else?" His answer: The city had become the metaphorical equivalent of a "sandbox," a place to store those unable to engage in "the serious things of life."[66]

In 1971, Sternlieb was interviewed by *U.S. News & World Report.* The following exchange took place[67]:

Q: Should the government discontinue its urban-renewal and
   model cities programs?
A: No. We've got to have a sandbox.
Q: Are you saying that facetiously or for real?
A: I am saying that for real because I don't want these people
   climbing up over the walls, and that's a tax that I am willing
   to pay.

In Sternlieb's view, the city had become a reserve for unproductive individuals supported solely by government programs that did little to ameliorate the problems to which they were directed. Long and Sternlieb thus seemed to use the urban crisis to isolate minorities and the poor from white society and to blame them for their condition. In response, Murray Bookchin wrote that "[n]o longer are the elements of the city cemented by mutual aid, a shared culture, and a sense of community."[68]

The riots highlighted the African American presence, the problems of the ghetto, and the consequences for the city and its suburbs. Through the sixties and into the early 1970s, race emerged as the central element of the discourse to such an extent that it became synonymous with the decay of cities. What characterized a declining city? Answer: a large black population concentrated in ghettos. What caused the city's crisis conditions and its virtual abandonment by white households and investors? Answer: a large black population concentrated in ghettos.

Nonetheless, these answers failed to capture the degree to which white society and, by association, the suburbs were implicated in the city's decline. They also failed to register the fear, even panic, that ensued as African Americans took to the streets to protest the conditions under which they had been forced to live. Racial prejudice and discrimination had consequences beyond that of the cities and not all of urban decline could be easily fitted into the racial mold. Decline was increasingly unruly.

CHAPTER 7

Crisis of Our Cities

Race was the dominant theme of the discourse during these years of riots and unrest, but it was not the only element of urban decline to be put into discursive play. The modern city was undergoing what would be viewed in retrospect as a profound transformation in economic function. Its once-defining factories were closing down, and manufacturing employment was shrinking. Simultaneously, new office buildings were being built for expanding financial and business services and for the administrative headquarters of far-flung corporations. Overall, though, most large cities experienced a net loss of jobs, and this worsened local fiscal conditions. City governments were blocked from implementing the most obvious solution: the annexation of suburban areas where people and jobs were on the rise. The out-migration of middle class households, moreover, increased the proportion of poor and minority households within the cities. Government responses, particularly urban renewal, were increasingly deemed inadequate.

Each of these problems had a racial dimension. African Americans experienced higher rates of unemployment and poverty, were more dependent on public services than white families who had left for suburbia, suffered most from the loss of good-paying, entry-level manufacturing jobs, and were prevented from relocating to the suburbs where housing, schools, and employment opportunities were better. Race infiltrated each element of the discourse and bound one to the other in a single, tragic story.

In addition, race anchored urban decline deep in the historical consciousness of American society and brought to the surface a discomforting combination of fear and guilt. When joined to the business sector's seeming rejection of the city as a site for investment, the failure of governments to mount effective solutions, the continued spread of physical decay, and the isolation of declining cities from suburban prosperity, race fueled a spreading sense of crisis. Commentators who had once been fashionably pessimistic now were scandalized by the once-revered industrial city. Hopes for a turnabout were replaced by condemnation. The contradictions of urban development were simply overwhelming; the modern city seemed on the verge of total collapse.

Urban crisis, the term of choice used by commentators to express their fatalism, was a euphemism for *race.* Any ambivalence that might have remained after Detroit and Watts was drowned out by the cities' purported self-destruction. By claiming an intractable crisis, commentators severed their moral ties to places in decline and thereby reneged on their social obligations. Suburban and rural America, many seemed to be arguing, were not responsible for these bankrupt places where people had either succumbed to despair or lacked the capacity to overcome their condition. The practical advice instead became extreme—abandon the city!

APARTHEID ON A METROPOLITAN SCALE

In 1968, John Kain, an economics professor at Harvard University, published a much-cited study of the economic changes faced by forty large metropolitan areas. Central cities had continually lost employment relative to the suburbs. In 1948, these central cities had 67 percent of the manufacturing employment in their metropolitan areas. By 1963, their share had been reduced to 48 percent. The central city share of wholesaling activity went from 92 percent to 71 percent; retailing, from 75 percent to 45 percent; and services, from 85 percent to 69 percent. At the same time, the central city proportion of population fell from 64 percent to 56 percent.[1] This loss of jobs eventually had a devastating impact on the fiscal stability of big city governments, heightened the tension between central cities and their suburbs, and undermined the good intentions of federal and local programs.

Such consequences were not part of Kain's initial analysis. Kain believed that the decentralization of jobs was simply the continuation of a long-term trend that had been interrupted by wartime controls. He was optimistic about the possibility of a massive relocation of industrial investment back to the city and, at the same time, realistic about continued decentralization: "[M]uch of the postwar dispersal of manufacturing (and probably by extension many other kinds of employment) was simply a delayed redistribution. It follows that employment dispersal should slow down as this backlog of relocations is worked off."[2]

Alexander Ganz, research director at the Boston Redevelopment Authority, provided an even more pro-city interpretation of economic trends. Large cities, for Ganz, still served two major, irreplaceable functions: the production of an expanding flow of goods and services and the absorption and upgrading of disadvantaged migrants. The picture he painted was rosy: "[S]ince at least 1963, large cities are no longer net losers of jobs."[3] In fact, business, government, and personal services were offsetting declines in manufacturing, the central city's share of rapidly growing industries was similar to that of the suburbs, productivity in manufacturing in cities was rising, and service-sector growth in the cities exceeded that of suburbs.

David Birch, another academic economist, published in 1970 a study for the Committee for Economic Development that replicated Raymond Vernon's work of eleven years earlier on the economic function of city and suburbs. Vernon had pointed to an increasing specialization of the city, and Birch agreed: "As a result of relocation, the central city, which was once a concentrated, self-contained economic and residential whole, now finds itself becoming a relatively specialized segment of a rapidly growing area." That specialization was services. The data, Birch suggested, support the Darwinian assumption that "some forms of activity survive better than others in a central city environment, and that services survive the best."

Although the reader might take this as evidence of the emergence of a new urban function, and thus of an economic upturn, Birch's analysis implied otherwise. Pointing out that economic specialization was taking place faster in the older, larger and more established central cities, he stated that "[t]he tendency for central cities to become elite service centers appears, like rheumatism and decaying teeth, to be a strong function of age." Thus, he could only conclude that "[t]he young cities of 1970 will become the older cities of 2050 and, in the process, more than likely will pass through the typical phases of growth, saturation, and eventually stabilization and decline."[4]

Not all of the commentators were so quick to adopt the parallel between urban decline and old age. Charles Abrams, for one, hypothesized that age was just a surrogate for that particular type of economic growth that had set industrial cities on a path to prosperity. The cities in trouble, he wrote, "are principally the older central cities that grew up in the first flush of America's industrial revolution, have now aged, and are being challenged by the suburban push on their peripheries."[5] Urban decay stemmed both from a change in the city's economic functions and from new types of investment that were appearing beyond its boundaries. To that extent, unlike old age, urban decay was not inevitable.

Confounding an understanding of changing economic functions was a simultaneous diversion of capital investment away from the cities. Business seemed to be less and less interested in expanding within the central cities: "Costs are seen as growing too high, labor problems too great, uncertainty too discouraging."[6] As early as 1961, George Sternlieb had presented the findings of a survey that asked whether business was abandoning the big city. He pointed out that many businesses had already reacted to higher city taxes, transit problems, and extremely inflexible city expenses by shifting investments outside the cities. "For example," Sternlieb wrote, "one major retailing chain reports that it expects to close 10 to 20 downtown stores per year as leases expire. At the same time, of the 348 new stores it has opened in the past five years, 308 are located in suburban shopping centers." He concluded that "a clear majority [of business executives surveyed] have no great faith in growth of downtown real estate values, while a sizable minority feel that long-term investments in the downtown area make little sense."[7]

Manufacturing plants were also leaving the city. The Campbell Soup Company had located twenty of its twenty-six new plants in rural areas, whereas previously it had invested in urban areas. In fact, its first plant and headquarters were in Camden, New Jersey, which later became one of the more devastated cities in the country. The policy of the IBM corporation was to locate its manufacturing and engineering installations outside the big cities. *U.S. News & World Report* concluded that "[a] revolt is developing against big cities— against their traffic jams, pollution, crime and costs. Industries are fleeing, taking workers with them. The escape is to small towns— even to wide-open spaces."[8]

By 1970, not only the owners of commercial and industrial businesses, but also many residential investors had come to the conclusion that the central city was no longer desirable. A major problem affecting cities in decline was abandoned dwellings, empty housing units for which even the owners often could not be found. Philadelphia reported approximately 25,000 residences, mostly two- and three-story rowhouses, standing empty. Baltimore had over four thousand houses in this condition, and Boston more than one thousand. In Chicago, 150 structures were being abandoned each month, while officials in Detroit put their estimate at ten buildings per week. A study conducted by the University of Pennsylvania and Morgan State College in Baltimore noted that "[i]nvestors want out because of declining prices, negative cash flows, fear of collecting rents, and vandalism." Sternlieb appears in this same article to provide the conclusion: "Real estate investors take a long-range look at things. They have simply lost faith in the future of the inner city."[9]

This disinvestment had a detrimental impact on the fiscal condition of local governments, particularly since it meant a change in both the composition of city taxpayers and the users of public services. The flight of middle-class white households additionally meant the loss of consumer disposable income and of tax revenues for the city government's coffers. Those entering the cities—mainly poor whites and African Americans —further diminished the cities' financial viability. The new migrants "deliver[ed] about $3 in tax revenues but require[d] about $8 in public services."[10] The expanding population of 'deficit citizens'—as William Foster, editor of *The American City,* called them—and the decentralization of middle-class households and industry left city governments without sufficient resources to meet their obligations.[11] By implication, those who resided in the suburbs were "surplus citizens" who needed little public assistance and were able to afford the taxes that made for fiscally sound government.

Fiscal instability was a racial issue; popular perception equated deficit citizens to minorities. Who else was "impoverished, unskilled, and uneducated"? Mayor Sam Massell of Atlanta noted the connection between race and governmental performance at an interracial luncheon in 1971. He told the attendees that "[w]e cannot consider black as our only interest when the economic base of our city is being threatened. It is political blindness not to get alarmed when the city's resources begin to diminish while the governmental needs of its citizens grow at an accelerated pace."[12]

The economist Bennett Harrison was one of the few to resist blaming inner-city minorities for fiscal problems. Fiscal instability was not, he maintained, directly attributable to black presence. Rather, "[i]t is poverty and the shortage of central city public services which repel the middle class and exacerbate the central city fiscal crisis, not race per se."[13] Separating race from poverty and white flight in this way was an heroic but futile act, however. Race was increasingly the glue that bound together all of the perceived problems of the declining cities. Admittedly, it was not the only issue contributing to the erosion of the tax base, but it was the only one common to all of the city's ills, including the increasing gap between governmental expenditures and revenues. Moreover, race engendered so much fear and indecision that it could not be suppressed.

Regardless of what variables one factored into the fiscal equation, its basic form still showed that city revenues could not keep pace with expenditures. The city was facing a "money problem," the sociologist Nathan Glazer explained; it "is forced to tax business heavily, while it must depend on new business to provide jobs and a tax base."[14] Higher taxes on business, though, particularly when compared with suburban tax burdens, discouraged investors from expanding or starting up businesses in the city. As the demand for services increased, taxes were raised, businesses left, the tax base shrunk, tax revenues fell, and needs went unfilled, with the cycle destined to repeat itself.

For elected officials, the city was its government; if the government went bankrupt and could no longer deliver services, most investors and households would leave and the city would ultimately have to be abandoned. Elected officials were "most worried about . . . the danger of municipal bankruptcy plus inflation and high taxes which often combine to force taxpayers to pay more for less services."[15]

Viewed from this perspective, the fiscal squeeze was not just the result, but also a cause of urban decline: High taxes meant disinvestment from property, the flight of the middle class, the closing of businesses, and deteriorating infrastructure. William Shannon agreed: "Real estate taxes, sales taxes, and nuisance taxes are already high in the cities. As they go higher, they push more people to the suburbs."[16] Supposedly, property taxes could not be raised, yet they had to be if city government were to maintain services and address slums, blight, poverty, and widespread unemployment. To raise taxes, though, was to accelerate the flight of the city's businesses and households, its taxpayers.

Bernard Weissbourd attributed this fiscal squeeze to the actions of the federal government, a theme that would become more prominent in the discourse later. Up to this point in time, the federal government had been viewed as part of the solution, not part of the problem. "A case can be made," Weissbourd wrote to the contrary, "that the wealth produced by the cities has been drained out by federal taxes and redistributed first to agriculture, second to suburbia, and third to the cities."[17] This argument, if broadened, encompassed the more specific belief that the larger society was exploiting—or at least ignoring—the cities. That in turn fixed attention on the suburbs. For many pro-city commentators, suburban insularity blocked ghetto dispersal and made it unlikely that the central cities would achieve fiscal solvency.

C. W. Griffin, writing in 1966, commented on the inseparability of race prejudice, ghetto formation, and stunted upward mobility for African Americans. He pointed to "millions of Negroes, Puerto Ricans, and other victims of prejudice trapped in our teeming big-city ghettos." Minorities were not being admitted to suburbia, and "[t]o attempt at this time to persuade middle-class whites to accept lower-class Negroes as neighbors and class mates for their children would be hopelessly utopian. It strikes at the heart of the American dream of climbing the social ladder and pushing one's children a rung or two higher."[18]

Whites continued to flee the central cities, their numbers dropping from 47.6 million in 1960 to 45.5 million in 1968, while blacks continued to enter them. Approximately 9.5 million blacks had resided in the central cities in 1960. By 1968, that number had grown to 11.9 million. A popular image to describe the situation was that of the doughnut. As portrayed by the editors of *Senior Scholastic*, "The dough (the more educated and above-average income group) is in the sprawling suburbs. In the inner cities is an increasingly deprived 'hole' of poverty and problems."[19]

The suburbs were an integral part of the popular understanding of urban decline. They prevented the dispersal of the ghetto population directly through exclusionary zoning and restrictive housing practices, and indirectly through housing costs in excess of what minorities could afford. Without opportunities for social and spatial mobility, blacks became locked in the ghetto, and the ghetto remained on its downward trajectory, pulling the city along with it. Mayor Coleman Young of Detroit indicated this when he commented that because "housing discrimination prevented most blacks from moving to the suburbs where the jobs existed, they were forced to remain jobless in Detroit, where they became heir to the various urban diseases—crime, drug abuse, poor health care, poor schooling and despicable housing."[20] Mayor Henry Maier of Milwaukee described the situation more colorfully before the Midwest Ecumenical Symposium in 1969: "Two caravans have passed on the urban highway: the Cadillacs of the rich heading for the green fields of suburbia; the jalopies of the poor headed for the hand-me-down housing of the inner city."[21] The suburbs had become a suburban noose, not just restricting but strangling the central cities.

The urban sociologist Herbert Gans suggested that the most harmful effect of suburbanization on the city was this "ever-increasing class and racial polarization of city and suburb." Polarization resulted not only in a restriction of housing choice, but also placed a "traumatic financial squeeze" on the city. Its major consequence was an "increasing economic gap between the urban have-nots and the suburban haves . . . resulting on the one hand in greater suburban opposition to integration and to solving the city's problems, and on the other hand in greater discontent and more ghetto rebellions in the city." This vicious spiral, Gans predicted, could eventually result in a massive exodus of urban whites and "might well hasten the coming of the predominantly Negro city." While this turn of events might be welcomed by many white suburbanites who could sever all ties to the city and by many Negroes who could then occupy the good housing left behind and take political control, the prospect had to be resisted. The city would be poorer, less able to provide services, and deficient in the political influence needed to obtain state and federal support. A predominantly Negro city was, to Gans, also morally repugnant: "[I]t would create apartheid on a metropolitan scale."[22]

Urban decay had become cumulative. As more desirable households left, urban deterioration spread and fewer resources were available to stem decline by eliminating the conditions that drove out the white middle class. Exodus grounded in racial prejudice and discrimination exacerbated the city's problems. Mayor Maier offered an insightful summation of these dynamics: "The metropolitan establishment brags: 'There are no slums in suburbia.' Of course not: The slums of suburbia are in the central city."[23]

Not everyone agreed that suburbanization was having a dual effect on cities: first, creating a geographically articulated class and racial polarization that thwarted social mobility and launched a vicious spiral of decline, and, second, depriving the central city of the leadership and tax revenues that would slow and possibly reverse decline by enabling local governments to undertake successful remedies. Edward Banfield of Harvard University viewed present conditions as typical of the logic of metropolitan development. By that logic, less well off immigrants enter the city and, as they became more affluent, migrate outward. Banfield believed that blacks eventually would also participate in this decentralization.[24]

Both Robert Weaver, a U.S. housing official, and Daniel Moynihan concurred. Weaver wrote in 1966 that "minority groups can be contained in the central city, where they will increasingly displace middle-income families, or they can, as earlier migrants have done, move out of the areas, as they progress economically and socially."[25] A hint of optimism was all that he was willing to show. Moynihan was bolder. He told an interviewer from the magazine *Challenge,* "I think by 1980 declining racial prejudice and rising Negro incomes will enable nonwhites to make the same trek to the suburbs."[26]

On the whole, commentators viewed suburbanization as both a contributor to central city decline and a mechanism of upward mobility in which all immigrants would ultimately participate. White and black out-migration from the cities was thus inevitable—a large minority presence was not considered permanent. The heavy migration of blacks into central cities simply accelerated what had been an existing trend. Suburbanization and urban decline were thereby tightly connected in the discourse and yet distanced from each other. The separation occurred when commentators posed the option of central city or suburb as a matter of individual—and an obvious—choice. This released white society from the twin crises, and responsibilities, of race and urban decay.

As for lost leadership and tax revenues, Gans took exception. No evidence exists, he stated, that would show middle-class families to be

more civic-minded than lower class neighbors. Moreover, suburbanites continue to exert political influence in the cities as a result of their
employment and their property holdings. As for their contribution
to tax revenues, "middle-class families are often a tax liability for the
city; they demand and receive more services, particularly more
schools, than their taxes pay for."[27]

One solution to suburban exclusivity and central city fiscal
decline was to dismantle the barriers facing blacks in the suburbs.
Another was to wait patiently for blacks to begin their ascent up the
escalator of prosperity. A third was to rely on the legislative and financial commitments of federal, state, and local governments to eradicate urban decay. With urban decay erased, the cities would no longer
repel affluent households and investors, the tax base would grow,
public services would improve, employment would expand, and all
would share in the good life. Yet, just when the riots focused national
attention on urban problems, the federal government—the government with access to the greatest revenues—began to turn away from
the crisis of the central city.

Neither our understandings of the riots nor the significance of the
related deterioration of the cities was independent of how governments responded and the political debates in which those responses
were encased. In the early 1960s, optimism about government intervention persisted. Urban renewal had many supporters, some even
smitten to the point of claiming success. *U.S. News & World Report*,
for example, captioned a picture of a building being demolished in
the following way: "Slums and old buildings across the country are
being demolished—the beginnings of a massive drive to halt decay in
major cities and to reshape urban America."[28] The caption could have
posed demolition as a sign of weakness and thus a precursor of future
difficulties, but it did not.

That optimism extended to the potential role of the federal government in placing its great moral and financial weight in service of
reversing urban decline. Just prior to his election as President, Senator John Kennedy told attendees at the annual conference of the
American Municipal Association that "[t]he cities of America, their
problems, their future must rank at the top of any realistic list of 1960

campaign issues."[29] His successor, Lyndon Johnson, gave in 1964 one of the most pro-city speeches of any U.S. president. In it he declared that "[i]n the next forty years, we must rebuild the entire urban United States."[30] Such commitment was unprecedented, and remains so to this day.

Even during the worst of the riot years, a commentator writing in *Commonweal* observed that "[t]he most deceptively attractive legacy of the 89th Congress is the widely held feeling that the city is about to be saved."[31] Many believed that the federal government would not allow the cities to decline further. Never had there been such a need, and never had the national leadership seemed so solidly in support of the cities.

At the same time, however, urban renewal seemed less and less a panacea. More projects than ever were underway, but urban decline had not abated, and the riots had made the cities even less attractive to investors. Slums were expanding in size and number, demolished housing units exceeded those being built, and the costs of the renewal effort became more and more daunting.[32] The promise had become tarnished by the formidable scale of the task. Making matters worse, no other solutions had such widespread political support.

Simultaneously, and around the country, grassroots rebellion welled up against the onerous costs imposed by urban renewal. The destruction of neighborhoods, the demolition of habitable homes, the uprooting of functioning commercial and industrial areas, and the dislocation of families created a backlash and resulted in numerous public protests against both urban renewal projects and inner-city highway construction. Blacks who lived in the blighted urban areas and slums adjacent to central business districts were disproportionately affected. A homeowner in the Watts district of Los Angeles called it "urban removal, not urban renewal," and another observer pointed to the "white highways running through black bedrooms," thereby tying together suburbanization, race, and urban decline.[33]

The disappointments of urban renewal and the deafening clamor of the opposition led most mayors and many city and national officials to lobby for greater federal involvement. Their goal was to frame urban decline as a national problem. During the early 1960s, both Senator Joseph Clark of Pennsylvania and Senator Clifford Case of New Jersey were outspoken on the point that state and local governments alone could not solve the problems of the city. Senator Clark, on introducing the Kennedy Administration's bill that would establish a Department of Urban Affairs and Housing, stated that "[t]he time has come to mature and sharpen our thinking about the national responsibility for metropolitan affairs in general and urban renewal in particular." He went on to say that "[i]t seems incredible that one of the world's oldest democracies, the world's richest industrial nation and the world's No. 1 power should permit millions of its citizens to live in poverty, disease and misery, but we do."[34] Senator Case argued that the scale of urban problems was so great that solutions could only be forthcoming if all levels of government worked together. Within the federal government, he continued, all urban programs should be reorganized under a single coordinative body as Kennedy had proposed.[35]

President Johnson created the cabinet-level Department of Housing and Urban Development. He appointed a black man, Robert Weaver, as its first secretary. Johnson also helped to establish the Urban Institute, a Washington-based think tank, the goal of which was to provide policy research on urban problems. During these years, Kenneth Clark called for an "urban Marshall Plan," and senators and members of Congress offered numerous bills in support. Despite the attention paid to urban problems, though, few new initiatives were forthcoming beyond a program known as Model Cities. It coordinated existing programs in neighborhoods with concentrated social, economic, and physical problems. While seemingly an advance over urban renewal, it was underfunded and never intended to replace it.[36] Urban decline had finally become a federal responsibility, but the national response was limited in conception and execution.

During the presidential elections of 1968, *Business Week* proclaimed that "[o]ther than Vietnam, no issue presses more forcefully on the candidate for President than the roiling mass of controversy known as 'the urban crisis' or 'the problems of our cities.'"[37] Once in office, though, the victor, Richard Nixon, redefined the urban crisis, a crisis that only a few months earlier had figured prominently in his acceptance speech before the Republican National Convention. The problems of the cities were now local problems requiring not expanded federal aid, but better municipal coordination among existing programs. Nixon established an Urban Affairs Council, headed by Daniel Moynihan, to develop policy and coordinate programs, and even to undertake new initiatives, but the essence of Nixon's urban policy was to avoid grand schemes and to delegate burdensome responsibilities to city governments. Nixon believed that "fears of doom are no longer justified."[38]

George Romney, Secretary of the Department of Housing and Urban Development, a year earlier had taken a contrary position. Despite the federal government having spent nearly $160 billion between 1960 and 1973 on inner city problems of poverty, slums, inadequate education, violence, and congestion, "none of this has made a dent on the over-all problem of the central cities."[39] Yet President Nixon was not swayed by the implicit call for action in his secretary's assessment. In a nationwide radio address a year later, he prepared listeners for his urban policy by reciting the many advances that had been made: crime reduced by more than half, fewer civil disorders, cleaner air, a halving since 1960 of the number of people in substandard housing, and city governments no longer skirting financial catastrophe. The implication was obvious: "The hour of crisis has passed. The ship of State is back on an even keel, and we can put behind us the fear of capsizing."[40]

Predictably, many city officials felt that the cities were being abandoned. Mayor Richard Hatcher of Gary, Indiana, commented at a 1973 symposium that "a great crisis exists in cities, but no one is being called to Washington to talk about that crisis. All that is coming from Washington is a great deal of silence."[41] The director of economic development in Milwaukee placed this silence in a broader perspective: "Perhaps our generation is so taken up with America's global supremacy that local concerns seem provincial and picayune. Perhaps a nation gazing at the moon can't glance at its own back yard."[42]

Some of these critics went so far as to blame the federal government for urban problems even while they were imploring it to pass new legislation and release additional funding. Numerous governmental programs, they argued, had exacerbated suburbanization and deprived the city of needed investment and middle-class residents. The federal interstate highway program had demolished neighborhoods in order to connect cities with one another, thus making it easier for white collar workers to hold jobs in the central cities while owning homes and paying taxes in the suburbs. The federal home mortgage insurance program had financed suburban homebuilding even while rejecting requests for mortgages from buyers in the cities. State and local governments were also complicit; state laws thwarted annexation and limited revenue sources for city governments, and local suburban governments engaged in exclusionary zoning and ignored public housing programs.[43] The government seemed not simply ambivalent but positively anti-urban.

Whether a national or a local problem, the urban crisis had not disappeared. The federal government's reassignment, indeed abdication, of responsibility had neither allayed anxieties nor removed urban decline from the national agenda. Urban economies were still weak, black families still faced discrimination and misery, local fiscal instability still threatened, and the suburbs remained a haven for those who opted, and were able, to flee the declining cities.[44]

DECLARING THE URBAN CRISIS SPURIOUS

The combined effects of fiscal and racial calamities generated alarm and fear. Not surprisingly, numerous commentators went beyond merely representing the cities as simply decayed. For them, the cities were doomed. What that meant was seldom clear. Implied was that central cities would soon be abandoned by all except those with no choices in the housing market or investors unable to liquidate their holdings. Some raised their voices in opposition to this pessimistic assessment. Yet, optimists were decidedly in the minority.

In the early 1960s and before the destruction unleashed by the riots, a few observers still clung to a view of urban decline as susceptible to being ameliorated by well-designed and fully-funded governmental programs. The litany of ills was long, but once isolated and with opposition eliminated, successful turnabout could be expected.

The chairman of the Committee for Economic Development offered his list: polluted air, sewage-filled rivers, heroin-using teenagers, racial tension and riots, school dropouts, economic and social ghettos, illegitimate children on relief rolls, helpless and hopeless city halls, and ugliness by day and terror by night. To this he added "the exodus of the economically self-sufficient, emotionally stable, and culturally advantaged . . . [who] . . . abandon the central city to the angry or spiritless poor."[45] (This commentator had no problem with moral distinctions.)

The cumulation of these various ills repelled capital investment and households, thereby leading to economic stagnation, fiscal shortfalls, and the persistence of decay. The architect and planner Victor Gruen wrote that "[w]ith very few exceptions, city cores are stagnating, and statistics registering the number of visitors entering the city cores as workers, shoppers, or participants in urban activities show a steady and increasingly steep downward trend."[46] Until people and investments remained in and returned to the cities, decline would persist. For Gruen, the only solution was the redevelopment of central business districts and the resultant return of people to the city.

Donald Canty, senior editor of *Architectural Forum,* believed that urban decay and stagnation were more than a matter of physical rebuilding. Ghetto residents suffered from a culture of despair. The primary reason for stagnation was "the failure of the city to produce a middle class out of the human ore of the poor."[47] The issues were social, not environmental. Urban renewal was not a solution to the urban crisis.

Yet, and even after the riots, many experts firmly believed in the possibility of renewal. As *Newsweek* noted in 1969, "[c]ity problems are being diagnosed in stupefying detail by squadrons of earnest academics, analyzed by banks of computers, brainstormed by urban planners, hashed out in countless public hearings and self-conscious 'confrontations' around America."[48]

Other experts took a different approach, one based on the inevitability of cities. Edmund Bacon, executive director of the Philadelphia City Planning Commission, pointed to the declining viability of the suburbs for middle-class households and the opening up of the suburbs to poorer people. Out of this, he believed, would emerge a better population mix in the cities and a reversal of past trends. David Wallace of the University of Pennsylvania pointed to an incontrovertible logic to the cities. "If we wiped out all our cities in the U.S. and started over," he said, "we would find cities rising where they are today, with only a few exceptions." William Wheaton, director of the Institute of Urban and Regional Development at the University of California, agreed. "That's where the action is. People want to be near the big cities. And industries want to go there, so jobs will be there."[49]

And, in 1971, the U.S. Conference of Mayors concluded that urban problems—lack of funding, unemployment, drugs, crime—were still very serious, "[b]ut guerrilla warfare in the cities—attacks on police, bombings and the like—appear to be subsiding." Mayor Harry Haskell of Wilmington provided this ironic comment on improvements in his city: "We haven't had a sniper shoot at a policeman for six months."[50] It was all a matter of perspective.

Nonetheless, the optimism of the early-to-mid-1960s did not compensate for the despair brought on by the riots. John Gunther, executive director of the U.S. Conference of Mayors noted that "for all their physical vigor, most of America's cities are in deep trouble." He went on to tell the editors of *Senior Scholastic* that "[t]here is no question that 'crisis' isn't too strong a word for what cities are going through."[51] Others would be more blunt, resurrecting a theme that had been part of an earlier phase of the discourse on urban decline—the city no longer served the purposes for which it had been established.

George Sternlieb had been making this claim for years. Because the city had lost its capacity to generate new economic activity or "act as an interface between the newcomer and the national scene," it was functionally obsolete. In the competition for middle class households and investors, "[t]here are very few things that [the city] currently does better than an alternative location," he argued.[52]

Joining Sternlieb in proclaiming the obsolescence of the modern city was Bernard Weissbourd. Unlike Sternlieb, though, Weissbourd rejected the notion that people had made a "free choice in a free enterprise market." Instead, he pointed to the pernicious effects of federal policies, the draining of the wealth of the cities by federal taxes, the acceleration of suburbanization and the undermining of mass transportation by governmentally-funded expressways. The cities did not naturally become obsolete, he claimed, they were made obsolete.[53] The architectural critic Jane Jacobs placed most of the blame on urban renewal and credit blacklisting in which banks withheld money for the purchase and improvement of residences and other buildings in specific areas. "[A]s the money goes, so goes our cities," she wrote in 1961, and additionally pointed out how this applied even more forcefully to black neighborhoods: "[n]early all neighborhoods that possess any appreciable Negro population, in all Northern cities, are automatically blacklisted for conventional mortgage credit." Credit blacklisting, urban renewal, and "our ignorance about how cities are built" were the bases of urban obsolescence.[54]

Wolf Von Eckardt, another architectural critic, also reflected on why the cities were obsolete. Federal policy had slowed the renewal of buildings and cities, but obsolescence seemed to be a matter of fashion and economics. "When city neighborhoods become socially obsolete because of their location, maintenance and up-keep expenses are cut. They promptly become physically obsolete as well. And they turn into slums."[55] The mobility of Americans was also central to these processes. People fled the old and the out-moded in search of the new. To put it more bluntly, the cities were obsolete because of suburbanization.

Obsolescence, of course, meant that the cities would eventually have to be discarded. Stewart Alsop, writing in *Newsweek* in 1971, claimed that the cities were finished as social institutions, as places where people would want to live. He quoted with approval Mayor

Moon Landrieu of New Orleans: "the cities are going down the pipe."[56] Landrieu's fellow mayor, A. J. Cervantes of St. Louis, put the situation just as unequivocally: "[w]e just can't make it anymore."[57] If the cities could not solve their problems, and no one else was willing, then the choice seemed obvious—relegate them to the landfill of history.

Urban America's vision of itself had turned apocalyptic and the single, doleful question was whether the cities could be salvaged. Catherine Bauer Wurster blamed the middle class for banishing the city from public consciousness. "[A]s long as that great dominant stratum of American society is not convinced," she wrote, "there can be little hope of restoring either the historic functions or the social balance of the central cities."[58]

Senator Robert Kennedy deployed a powerful metaphor to express his position: "[w]e confront an urban wilderness more formidable and resistant and in some ways more frightening than the wilderness faced by the Pilgrims or the pioneers."[59] The metaphor, however, could be read in quite different ways. Either the cities had devolved into a primitive state and thus had fallen off the path of progress, or they were a new frontier that would, just as the Pilgrims had tamed what became the Massachusetts Bay Colony, be brought into the civilized world. Even images of doom were undisciplined.

By the mid-1970s, possibly because expectations of doom and obsolescence failed to lead to the city's disappearance, a number of commentators turned away from the existence of the urban crisis to dwell instead on which city was the worst. Arthur Louis, an associate editor of *Fortune* magazine, attempted to replicate for cities an article by H. L. Mencken in a 1931 issue of the *American Mercury* that had set out to determine the worst state. Louis used twenty-four indices of crime, health, affluence, housing, educational and professional achievement, atmosphere, and amenities to rank the fifty largest cities in the country. Newark (New Jersey) stood "without serious challenge as the worst of all," followed by St. Louis, Chicago, Detroit, and Baltimore, in that order. As objectively measured, the best cities were Seattle, Tulsa, San Diego, San Jose, and Honolulu. The old, industrial cities of the Northeast and Midwest generally ranked the lowest, while newer cities in the West and Southwest sat atop the list. The message, of course, was that the cities on the bottom were soon to become noncities.[60]

A few commentators did speak against the grain of obsolescence. One was an assistant secretary within the Department of Housing and Urban Development. Samuel Jackson told the American Bar Association in 1970 that "our cities are not obsolete, but they are being severely threatened by forces that could render them obsolete."[61] Lewis Mumford noted that trend was not destiny. He wrote in the *Architectural Record* that "[t]hose who assume that a curve extrapolated from past observations must be followed into the future are in effect worshipping the past as if achievements were immortal and its errors incorrigible."[62]

During this period, commentators addressed not only what was happening and would happen to cities, but also debated how the urban crisis itself should be represented. It is one thing to declare the city to be decaying, another to label it obsolete, and still another to question the bases on which those judgements were made. The latter requires that the debate be shifted to a wholly different ground. Emerging in the early 1970s, this new direction was built mainly, but not solely, on a single book: Edward Banfield's *The Unheavenly City*.

In this book, Banfield argued that the urban crisis did not exist. Sure there were problems, but they had been with us for a long time. Moreover, commentators who lamented their existence had failed to see that the problems currently facing the city were less severe than in the past and were more than compensated for by other advances in city living. The gist of the book was an interpretation of the urban crisis that situated the lower class at the core of decline. For Banfield, race was not a primary issue. Rather, within cities certain groups of people had lost the capacity to defer gratification and had become psychologically enfeebled. They were mainly found in female-headed families. Others would soon find jobs, apply their schooling, escape poverty, move out of the ghetto, and cease rioting; but this present-oriented lower class would persist as an insuperable burden. Little could be done to redeem the lower class, Banfield thought; most government programs were misguided and simply raised false expectations. Drastic measures were called for, including breaking the cycle of poverty by placing the children of these families in foster homes.[63]

The book was vehemently attacked and righteously defended. The sociologist Richard Sennett lamented the ascendency of the "hard-headed realists" who were proposing that we could not change the conditions of the cities and instead would have us ride the "new wave of tough-minded passivity."[64] Ruth Beinart, writing in *Commonweal*, compared Banfield to Cotton Mather, the primitive Puritan preacher. She noted the broad acceptance of Banfield's argument in the face of a seemingly intractable crisis: "Banfield's sophisticated cynicism has appeal, undoubtedly."[65]

The implications being drawn were not simply that we needed to be tough and cynical. Other commentators understood Banfield's argument to be a call for indifference and for the abandonment of our moral obligations. The former mayor of Minneapolis, Arthur Naftalin, concluded that the cumulative effect of declaring the urban crisis spurious and counseling us to "do nothing" was to relieve us of any responsibility for urban problems—classic conservative doctrine.[66] Sennett, for example, had called Banfield and other like-minded individuals "pragmatic conservatives" and decried their penchant for "benign neglect."

To the extent that the lower class was popularly believed to be made up mainly of African Americans, other commentators noted a strong strain of racial prejudice. Duane Lockard of Princeton University accused Banfield of an invidious form of racism. The deemphasis of discrimination in Banfield's book and the ignoring of institutional racism was simply too self-conscious for Lockard. To deny race as a dominant force in American society seemed to him a subterfuge.

Banfield defended himself by arguing that the criticism was either unfair because it was not scholarly—and thus ideological—or that the criticism involved a misrepresentation and misunderstanding of his argument. In fact, he accused his critics of playing rhetorical tricks and thus of engaging in politics. At no time did he withdraw from his positions.[67]

The critics were most upset by the possibility that Banfield's ideas would be adopted in Washington and used to dismiss the city from federal policy debates, thus leaving urban problems to fester.[68] *Time* magazine noted that the book had found favor with the Nixon administration, an administration that had already declared its belief in the spuriousness of the urban crisis and that, in any case, the federal government had only a minor role to play in the renewal of declining cities.[69]

Banfield also had his intellectual supporters. The editors of *Time* magazine provided praise: "Banfield has commendably deflated a certain amount of hysteria on the subject of the cities; he has shown that apocalypse does not lurk around the corner." James Wilson, professor of government at Harvard University, was less equivocal. "Whether you agree with it or not," he wrote, "it is now the only serious intellectual book that has been written about urban problems."[70]

A number of other commentators joined Wilson in praising the book for its candor and willingness to confront uncomfortable truths. Theodore Marmor wrote an equivocal assessment. He noted that detractors overwhelmed in numbers the supporters of Banfield's position, and that Banfield had been maligned mainly for being reactionary, academically dishonest, and an apologist for the status quo. He also commented on Banfield's inflammatory rhetorical style; Banfield had titled one chapter "Rioting Mainly for Fun and Profit." But holding Banfield "to the position that truth and bad consequences are unheavenly partners" was unfair, Marmor claimed, and, overall, "another chance was lost to discuss seriously the problems of urban America and their possible cures."[71]

The prominent neoconservative Irving Kristol offered more substantive and direct support. *The Unheavenly City,* Kristol wrote in *Fortune* magazine, is "easily the most enlightening book that has been written about the 'urban crisis' in the U.S. It is part of a healthy revisionist trend in the social sciences" that also included the work of Daniel Moynihan and Jay Forrester. Moreover, Kristol went on, "If Banfield's book receives the serious attention it merits, it might help us slow down this vicious round of inflated expectations and demoralizing realization."[72]

Kristol's praise was perfectly understandable, given the position he and others had been developing during the time that Banfield was writing his book. In 1967, within a review of a book edited by James Q. Wilson, titled *The Metropolitan Enigma,* Kristol pointed out that most of the authors were skeptical about the phrase *urban crisis* and that "what we call the 'urban crisis' is mostly just a euphemism for problems created by the steady influx of Southern Negroes into northern and western cities." Urban problems were not peculiarly urban. To the contrary, racial problems were peculiarly urban. Moreover, the United States was really a nation of suburbs and exurbs, not cities.[73]

In the same year, Kristol claimed that an historical and factual perspective on urban problems would demonstrate that the conditions of the city were better than ever. Substandard housing units had declined, the proportion of poor in cities had been halved, the percentage of population in cities had remained stationary since about 1920, and "[t]he overwhelming majority of Negroes and Puerto Ricans on New York's Upper West Side, when polled, report that they *like* living in the area, and that their squalid housing represents a clear improvement over their previous living conditions."[74]

Moynihan, then director of the Harvard–MIT Joint Center for Urban Studies, asserted in 1966 that "American cities are more livable today than they have ever been. To say that they are about to collapse is nonsense."[75] During an interview in *Challenge* magazine, Moynihan made his position more specific: "Our cities are cleaner, healthier and safer than practically all those abroad. The housing is better, transportation is more efficient, and the general standard of living higher." The crisis existed, first, because people had not recognized this progress and, second, because whites had been displaced from the city. The last point was an indirect reference to racial fear. Moynihan then removed any uncertainty about what he meant: "White America talks about an urban crisis because it fears that our large cities will become increasingly characterized—if not dominated—by huge lower class Negro populations."[76]

An editorial in the Jesuit magazine *America* also called for more historical perspective. It argued that although problems existed, they were exacerbated by the "revolution of rising expectations." Because of the mass media, "the poor are no longer reconciled (if indeed they ever were) to living in subhuman squalor." Still, the editors recognized that even though cities were a disgrace in the past, this did not justify allowing them to remain a disgrace.[77] Even though perceptions were distorted, intervention was still necessary.

Kristol summed up his position, and that held by many others, when he wrote that "[w]hether one wishes to call it an urban crisis really depends on whether one (a) regards it as intolerable, and (b) can envisage some kind of governmental action that would radically transform the situation."[78] Of course, a tough-minded urban realist—particularly the ones to which Sennett had referred—believed the first (conditions were intolerable) and rejected the second.

Banfield, Kristol, and fellow travelers were opposed to any interpretation of the urban crisis that led to calls for government intervention. Simply put, governments had no ameliorative role to play. Thus, these commentators recognized and then quickly dismissed the urban crisis. Other commentators, though, used the forecast of doom to justify an activist government and greater federal aid to the cities. Both positions differed from but were not contrary to the argument that government intervention itself was partially responsible for the urban crisis, a position that was given its most popular presentation by Jane Jacobs.

Jacobs's book, *The Death and Life of Great American Cities,* had appeared in the early 1960s.[79] In it, she attacked the large-scale urban planning that had cleared slums and replaced them with sanitized urban design. She criticized its insensitivity to how people actually lived within cities and its fixation on physical renewal as the solution to urban decline. Planners, large developers, lending institutions, and governments were part of the problem. Needed instead was a recognition of the vibrancy of street life, the diversity of economic activities and social groups, and the importance of daily personal interaction for creating a sense of community. By making cities livable, we would be allowing them to prosper.

Jacobs's call for small-scale, indigenous redevelopment of cities did not find favor with those who placed their hopes in planning and the federal government. Edward Logue of the Boston Redevelopment Authority rejected her argument. "Our cities are in deep trouble," he said, "and large-scale financial aid is essential."[80] Mumford called Jacobs's proposal "home remedies for urban cancer," thus capturing metaphorically the discrepancy between the seriousness of the problem and the ostensible superficiality of her solution, while Herbert Gans noted that Jacobs had missed the key factors in the emergence of urban slums—poverty and racial discrimination.[81]

Supporters, on the other hand, praised her critique of an arrogant and elitist urban planning, her personal perspective on urban life and championing of neighborhood values, and her social sensitivity. For the many planners, architects, and community activists of the sixties who were searching for community in an increasingly repressive America, Jacobs's book became a bible.[82]

Nevertheless, Jacobs, like Banfield and others of his ilk, had crossed an invisible line that had confined the discourse within the boundaries of hopeful solutions realized through large-scale government intervention. She placed her hopes for the prevention of slums on the absence of a modernist planning that only undermined diversity and social interaction and drove the stake of financial calculations through the heart of human values. Jacobs thus reinforced a long tradition of neighborhood advocacy and grassroots organizing, but her argument ran counter to that of the commentators who occupied the center of the discourse. For them, it was difficult to envision a future for the cities, and thus the passing of the urban crisis, in the absence of massive governmental action.

THE INFERENCE IS INESCAPABLE

The period from the early 1960s to the early 1970s was one of deep angst about the cities, an angst whose real source was racial fear and guilt. This could not always be publicly or personally acknowledged. The newly elected mayor of New York City, John Lindsay, wrote in a guest editorial in *Saturday Review* in 1966 that "[o]ur cities exact too much from those who live in them. They are not only expensive places in which to live or work; more and more, the price of city living is being paid by a sacrifice of fundamental personal freedoms."[83]

The editors of *Time* magazine in that same year remarked that "[m]en have been city dwellers for 50 centuries, but barely two centuries sufficed to bring U.S. cities to a desperate crisis."[84] The "fundamental personal freedoms" evoked by Mayor Lindsay and the desperation alluded to by these editors were references to the fear that whites and many minorities felt as they were told time and again about crime and unrest in decaying cities, and as they searched unsuccessfully for solutions.

The minority presence in the city, the depth of minority frustration, and unsettling images of burning buildings, overturned automobiles, and police in riot gear created a great sense of personal insecurity, guilt, and helplessness within white, middle-class society. All other dimensions of urban decline were made peripheral by the riots. The ghetto expanded in public perception to encompass neighborhoods, industrial areas, and business districts. Urban problems became synonymous with the *urban crisis,* as the central city—once simply the city—became the inner city.

Rather than the deterioration of the environment as represented by slums and blight, urban decline became equated with obstacles to "the common concerns of the people who choose to live in large central cities—migrating to the city, forming and maintaining (or failing to maintain) a family, educating the young, finding a job and a home, coping with crime, moving about on the highways and buses, breathing the air and drinking the water, and last—but certainly not least—looking at the buildings and other artifacts of an urban culture."[85] Urban decline went from being a problem situated in the environment and the economy to a problem of everyday life, with roots in the values and beliefs of the nation's citizens. Commentators who held these views transformed the shame of the cities into a human frailty.

A racism whose existence was unquestioned, but whose eradication was unlikely, deepened urban decline. For much of white society, pleas and demands for the tearing down of racial barriers only heightened anxiety. Two economists established the "bottom line" when they wrote that "the poor are found less frequently in the central city; it is mainly the Negro poor that are found there. The inference is inescapable: *central cities are poor largely because they are black, and not the converse.*[86] The ghetto was responsible for the decline of central cities and racism was responsible for the ghetto.

Constantinos Doxiadis, the Greek engineer turned city builder, provided a concise summation of the historical events that had led to this situation: "[T]he problem [of the cities] which started as a structural problem turned into a problem of succession of economic and social classes, and finally has turned into a racial problem."[87] Any enduring solutions had to break up the ghettos or erode the foundations of the racist practices that perpetuated them. Either path was bound to threaten white society.

The city had become a locale in which social and racial problems were concentrated, a place where their most perverse consequences were experienced by those who could not flee to the suburbs. Decay bred decay in a seamless, downward spiral, with race providing the gravitational pull. Jay Forrester even developed a mathematical model to demonstrate that the path of economic development for cities led to the in-migration of more and more of the lower class. He showed in his book *Urban Dynamics* that policies to ameliorate the condition of the poor were counterintuitive and counterproductive. The current predicament of the cities was viewed as virtually irreversible in the short run and a result of policies meant to stem decline. Forrester's computer runs demonstrated that even "intuitively sensible policies can affect adversely the very problems they are designed to alleviate."[88] Thus, not only were solutions rare, but any ameliorative intervention would likely only make matters worse. Here was a clear reason why abandoning the cities was preferred to reforming it and why white society could take this position and remain free of moral discomfort.

Forrester's understanding of urban dynamics was summed up neatly in the article on the "gilded ghetto." The authors wrote that "[t]he ultimate result of efforts to increase Negro incomes or reduce Negro unemployment in central city ghettos may be simply to induce a much higher rate of migration of Negroes from Southern rural areas. This will accelerate the already rapid growth of black ghettos, complicating the already impressive list of urban problems."[89] In the face of crisis, then, Forrester and others offered a Banfield-esque stratagem as solution—Be a realist and act conservatively. (That the second did not follow from the first did not seem to bother them.) This meant an end to "massive programs of external aid." Instead, they favored giving free rein to the private sector.[90]

The edges between the pessimists and the optimists had blurred. Now, the optimists could find few signs of hope, and the pessimists were convinced of their own correctness. Given the fervor of events, ambivalence toward the cities was too emotionally subdued to be appropriate. One of the pessimists, George Sternlieb, offered this advice in 1971: "Remember, the city isn't dead yet—though it is pretty far gone—and I would say in terms of putting money in it the city is no longer a good bet."[91] Albert Mayer, hopeful and still searching for solutions to the urban crisis, wrote (though badly) that "[a]s an observer and a hopeful re-former of the urban scene for many years, I have gone through as many years of alarm and elation. I have known continuing and recurring alarm at the intensifying deterioration of our cities and the accelerating expansion of urban decay and disorder."[92] Mayer's optimism was scarcely an antidote to Sternlieb's pessimism. The contradictions were so overwhelming that even the most dedicated of urbanists struggled to draw forth hope, much less praise, for the modern city.

The angst and resignation of these commentators was in sharp contrast to the mood of the architects, planners, and urbanists who attended a 1973 symposium on urban America. In attendance at the symposium was John Breslin, the book editor of *America* magazine. He reported on the tenor of the brief opening remarks of the speakers: "[E]ach strove to outdo the other in expressions of optimism about the fate of the cities, with the sole exception of Dr. [Paolo] Soleri, whose contemplatively pessimistic tone and visionary approach frequently singled him out from his action-oriented colleagues." Critics attacked that optimism at its basic premise. Breslin continued: "As the discussion wore on . . . the enormous social and political problems that underlie the plight of the city came bubbling to the surface. Charges of irrelevance, heavily laced with ideology were hurled at the panel members because they did not spend their time roundly condemning American capitalism with all its works and pomps."

Resolving such conflicting views was impossible and Breslin ended his commentary with two themes, one central to the whole historical sweep of the discourse on urban decline and the other peculiar to this period. He wrote: "Two other obstacles remain intractable: the deeply ambivalent feelings Americans have about the city as a place of promise *and* peril, and, more immediately, the current Administration's disinterest in facing the urban problem head-on."[93]

Optimists, lacking solutions and saviors, sounded alarmingly like pessimists of an earlier period. Even Jeanne Lowe, an avowed lover of cities, began her 1967 book on urban renewal with the sentence, "As almost every American knows, our cities are in serious trouble."[94]

A Double Reversal of Fortune

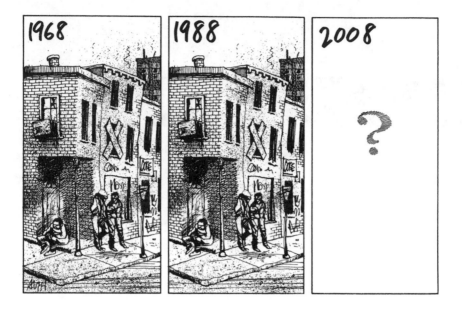

CHAPTER 8

Rising from the Ashes

Neither those willing to abandon the city nor those holding to its central importance in American life had reckoned with the potential for an urban fiscal crisis to exacerbate "The Negro Problem." At the same time, the fiscal crisis marginalized race within the discourse. Social issues dominated in the sixties and early seventies, but the fiscal crisis facing the large industrial cities during the mid-seventies' recession pushed economic issues to center stage. Decline, along another dimension than race, became a problem of nationwide proportions. Despair deepened and resignation from the cities spread, though both were soon to be followed by an astonishing reversal of conditions. Out of racial unrest and fiscal crisis emerged the urban revival of the 1980s and 1990s; cities seemed once again to be places of prosperity and the good life. But only those commentators without any sense of irony, or any skepticism, viewed the renaissance as real and enduring.

During these years, attitudes toward the city were unstable. Consequently, the practical advice contained within the discourse swung from one extreme to another. The twin crises of race and fiscal collapse suggested abandonment of the cities and a severing of all ties between them and the rest of the country. Yet, the redevelopment of neighborhoods and the surge in office and retail construction pointed to a return to the city and a renewed dedication to urban living. The attraction and optimism faded, however, as the economy soured in the early 1980s and enduring weaknesses floated to the surface. The Los Angeles riots in early 1992 returned the discourse to an earlier gloom.

The riots compelled Americans, once again, to ask what they as a nation should be doing to solve the problems of the cities. The resultant governmental response was predictable: much rhetoric, little action. Elected officials, academic experts, and urban commentators simply lacked a sense of how to center cities in the public consciousness. As the century drew to a close, little progress had been made in confronting the root causes and symbolic depths of urban decline.

DRAMATIC SHIFTS, SUBSEQUENT SLIPPAGE

In the popular literature, the 1950s are often depicted as a decade of quiescence, the 1960s as years of turmoil and experimentation, and the 1970s as a time in which the United States experienced a profound restructuring of its global economic position, political leanings, and cultural inclinations. The recession of 1973–1975, the worst since before World War II, marked a boundary between an earlier prosperity and a subsequent precariousness. Like the Cold War, the postwar era as an "historic moment" seemed to have ended.

Deviations in trends, of course, look less abrupt as perspective lengthens. What were once novel courses and startling reversals often become, in retrospect, modifications or cumulative effects of past trends. In the almost thirty years from the recession of the early 1970s through to the next century, the discourse on urban decline shifted dramatically from crisis to revival, subsequently slipping back to resignation and ambivalence, and then, once again, returning to a hope that decline had ceased.

One of the most striking of events, because of its political reverberations and impact on the daily lives of millions of American households, was the transformation of the national economy. The 1973–1975 recession inaugurated a major industrial restructuring.

An oil shortage sent prices skyrocketing and amplified what might have been a mild trough in the business cycle. Manufacturing was the hardest hit, experiencing a rash of plant closings in major industries such as steel, automotive assembly, and rubber. Business and personal services expanded after the recession ended, but goods production remained moribund. Numerous commentators pointed to high-technology and advanced services as the new economic wave that would enable the United States to rebound from the demise of its manufacturing base.

Foreign competition was one of the factors driving the shift from manufacturing to services. The Japanese invaded the automobile and consumer electronics markets, and the Germans, Koreans, and Scandinavians also proved to be worthy competitors. Many large corporations expanded their global operations; U.S. multinational firms relocated labor-intensive operations to low-wage countries. Additionally, the rise of newly industrialized countries cut into U.S. foreign and domestic markets. By the late 1980s, heightened international competition, the erosion of manufacturing dominance, and the weakening of the dollar on international currency markets led to the country's worst trade deficit ever, a balance of payments problem that included the flow of foreign capital into the United States to buy up vast amounts of real estate, purchase corporations, and set up branch plants.

Bracketed by recessions in 1973–1975 and 1981–1982, the economy was relatively robust in the latter half of the 1970s. Nonetheless, this growth did not translate into a revenue-rich and venturesome national government dedicated to assuring social welfare. President Richard Nixon had engineered a withdrawal of the federal government from the problems of big cities, and Gerald Ford did not deviate from this path. Even Jimmy Carter, a Democrat, did little to reinvigorate an attack on urban problems, despite featuring a national urban policy and instituting new urban programs. In fact, he turned the initiative for redevelopment over to a partnership of developers and local officials and thus paved the way for Ronald Reagan to crystallize a conservatism that denigrated big government and championed the private sector. His successor, George Bush, continued an agenda that excluded cities, the poor, and minorities. Even President Bill Clinton in the

1990s found little political capital to be made in pushing for a national urban policy, a sorry comment on how both Republicans and Democrats had come to view the cities as electorally insignificant.

The conservative turn of national politics in the 1980s was characterized by a massive military buildup and a virulent attack on social programs and aid to cities. Income and corporate taxes were cut, benefiting mainly the rich; social security taxes were raised. The overall result was to deepen a gigantic federal budget deficit, hardly a goal compatible with conservative austerity. The cessation of many federally funded urban programs, two recessions, and high interest rates in the 1970s laid the groundwork for the chronic fiscal difficulties of local governments that extended into the 1990s, not to mention a federal government resistant to new social policy initiatives.

The fiscal problems of governments were dispelled by the stock market surge of the 1990s. The economy boomed and tax revenues grew. New types of businesses—dot-coms—became the focal point of investment, both measured and speculative. Moreover, rising immigration provided low-wage workers for an expansive economy. Government deficits slipped off the policy agenda. The conservative cast of government, however, meant not renewed welfare programs and a rededication to cities, but tax cuts and calls for the privatization of public services.

Prior to this, in the 1970s, U.S. economic dominance in the "Free World" eroded, as did the country's global political influence. Vietnam had disoriented American foreign policy, and the Iranian hostage crisis during the Carter Administration weakened it further. The United States looked to be a declining world power. President Reagan responded by sending troops to Beirut, invading—on a trumped-up pretext—the small Caribbean island of Grenada, and funding the counterrevolutionaries in Nicaragua in order to bring down the Marxist Sandinista government. President George Bush engaged the country in a regional war in order to oust the Iraqis from Kuwait, protect Saudi Arabia, and maintain U.S. access to and control over oil production. Reagan and Bush, though, claimed responsibility for the breakup of the Eastern Bloc in the late 1980s and early 1990s as popular revolts ousted communist dictators in Poland, East Germany, and Rumania; and the Soviet Union fragmented into the

Commonwealth of Independent States. With the demise of the Cold War, capitalism and American-style democracy had ostensibly triumphed. Worldwide popular reaction against its globalist pretensions, however, tainted celebration.

Conservatives, of course, were not satisfied with attacking big government and defeating communism across the globe. Many were also directing their attention to peoples' private lives. The New Right, along with the Moral Majority (religious fundamentalists with political aspirations), attacked the permissiveness of the schools, the rise of secular humanism, abortion rights, and the erosion of the "traditional" American household. Their targets were liberals and feminists, civil rights activists and environmentalists, free-speech advocates and radical professors. The intent was to return the country to basics: God, family, hard work, respect for authority, and knowledge of the "classic" texts. Welfare reform that made work mandatory and put limits on how long a family could receive government support was one of the conservatives' major victories. Liberalism, at least the reformist strain so vilified in the 1980s, was no longer in vogue.

Right-wing economists championed policies that would reduce taxes and dismantle regulations and other hindrances to capital investment. The goal was to shrink governments while their counterparts in the private sector downsized corporations, making them "leaner and meaner," as their critics phrased it.

By the late 1980s, that program seemed to be reaping its claimed benefits in American cities, but mainly in property development. A massive building boom erupted, based mainly on new office construction in central cities and beyond, suburban commercial and residential development, and the renovation of inner-city neighborhoods. The shift to a service economy fed an expanding office market, and office employment spurred the demand for residences close to central business districts. Inflation drove up the price of new housing, generating capital gains for current homeowners but also expanding the number of households who could not afford to buy homes. Foreign capital flowed into real estate, and banks lent freely to developers. By 1990, the office boom had subsided, gentrification had waned, suburban growth was slowed by its own success, and many development projects built on fictitious financial projections had gone bankrupt.

Commercial banks were faced with a surge of foreclosures, and numerous savings and loan associations had to be rescued by the federal government, adding another giant burden to the already massive deficit.

The crash of the building boom was only one symptom of a recession that lingered through the early 1990s. Unemployment rates settled at politically unacceptable levels, trade imbalances persisted, the federal deficit grew and grew, and despite falling interest rates, the economy remained sluggish. All of this boded ill for the cities and the areas immediately outside them. The riots that occurred in south-central Los Angeles in April of 1992 struck another blow against what had been an improving attitude toward the cities.

Soon forgotten, the riots and the return of race to the discourse were overwhelmed by a dramatic rise in stock prices and the wealth it generated. Developers spurred new investment in downtown real estate, gentrifiers reappeared, and the number of jobs expanded without interruption for about ten years. Prosperity so diluted decline that decline only rarely figured in the public discourse concerning the country's cities.

As we look back on these events, the shift in the discourse from the morass of race to the ledgers of fiscal affairs seems less shocking. Though some cities, such as Camden (New Jersey), still experienced riots in the 1970s, racial unrest in that decade was challenged for the center of debate by economic decline and the enduring fiscal difficulties facing local governments. A new crisis loomed on the horizon. Commencing with the financial agonies of New York City in 1974 and 1975, that crisis vied with "The Negro Problem" for discursive dominance. By 1975, the fiscal crisis commandeered the discourse, recentering it around the economic restructuring that had eroded the urban manufacturing base and shifted capital investment and population from the older industrial regions of the Northeast and Midwest to the newer post-manufacturing regions of the South and West. The Los Angeles riots and rising rates of inner-city violent crime and drug abuse returned the urban debate to its racial ground. The fiscal crisis became a secondary concern.

Substantive themes of earlier years were augmented by new understandings. Two of the more novel were the introduction of regional and, later, global considerations. Added to the themes of internal decay and central city–suburban competition was the regional shift in jobs, investment, and people that exacerbated the decline of the old manufacturing cities in the Northeast and Midwest. Other commentators acknowledged the rise of immigration, the expansion of multinational firms, and global cities. The urban story was no longer confined to the metropolis, but extended across state boundaries.

Suburbanization continued, but at a slower pace. In fact, nonmetropolitan areas momentarily passed cities and suburbs as the fastest growing. That being said, metropolitanization and sprawl never disappeared as issues. City populations, though, began to stabilize, and stirrings of a back-to-the-city movement continued from the late 1970s through to the end of the century (recessionary periods being the exception). Combined with new office investment in central business districts, the retention and attraction of middle-income households in declining cities led to significant infusions of capital in their commercial districts and neighborhoods. Decline seemed to be finished. *Revival, renaissance,* and *revitalization* were the new buzzwords. Perceptive observers recognized the simultaneous existence of growth and decline, the burden placed on the poor by this new round of reinvestment, and the failure of new investment to deflect the downward trend of aggregate indicators. A "dual city" of rich and poor came increasingly into focus.

This more sophisticated sense of geography and development was part of an increasingly systematic depiction of urban conditions. Analysts devised statistical techniques to measure urban decline and distress, along with numerous schemes to rank cities on the basis of their "livability." The discourse on decline was becoming more analytical and, it seemed, less emotional. By the late 1990s, the strident accusations of crisis had ceased. Urban decline was confined to the collective memory. Something approaching euphoria replaced cynical resignation. In 1975, however, there was panic.

REVERSING THE TIDE

For a long time, observers had recognized that central cities faced a financial squeeze. Anchored primarily to property taxes, revenue bases were being depleted by the out-migration of businesses and middle-income households. Simultaneously, changes in the social composition of cities left them with residents whose incomes were relatively low, whose buying power was less than those who had fled, and whose needs for education, health, law enforcement, and housing were ostensibly greater. The concentration of low-income and elderly households burdened cities in ways unknown to the suburbs, weakening financially strapped local governments. Public services and the construction and maintenance of public infrastructure were two of the victims.

The squeeze became a crisis with the 1973–1975 recession. Industrial output declined, unemployment reached a postwar peak of 8.2 percent, and the gross national product fell 7.4 percent, nearly double its previous postwar high. By March of 1975, the economy had been in a slump for sixteen months, longer than any time since the depression of 1929. Arthur Okun, an economist at a think tank in Washington, D.C., noted that "[t]he economy has now deteriorated to a point most of us have not seen in our adult lives."[1]

The recession hit city governments especially hard. A study released by the Urban Institute noted that of cities over one-half million population, more than half of those had insufficient or severely strained financial resources and were losing population. Inflation made services more costly and provoked union demands for wage increases. Unemployment added to overburdened public services. Federal tax policies were more hindrance than help; the federal code "tilted the terms of economic competition in favor of suburban development . . . [thereby] . . . precipitating decline of the central city tax base."[2] The result was that many cities were brought to the brink of fiscal crisis. Once there, they faced the possibility of bankruptcy. None experienced this as dramatically as New York City.

As the country's largest city, and a city that could rightfully claim world status, New York's flirtation with default was a major media event. Here was the potential for urban decline in one of its clearest forms—actual bankruptcy of the city's government. The City's 1974–1975 fiscal year budget was set at $11.9 billion, second only in size to that of the federal government, and its deficit was at $726 million.[3] Between 1974 and 1976, the city government found itself unable to use the bond market to meet its financial obligations. For years, it had borrowed to pay operating costs, not just to fund capital expenditures. Faced with an international recession, investors refused to participate in this practice. The bond market was closed to New York City. Ken Auletta, a newspaper reporter, summed up the situation: "Federal aid has dried up, years of fiscal gimmicks have sapped our credit, and optimistic slogans have served as a narcotic, inducing us to avoid the painful choices we and our leaders must begin to make."[4]

Throughout the summer of 1975, a weekly and then daily drama unfolded. Obligations would become due, money would be unavailable, and at the last minute a temporary solution would surface. Financial institutions and the federal government finally imposed a less ad hoc procedure. New York City would enter a period of extreme austerity, laying off workers, cutting back services, and raising taxes. The federal government would guarantee loans to the city, a commitment arrived at only after President Ford had rejected numerous proposals. (After one of these rejections, the front page of a major New York City paper carried a now-famous headline: "Ford To City: Drop Dead!") In addition, bankers would sit on boards that would oversee—some said govern—the city government. The local public-sector unions also became involved, using their pension funds to purchase city bonds.

Only these unprecedented institutional arrangements saved New York City from default. The newspaper reporter Jack Newfield noted that "[u]nder the three-year financial plan and debt moratorium, the banks have been saved, and the city has been condemned."[5] The overall result was to place the burden of fiscal crisis on working people and the poor and to erode city services in ways that discouraged investment and continued to drive off middle-income households.

New York City was not alone; its woes were contagious. The director of the Municipal Finance Officers Association claimed that "[u]ncertainty over the New York City situation has contaminated the minds of investors throughout the Northeast."[6] The flow of investment into the cities, both for public and private projects, was slowing, and the perception that the nation's largest city was at risk had a dispiriting effect on the municipal bond markets. Many cities were near bankruptcy. Charles Kimball, chairman of the Midwest Research Institute, echoed this fear, commenting that "[n]one of us can escape the very real financial crises that threaten New York City."[7] Cleveland, Philadelphia, Newark, Boston, Detroit, and other large cities confronted deficits and unfavorable bond ratings that could only be eliminated through service cuts and tax hikes.

The larger the city, in fact, the higher the tax burden and the greater the debt. Taxes per capita in cities over one million in population were twice as high as in all cities, and their debt per resident was two and a half times the national average.[8] In addition, the larger, declining cities had higher personnel costs, more generous pension plans, and larger long-term debt than growing cities, thus necessitating more intensive efforts to raise funds to meet higher spending levels. And a deep recession exacerbated the earlier deficiencies of the declining central cities. The existence of dependent populations became more pronounced, and two rationales for fleeing to the suburbs became even more compelling: poor city services and tax avoidance. Minorities, the elderly, and the poor were too weak politically to resist austerity measures. The higher tax rates needed to balance the city's budget, moreover, contributed to its undesirability.

Pierre de Vise of the University of Illinois provided empirical documentation of this fiscal dilemma: "The average property tax cost in a Chicago industrial suburb is about 40 cents per square foot, and inside Chicago it's about $1.80."[9] Such a discrepancy was not only seen as driving businesses to relocate to the suburbs, but also as an indictment of the excessive costs of working and living in central cities. Combined with the fiscal difficulties faced by urban governments and lingering social problems, tax disparities made cities less desirable and more dependent on state and federal aid. As then-mayor of New York Abraham Beame indicated to the annual meeting of the American Business Press in 1976, "When the commercial base of our cities erode (sic), our cities do not vanish, they merely become more dependent on public revenue."[10]

At the height of the crisis, pessimism was the norm. Jason Epstein concluded that "[t]he prevailing wisdom is that New York and the other older Eastern cities are finished anyway. The country's future has shifted westward. . . . As New York once carelessly discarded its own marginal neighborhoods, so America may have decided that New York itself can now be junked."[11]

Roger Starr, formerly of the New York City Housing and Development Administration and later at New York University, suggested that "planned shrinkage" was the solution to the fiscal crisis. "The central fact of New York's financial crisis," he wrote, "is that the city government does not have enough wealth to sustain the city at the level to which its citizens have become accustomed."[12] City services would have to be reduced in parallel with falling population. Specifically, Starr advised, the local government should cut back services in those areas of the city being abandoned, usually the worst slums. Present inhabitants would be encouraged to move to neighborhoods where the services were better. Urban triage would, in effect, scale down the city.

Critics argued that the costs of this change would be borne by minorities and the poor who still occupied abandoned neighborhoods, but Starr thought otherwise. "The poor," he wrote, "who need the greatest service from the city government, would be worst hurt by a failure of the city to use its resources economically." For Starr, "[b]etter a thriving city of five million than a Calcutta of seven."[13]

William Baer, an urban planner at the University of Southern California, went beyond planned shrinkage. He chastised those who refused to admit that older cities and neighborhoods could die and pointed out that some cities were so deteriorated as to be "terminal," beyond redemption. Urban death, he claimed, was "very much in the natural order of things, to be taken in stride." To Baer, the fiscal crisis following on the racial crisis signaled the death of cities. The old industrial cities were simply no longer viable. "The major urban issue facing our nation in the next decade is not the cost of dying sectors of our cities, but the incidence and the timing," he wrote.[14]

Disagreement came from an editor for *U.S. News & World Report*. His position evoked the earlier argument by Roger Starr. The budget deficits, threats of bankruptcy, and diminishing revenue sources, Marvin Stone wrote, simply meant that "big cities, rather than being left to die, should be allowed to shrink to manageable size."[15] Mayor Beame also reacted incredulously: "The current crop of Cassandras seems to take a special delight in projecting negative trends to absurd lengths, concluding that cities are dying and will soon be dead." Then he counterattacked with an equally extreme position: "Whoever buys the conclusion, buys the end of the United States, for neither the suburbs, nor the countryside can replace the assets of our great metropolises."[16]

For Starr, Baer, and others, the fiscal crisis was the final blow after decades of pummeling. With the city government no longer viable and the urban population possessing low skills and high needs, there was little reason to expect or want large cities to endure. An article in *Business Week* noted that "[t]he U.S., some urban experts believe, may become the world's first industrialized, urbanized country without important cities."[17] To the extent that industrial development and urbanization had become separated from the presence of "important cities," their disappearance seemed both inevitable and without dire consequences. Baer's natural order of things provided a rationale for acceptance of this state of affairs, one that skirted accusations of racism and an anti-urban bias and cast fiscal crises and urban decline as unavoidable.

Other commentators preferred to see the problems of the city in historical perspective, some looking toward the past, others to the future. One historian repeated the views of neoconservatives a few years earlier, that, from the proper perspective, things were not as bad as they seemed. He wrote that "the present city, for all its problems, is cleaner, less crowded, safer, and more livable than its turn-of-the-century counterpart. Its people are more prosperous, better educated, and healthier than they were seventy years ago."[18]

Alexander Ganz of the Boston Redevelopment Authority and Thomas O'Brien of the Office of Planning and Management for the Commonwealth of Massachusetts opted to look to the future. They predicted an economic restructuring of the cities, a restructuring that would be fully recognized only years later. Writing in the early 1970s, they argued that the strong growth of services in the central cities, renewed capital investment, and the retention and even return of the middle class had strengthened the city. "Newly emerging factors of strength," they wrote, "are reversing the tide which ran against job opportunities and the attractiveness of living in our large cities."[19] The lack of an economic function, a basic cause of urban decline, was disappearing. What remained of decline's causes—minority populations, the unemployed, and fiscal weakness—would be swept away with enlightened public policy and economic prosperity. As the economy cycled out of the recession, the fiscal crisis would lose its position at the core of public anxiety about cities.

Neither the fiscal crisis nor decline's consequences disappeared with the return of economic prosperity. The fate of cities was not simply a matter of business cycles. Something much more profound was underway—economic restructuring—and its consequences were not wholly beneficial.

For almost all of the older industrial cities, the end of the 1973–1975 recession did not initiate a renewal of growth. At the fulcrum of their continued economic and fiscal problems was the shrinkage of manufacturing activity. Cities like Detroit, Youngstown, Philadelphia, and Cleveland remained in economic doldrums through to the mid-eighties. Cities in the South and West that had not been built on goods production did much better. Their service industries expanded without a corresponding loss of manufacturing jobs. High-tech industries (e.g., micro-electronics) fueled development in Denver, Atlanta, and San Francisco; and military spending generated economic expansion in San Antonio, Los Angeles, and San Diego.

By the 1980s, even cities in the Northeast, such as Boston and New York, had robust economies. Two writers for *Business Week,* commenting on the development of computer software, robotics, and medical technology, noted that one of the cities most devastated by the demise of manufacturing—in particular, steelmaking—had rebounded. "[A] vibrant new Pittsburgh is already rising from the ashes," they claimed. James Howell, an economist for the First National Bank of Boston, also noted that former declining cities that had once relied on traditional manufacturing had now shifted to high-tech, service, and defense industries and were doing well. "Northeastern cities, the basket cases of the 1960s and 1970s," he wrote, "are healthy again."[20]

Cities that were able to move away from a reliance on old-line manufacturing, particularly when focused on a single industry, underwent an economic resurgence. In fact, the cities that thrived, it seemed, were those that had combined diversified local economies with strong business leadership, cities like Memphis, Phoenix, and Portland, Maine. In 1987, Ford Worthy noted in *Fortune* magazine that "[a]s the service sector continues to outshine manufacturing, as tomorrow's technology replaces today's, U.S. cities are fast learning to adapt. Some have emerged from the process as veritable boom-towns."[21] That optimism was echoed by the editors of *U.S. News & World Report*. They observed that "[d]espite the regional rivalries and worries over finances, urban experts believe that many cities in the 1980s will make progress in their switch from being centers of gritty industry to being magnets for trade and leisure." In fact, "[t]hose that are able to make the transition the fastest will be the leading communities of the next decade."[22]

The transition seemed to have been made most quickly by those cities that developed their knowledge-intensive industries: financial and business services, insurance, education, and media. Here, cities were able to build on their vaunted concentration of diverse activities to enable new ideas and innovation to percolate through the local economy. Such declining cities as Boston, New York, Chicago, and Philadelphia were even listed as the "best cities" to find knowledge workers.[23] Later, in the 1990s, dot-com firms (doing business on the World Wide Web) would also become a significant component of the new urban economy, along with tourism and firms that merged media and computer technology. Cities were rediscovering their competitive advantages as information-generating, tightly integrated, innovative, and knowledge-based economies. They were no longer, economically speaking, "forgotten islands."[24]

Fortune magazine in 1997 produced a list of the nation's most improved cities. At the top of the list was New York City, followed by Denver–Boulder, Boston, and Seattle. Also in the top ten was Cleveland, one of the most distressed cities of the 1970s. In these cities, business was thriving, crime was down, schools were improving, and the quality of life was high. Nationally, the stock market was booming. The conclusion: "Today, it's rare to find a city that hasn't shown some improvement during these heady bull-market years."[25]

The growth in knowledge-based (specifically, financial) industries shifted the economic function of central cities. No longer were cities producers of and marketplaces for goods. Increasingly, they were the locus for "advanced services" involving finance, insurance, corporate management, law, communications, and information processing. The quintessential advanced service cities were New York, Los Angeles, San Francisco, Denver, and Houston. "Especially in the booming [Southern] Rim cities," Kirkpatrick Sale wrote as early as 1974, "service employment has enormously increased, in fact by more than 70 percent over the last twenty years, as against 6 percent in the older cities of the Northeast."[26] The older, industrial cities—Detroit, St. Louis, Baltimore—were left behind, still weak and still threatened by the prospect of further urban decline.

Although corporate and business functions were concentrating in a few major cities, corporations were still moving to the suburbs and to small cities within metropolitan areas. Edward Kelly, president of the Cleveland-based Industrial States Policy Center, blamed the corporations for the decline of older industrial cities in the 1970s. "[C]orporate prosperity," he wrote, "was decreasingly based in the cities." Clearly, "[b]y exporting jobs, and by automating, large corporations effectively severed the connection between their prosperity and that of urban America."[27]

Corporations wanted less congestion, cheaper labor, more favorable tax rates, and lower living costs. Their out-migration in the 1980s, moreover, pulled along a second wave of businesses—law firms, advertising agencies, and accounting firms—to service them. "The nation's huge metropolises are losing out to their smaller, more easy-going neighbors in attracting new businesses that add tax revenues and create new jobs," one commentator observed.[28] The prosperity of these new business centers came "partly at the expense of big cities, whose lifestyle is frenetic and costs are high."[29]

Consequently, jobs became more plentiful in the suburbs than in the inner cities. Between 1982 and 1985, employment growth in the suburban periphery of Atlanta was twice that in the central city. Compared with the urban core, suburban increases were almost five times greater around St. Louis, Chicago, and San Francisco, and nearly seven times greater around Detroit, than in their central cities.[30] The more rapid expansion of suburban service industries was the key element in what came to be a metropolitan discrepancy between where employment opportunities were located and where jobs were most needed. The director of a job creation project in Detroit noted that "[t]he largest number of jobs is being created in the suburbs, where unemployment is the lowest. In the city, where the unemployment problem is the greatest, we find the least number of jobs being created."[31]

Elected officials focused more and more on enhancing the city's labor force through improvement of the schools and creation of more livable environments. *Fortune* magazine in late 1989 celebrated the perception that the large cities that managed to do well economically were those that invested in infrastructure and created a local climate conducive to business investment. Qualified workers and pro-business city administrations were touted as the keys to economic revitalization.[32]

Economic resurgence, moreover, was increasingly a function of international linkages. Cities were becoming "globalized" and the forces shaping them even more distant. Two commentators offered the following observation in *The Progressive* in 1979: "The new prosperity is based on great wealth amassed elsewhere, on the decline of America's manufacturing strength, on the automation and export of skilled jobs, on the rise of a growing class of working poor, and on the transformation of this nation's once flourishing and then degraded cities into global headquarters of multinational power." "Capitalism's leap into a fully globalized economy," they asserted, gave the appearance of a renaissance, even though cities continued to experience "the uprooting of their neighborhoods, the degrading of their schools and hospitals and other public services, the shrinking of the middle classes, and the spreading blight of public cynicism."[33]

The fiscal difficulties faced by cities in the middle to late 1970s, difficulties that lingered into the early 1990s, could be traced to an underlying shift in economic functions that struck the older cities of the Northeast and Midwest particularly hard. Many of these cities had been able to replace only a portion of manufacturing loss with business and financial services.[34] Some were able to rebound from fiscal crisis and the precipitous decline engendered by subsequent recessions. Those cities that could not stanch job loss continued to experience all of the ills associated with the postwar decay of cities.

MARCHING ACROSS THE COUNTRYSIDE

Population loss continued to plague the older central cities in the 1970s and 1980s. Suburbanization persisted as a theme, despite evidence of its diminution and even glimmers of a possible reversal. Black suburbanization accelerated, growing 40 percent from 1970 to 1978. The 1990s, however, brought a cessation of population decline, and even some growth, as a new wave of immigrants flocked to both old and new cities. Regional shifts continued.[35]

In 1976, many cities were still shedding residents. "People are continuing to move away from the nation's big cities in favor of life in smaller communities and the wide-open rural regions," *U.S. News & World Report* claimed.[36] Seven of the ten largest central cities in 1976 lost population, and fourteen of the largest twenty. Those gaining population—for example, Houston, San Diego, and San Antonio— had a common characteristic; they were all located in the West or the South, the region now labeled the Sunbelt. The cities that were shrinking the most were in the Northeast and Midwest, places like Dayton, Cleveland, and St. Louis—the Snowbelt.[37] No longer was migration a simple movement to encircling communities. People were migrating to the suburbs, to cities and suburbs in the Sunbelt, and to nonmetropolitan areas. Regardless of destination, the net flow was away from central cities.

George Sternlieb and James Hughes, both at Rutgers University, noted in 1980 that of affluent migrating families (those with incomes of $15,000 or more in 1975), "three central city families migrated to the suburbs for every family that went the other way."[38] A graphic presentation in *Black Enterprise* indicated that between 1975 and 1980, suburbanites and those living in rural areas were less likely to move out of their communities than those who lived in central cities. As a result, "[d]uring the 1970s, the population of suburban areas rose by 17.4 percent, or 14.5 million people," and the proportion of those living in the suburbs went from 41 percent to 43 percent, while population losses in the central cities were substantial: "New York City alone lost more than 860,000 people, a drop of almost 11 percent."[39]

"America's rush to its suburbs" was not without its irony.[40] Inner-ring suburbs—older, denser, and more likely to attract minority populations—became more and more distinct from the newer and "whiter" outer-ring suburbs. In 1980, the historian Richard Wade predicted that "[t]he crisis of the inner cities will move to the inner suburbs in the 1980s."[41] By 1987, that prediction seemed to have come true. One sociologist "pointed out that America's older, inner-ring suburbs are increasingly facing the same problems that were once exclusive to the inner city: growing crime, a mass middle-class exodus, decreased revenues from an eroding tax base, inundation by the poor, and increased rates of unemployment and public assistance."[42] Under such conditions, higher rates of migration to nonmetropolitan areas and small towns was not a total surprise.

In the early 1970s, three times as many people moved into small towns and farm regions as moved into metropolitan areas. From 1970 to 1973, nonmetropolitan areas grew by 4.3 percent, while large cities and suburbs grew by 2.8 percent. From 1975 to 1980, more people moved out of metropolitan areas than into them.[43]

"More and more Americans are getting fed up with big cities—their high living costs, zooming crime rates, breakdown of services," reported *U.S. News & World Report*.[44] Industries were leaving for rural areas where costs were lower and surroundings more pleasant, the young and the elderly were searching for a simpler life, and the spread of community colleges and junior colleges was making many small towns more desirable. The president of the College of Idaho crystallized an often-mentioned reason for these population shifts: "This is the great American dream—fresh air and wide-open spaces."[45] John Herbers, a correspondent for the *New York Times*, resurrected almost as common a reason, and one with the same sense of inevitability. He wrote that "[t]he advance of technology, the change from a manufacturing to a service and information-based economy and the accumulation of private wealth have made it possible for people and commerce to settle pretty much where they please"—and they preferred the countryside.[46]

For some, postwar suburbanization was merely a transitional phase between compact pre-war cities and metropolitan areas that would be organized into urban villages—low-density communities with urban services and open space—spread throughout outlying suburbia. By the late 1980s, developers were touting the "village" scheme and providing a new type of suburban place, one that referred nostalgically to a bygone small-town era. As Thomas Hine, an architectural critic, noted, these urban villages are "carefully tended, extremely harmonious, more intensely Main Street than anything that ever ran through the center of an actual town. Sinclair Lewis might not recognize it, though Walt Disney probably would."[47]

Suburbanization was taking a form quite different from that produced by the earlier "bedroom" and "industrial" suburbs. Suburban communities were being transformed, not into low-density "anticities" without centers and geared solely to consumption and the raising of families, but into full-service places. Herbers noted in 1986 that "[t]he once-mighty cities have come apart, and, in effect, pieces of them are marching across the countryside."[48]

The journalist Joel Garreau in the early 1990s labeled this new urban form "edge city" and positioned it between a frontier countryside and an overbuilt, congested, and less prosperous metropolis.[49] In the 1980s, places like Tyson's Corner outside Washington, D.C., and Camelback Corridor near Phoenix went from residential enclaves to mixed-use developments with retail malls and hotel–office complexes, thus providing all the necessities of earlier cities and serving as regional employment centers. Garreau portrayed edge cities as clear alternatives to and eventual replacements for the older central cities. That they did not halt low-density sprawl was another quality that distinguished them from the older central cities.[50] Regardless, Americans were once again expressing their dissatisfaction with cities by moving to the edge.

These population movements within and between metropolitan and nonmetropolitan areas paralleled a regional shift from the Northeast to the South and West. Beginning in the 1970s, the Northeast and Midwest began to experience a loss in population. The white population had been declining since 1940, but that loss had been more than balanced by an influx of African Americans from the South. Between 1970 and 1974, though, both groups fled the Northeast at rates that created an overall population decline.[51] Of the twenty largest cities, only six had population gains between 1970 and 1976, and all six were in the South and West. With the exception of Atlanta, which had a decline, the fastest growing cities were all in these regions. Of the one hundred largest cities in 1975, all of the ten fastest growing ones were in the South and West. Nine of the ten cities having the highest rate of shrinkage were in the Northeast and Midwest. In 1985, the reporter George Jones noted that "[s]ince 1945, they [the beleaguered cities of the industrial North] have been losing jobs, people and political power to the South and West."[52]

This regional shift slowed in the 1980s. Sunbelt cities began to lose population to their suburbs, and a more buoyant economy in the Northeast meant more growth there, and less out-migration. One magazine staffer noted in 1981 that "[a]fter two decades of phenomenal growth, the [Sunbelt] is awash with many of the same problems of the Northeast."[53] There were environmental problems in Houston, a deluge of immigrants in Miami, a shrunken tax base in New Orleans, and traffic congestion in Atlanta. Nonetheless, the U.S. Department of Commerce predicted that metropolitan areas in the Sunbelt would grow faster than those in the Snowbelt through to the year 2000. Los Angeles would surpass New York as the largest metropolitan area, and San Francisco would surpass Bridgeport (Connecticut) as the wealthiest.[54]

Population movements from central cities to suburbs, suburbs to nonmetropolitan areas, and the densely populated Northeast to the South and West also fueled the expansion of "strip cities." With the exception of the "BosWash corridor," the remaining twenty-five strip cities grew by 13.1 percent between 1970 and 1978, exceeding that of all metropolitan areas (6.5 percent) and nonmetropolitan areas (10.3 percent).[55] By 1983, there were twenty-eight strip cities and, absent those in the East and Midwest, they grew by more than 20 percent between 1970 and 1980. Calvin Beale, a demographer for the U.S. Department of Agriculture, noted that "people will continue to move from the central cities and older suburbs to fill the in-between places," and the geographer Brian Berry observed that "[u]niform, low-density urbanization is spreading across vast tracts of the country."[56]

Throughout the twentieth century, urbanization and later suburbanization dominated the demography of development, the first creating the large central cities and the second leading to their decline. Here, though, were new phenomena that needed explaining. Berry labeled these trends *counterurbanization.* Population deconcentration was leading to smaller size settlements, decreasing population densities, and increasing local homogeneity as people of similar backgrounds and stations in life occupied a common community. The decline of heavy industry in the older cities was a key factor. In addition, declining fertility rates, a fall in immigration, and the regional convergence of incomes also contributed. This new settlement pattern, despite being nationally integrated, lacked the large central cities that once had dominated the landscape.[57]

Two demographers from the Bureau of the Census commented on the rapidity at which the rate of growth of the older cities had slowed and suggested that the United States might be "witnessing a basic demographic reversal." Looking at urban areas, rather than central cities, they noted that "[i]n the 1950s only one area in 20 lost population; in the 1970s one in six did." Moreover, they expected these trends to continue as rural areas retained their attractiveness for new investments, as population continued to follow jobs, and as the function of the cities as employment generators waned further.[58]

Urban decline, though, was still a matter of population and employment loss. Pierre de Vise had a simple, two-part explanation. First, regarding counterurbanization, "Americans have always preferred small-town living." Second, with regard to the diminution of economic function, he noted that "[w]e no longer need large cities. We developed these behemoths like New York, Chicago and Philadelphia on the basis of a late nineteenth-century transportation and technology" that was no longer viable. He forecasted unabated decline: "Given the greater mobility of Americans, the growing viability of small cities, and the preference many people show for places with warmer climates, the migration will go on."[59] Size—once pursued by civic boosters—had become an "albatross around the neck of the cities who were trying to make it their main course."[60]

The "doughnut" metaphor of the mid-1960s was resuscitated to characterize the ongoing decline of the city and the growth of outlying areas. "Over the years," observed the historian Charles Trout, "Americans have witnessed the creation of doughnut cities: There may be a hot time in the old suburbs tonight, but downtown where proud central business districts used to be, there are silent, gaping holes."[61] The emptiness of the central city was juxtaposed to the substance and value of suburbs and nonmetropolitan areas. "The image is not new," Long and DeAre wrote. "What is new," they continued, "is the expansion of the region of population loss (the 'hole' in the doughnut) to include the inner suburbs. The hole has grown largest in the urban areas where the doughnut pattern has prevailed longest."[62]

The population movement that created the doughnut pattern also changed the rankings of the nation's largest cities. In the early 1980s, Los Angeles passed Chicago for second place in the urban hierarchy, and Philadelphia fell from fourth place to fifth. Of the ten largest cities in 1982, three were located in Texas and six outside the Northeast and Midwest. In fact, none of the top-ten cities in the Snowbelt gained population, with the exception of New York, which had a miniscule 0.21 percent increase between 1980 and 1982.[63]

The striking variations in urban growth from one region of the country to the next were even more pronounced in 1990. The ten cities of over 100,000 people that had had the largest percentage increases in population over the preceding decade were all in the West or Southwest. Moreover, all were in either California, Texas, or Arizona. Of the top-twenty such cities, seventeen were in these three states. Even more telling for the fate of urban America, fifteen of the top twenty were *suburbs* of central cities. Nevertheless, there were few dramatic changes in the top-ten largest cities: Los Angeles, Houston, Dallas, and San Antonio moved up one notch; San Diego moved up two; Chicago and Detroit fell one notch; and Baltimore fell three places.[64]

In response, one commentator pointed out that city dwellers now "accounted for only 29 per cent of all Americans; suburbanites, 48 per cent, and rural residents, 23 per cent."[65] The United States was seemingly less and less an urban nation, and the trend was unlikely to change: Only 13 percent of Americans considered cities the most desirable places in which to live. For older industrial cities, there was an ironic side to this population loss and slippage down the hierarchy: "Pollution, congestion and crowded housing have all eased a bit, say urban experts, as industry and residents have moved to areas beyond the urban cores."[66]

The loss of population during this period not only indicated a declining attractiveness to households and investors but also had repercussions for federal and state assistance. Much urban governmental aid had become tied to population size, and any shrinkage in number of people meant a loss of intergovernmental revenue. Elected officials in the large cities complained about Census undercounts of minorities. Myron Magnet, writing in *Fortune,* chided urban officials: "Declining localities will always complain." He further noted that the Census is "guilty of bringing bad news to the nation's older cities, which have shrunk grievously over the last decade: New York by 11.1%, Detroit by 21.3%, St. Louis by 27.9%."[67] One Census Bureau official stated that "[t]he trends are there and have been there for some time. We did not discover them. Cities, particularly in the Northeast, are losing population, and both the politicians and the public better get ready to face what that means."[68]

Big cities were becoming smaller and their metropolitan dominance more and more tenuous. Cities needed to be "rebuilt to be more efficient and livable places" if they were to recapture some of their appeal and be competitive with the suburbs.[69] Even the establishment of financial centers within the large cities during the 1970s and early 1980s was seen as insufficient to reverse decades of decline. In fact, some viewed these changes as merely hopeful illusions. "Large cities do continue to serve as financial centers and money warehouses," noted one economist, "but even this function is declining due to technological advances."[70]

DECLINE HAS GONE TOO FAR

The discourse of the mid-1970s to early 1980s was fascinated by, even fixated on, the full litany of postwar urban ills: white flight, an expanding poor and minority population, falling tax revenues, rising crime, unsatisfactory schools, a lack of jobs, and unsuitable housing, among many. In early 1975, for example, the editors of *U.S. News & World Report* stated their belief that "[t]he downward slide of American cities—and not only the oldest and biggest ones—is accelerating again."[71] That same article quoted one of the most ubiquitous urban commentators of this period, George Sternlieb. His opinion was that "[t]he mood in the cities has changed from resentment and sullen resignation. Five or six years ago, we thought aging cities could survive if they came to political and economic terms with the suburbs. But now the decline has gone too far. . . . Our society had decided it's cheaper to turn our old cities over to the poor and buy them off with welfare."[72]

Such dire predictions and negativity were compatible with an urban imagery that had been in vogue through the 1960s. For Judah Stampfer, the city was a jungle. "The very word," he wrote, "is repeatedly used to describe American city life: the asphalt jungle, the blackboard jungle—concrete as a cancerous quicksand." Rather than being a locus of civilized life, the city had become by 1975 a "catch basin of population and an urban wilderness."[73]

The urbanist Lowell Culver joined a series of metaphors to describe the depths of decay that had ensued by the mid-1970s. The city was undisciplined, lacking coordination and decision-making responsibility. It was also unheavenly, a city without moral direction or personal discipline. Certain "inhabitants who, out of greed, mental derangement, hatred, personal frustration, or estrangement from life, spread fear throughout the metropolis, threatening normal relationships between people and endangering efforts at developing satisfactory accommodations between blacks and whites."[74]

Other commentators built on the notion voiced by Stampfer that the city was a living organism, one that had aged beyond revitalization: "Like an old man who can no longer walk, the cities totter." So wrote Ellis Cose in 1977, a columnist for the Chicago *Sun-Times*. His concern seemed genuine: "It is painful to watch an aging city. For cities tend to die a section at a time. They tend to hang on desperately, becoming accustomed to the agony, fearful of the night, waiting for the sun to shine again."[75]

In 1976, Irving Howe, a social critic and author, visited Detroit:

> My mind is haunted by what I saw there: whole blocks looking as if they had been bombed in the war, buildings rotting or destroyed, a devastation of once-busy streets, the abandonment of even the pretext of care. During one visit I was in one downtown area on a Saturday afternoon: utterly eerie, large buildings and stores, but no one on the streets. A deserted city: chilling, frightening.[76]

For change to occur, resources had to be gathered and a will to reform set in motion. A Mt. Holyoke College historian perceived only anomie in 1976. While numerous cities over the centuries had risen from the destruction caused by armies and conflagrations, he wrote, "The smoldering ruin of urban decline does not, it seems, strike similar sparks of determination from its victims." Rather, "[f]ailing the reincarnation of Mrs. O'Leary's cow, today's cities will very likely continue to suffer citizen apathy, segmented reform, the persistence of self-interested bureaucracies and an exodus to the suburban crab-grass frontiers."[77]

Mayor Lee Alexander of Syracuse, New York, pointed directly to the dilemmas. Alexander suggested that "[c]ities in modern America aren't brought to the edge of despair by the problems they face but by the solutions that cannot be implemented because there isn't enough money."[78] The ability to solve problems—and the resources—had fled to the suburbs. Hope in the mid-1970s seemed quite inappropriate. Ellis Cose expressed defeat in the face of this new complexity: "There are many causes for the problems; and they are all intertwined; and there is not even such a thing as a 'central city.' For there are cities within cities."[79]

One of those "cities within cities" was a culture of drug use that fueled a startling rise in violent crime in the 1980s. Between 1980 and

1992, murders, rapes, and robberies in the United States went up from just under 600 per 100,000 population to 760 per 100,000 population. Violent crime rates were highest in the cities: 1,942 in Newark, 1,890 in Miami, and 1,523 in Baltimore—all more than twice the national average. Inner-city neighborhoods—places like south-central Los Angeles, north Philadelphia, and the west side of Chicago—were particularly notorious. The sale of crack cocaine had engendered a criminality that not only made murder the leading cause of death of young African-American males, but also led to the country having the highest incarceration rate in the world.[80]

Crime, of course, made cities less attractive. Not until the mid-1990s did the problem subside. In the interim, as one national magazine suggested, "city after city tolerates its own Beirut, a no man's land where drug dealers shoot it out to command street corners, where children grow up under a reign of 'narco-terrorism' and civil authority has basically broken down."[81]

Yet, even in the bleakest of times, many commentators refused to dismiss the possibility of recovery. The editors of one national magazine noted that even though the most avid city boosters predicted no quick reversal of fortunes, "they see at least a slow and painful recovery, step by step, to make big cities a place of work as well as social betterment and pleasure."[82] Taking a comparably equivocal position was Rene Dubos, a professor emeritus at Rockefeller University. He labeled himself a despairing optimist. Although the city was associated with a multiplicity of evils, without it, human intercourse would be stifled. "Our time," he wrote, "is characterized not by a retreat from cities, nor even simply by efforts to correct their present ills, but rather by an eagerness to rediscover and cultivate certain positive human values that only urban life can provide."[83] As usual, Sternlieb offered a more cynical version: Cities were going to survive, but as centers of consumption, "the city of fun and games, not industry."[84] Presciently, this summed up the cities of the 1980s and 1990s—urban conspicuous consumption hiding tenacious inequalities and unrelenting, but clearly diminished, decline.

BECOMING MORE EXCITING

Just about this time, in the late 1970s, the sense of urban decline was tempered, and partially erased, by a belief that middle-income families were returning to the city. The percentage of people living in the suburbs was no longer increasing as rapidly in the late 1970s as it had since 1950, and the out-migration from cities was slowing. Moreover, as two reporters for *U.S. News & World Report* observed, "People who might have moved from cities are staying put."[85] Their observation was supported by an Urban Land Institute study that found "significant resettlement of middle- and upper-income families in about three-quarters of all U.S. cities with populations over 500,000."[86]

Such evidence gave rise to the usual array of overly optimistic and, in reaction, dissenting pronouncements. Everett Ortner, the managing editor of *Popular Science Monthly,* in 1977 claimed boldly that "[b]ack-to-the-city is an important movement that is going on in virtually every city in the country."[87] One did not have to look far, however, for a contrary view. The editors of one national magazine were not yet convinced of any reversal of urban fortunes. The back-to-the-city movement, they wrote, "is still too small to offset the population loss from larger families headed for suburbia."[88]

The possibility of a reverse migration—a counter-counter-urbanization—was spurred by the redevelopment of neighborhoods adjacent to central business districts, a process eventually termed *gentrification,* and by a boom in downtown office construction. Fells Point in Baltimore, Adams-Morgan and Capital Hill in Washington (D.C.), Mt. Adams in Cincinnati, Queen Village in Philadelphia, and Brooklyn Heights and SoHo in New York City were some of the more widely recognized examples of places to which the more affluent were returning. Middle-income households were moving into these neighborhoods, not to the suburbs, rural areas, or the Sunbelt. Louis Masotti, a sociologist from Northwestern University, claimed that "[p]eople realize that suburbs aren't Shangri-La any more. At the same time, the cities are becoming more exciting."[89]

Part of this excitement had to do with the expanding ethnic diversity of the large cities as new waves of immigrants arrived in the country, a phenomenon that stemmed from the evolving connections that cities had to global networks. In 1990, *Newsweek* reported that "[m]ore immigrants now come to the United States than ever before. About 10 million poured out of the '80s, more even than the 8.8 million who arrived between 1900 and 1910."[90] These immigrants, however, were not the Europeans of the turn of the century but predominately Asians and Latin Americans.

Many immigrants headed for the big cities, but not necessarily the ones to which they had previously migrated. Mayor Frederico Pena of Denver commented that the immigrants "first impression of their new home is likely to be shaped by the skyline of Los Angeles, not the majestic Statue of Liberty."[91] Los Angeles, San Diego, Phoenix, Miami, El Paso, and Houston, and other Sunbelt cities were the new destinations, not the older cities of the Snowbelt. Nonetheless, New York City retained its status as a major immigrant city; nearly 20 percent of the residents of the metropolitan New York region in 1990 were foreign-born. However, in Los Angeles, the percentage of foreign-born was closer to 40 percent, and in Miami, over 30 percent.[92]

Immigrants helped to reverse population decline and changed the racial composition of many central cities. Boston had its first population increase in forty years. New York, Miami, Atlanta, Chicago, and Seattle gained residents, while the rate of loss slowed significantly in Milwaukee, Cleveland, and Detroit. Buffalo was the exception. Its population dropped by almost 11 percent, more than even in the 1980s. By the late 1990s, respondents in twenty of twenty-one big cities believed that their central city population would grow in the next dozen years.[93]

With the white population still declining in the cities, the non-white minority increased its presence. Seventy-one of the largest one hundred cities lost white residents in the 1990s, and by 2000, nearly one-half of these cities had more African Americans, Hispanics, and Asians than whites. Of course, if the past has any relevance, having (more) non-white cities bodes ill for the overall perception of cities by the white majority.[94]

Amid the good news about population growth in the cities, middle-income households were still fleeing to the suburbs. In the summer of 1986, *Newsweek* discovered a suburban movement precisely by those households that had participated in the gentrification of the city only a few years earlier. Writer Landon Jones declared that "[t]he news today is that [baby boomers] are behaving like their parents. They're looking for a nice house in the suburbs."[95] Noted Sternlieb, "Americans are voting with their feet, and they're voting statistically to live in the boonies. . . . [T]hey just don't want to put up with the problems and risks of city living."[96] In America, the cities can never seem to win.

Sternlieb, of course, was hardly an advocate of the cities and always consistent in his prognostications of doom and gloom. Nevertheless, as the nineties came to a close, such unequivocal dismissal of cities was less and less the central theme of the discourse. The growth in downtown employment, signs of middle-class return, a significant drop in crime rates, the gentrification of inner-city neighborhoods, the emergence of new immigrant neighborhoods, and a renewed interest in an "urban lifestyle" all fed the expanding euphoria of revitalization and boosterism.[97]

As the next chapter shows, the elation was neither long-enduring nor widespread. Yet, it served to shift the center of gravity of the American ambivalence toward cities. A focus on growth temporarily dispensed with the contradictions that brought poverty along with wealth and congestion with commerce. The result was a corresponding shift in the practical advice contained within the discourse. During the fiscal crisis of the mid-1970s, with racial unrest lurking close to the surface of events, one could hardly experience the discourse without also thinking about the dangers of the city and the need to keep one's distance. With the economic resurgence of the 1980s and 1990s, one could not be so sure that the cities were about to perish or that fortunes could not be made there. They were still cities, with all the negativity that the label implies, but were they still in decline?

CHAPTER 9

Not Excessively Inconvenienced

From the late 1970s until early in the first decade of the twenty-first century, the large, once-industrial cities belied their reputation. New urban conditions seemed inconsistent with those that had held sway since the 1930s. Growth was once again a possibility, and decline was in retreat. The dismal state of American cities, one commentator suggested, was "the least fashionable problem of the 1980s and 1990s."[1] Glimmering new office towers, retail malls, restaurants, waterfront apartments, entertainment districts, and marinas sprouted up virtually overnight to transform seedy downtowns. Dilapidated neighborhoods gentrified, and their new residents shopped and dined in bustling neighborhood shopping areas. There were skeptics, of course, but was this not a reversal of long-term trends?

An observer with any sense of urban history would have pointed out that growth frequently exacerbates social and economic disparities and does less to dispel decline than to reframe it. In fact, poverty was spreading amid deepening inequality. The underclass was growing and homelessness increasing, and both spoke to the pervasive marginalization of many city residents from this new prosperity.

Relatively speaking, the cities prospered in the latter years of the seventies, again through most of the eighties, and once again during the nineties. In between, recessions cast cities in the shadows and brought back memories of the devastation that had wracked them in the sixties and seventies. These periods of economic contraction led commentators back to the decline of cities, not just as naysayers casting a skeptical light on other people's euphoria, but as clear-eyed observers of the unavoidable. The troughs of urban development highlighted the continued presence of drug use, poverty, racial tension, and crime. The riots in Los Angeles in 1992 and in Cincinnati in 2001, along with staggering crime rates in the early 1990s, confirmed what these commentators had been claiming all along—the fate of cities was precarious; decline had not disappeared.

A STUNNING COMEBACK

The difficulty of achieving consensus on the meaning of demographic evidence has always enabled commentators to emphasize one trend over another. Yet, through most of the 1980s and 1990s, the discourse on urban decline shrank to insignificance. Revival, revitalization, renaissance, and rediscovery were dominant themes; decline was thrust to the rear of the public stage. This was an abrupt shift in emphasis from the 1970s.

As early as 1978, Horace Sutton claimed that "a monumental renaissance" was underway as Americans fell in love with their cities—again.[2] *U.S. News & World Report* noted that "little more than a decade ago, U.S. cities were torn by riots that erupted despite a flurry of federal programs aimed at easing urban woes. . . . Now . . . the outlook for many of the nation's big urban centers, ironically, is upbeat."[3]

In these last years of the decade, commentators were inclined to predict a rosy future. Neal Peirce, a veteran political writer, was most effusive. He wrote that "the inner cities of America are poised for a stunning comeback, a turnabout in their fortunes that could be one of the most significant developments in our national history."[4] By the 1990s, Peirce's prediction seemed to have come true. Many once-declining cities were thriving. Even Cleveland, a city that had suffered some of the worst losses of residents, jobs, and businesses, was no longer a "national synonym for urban collapse," but, under corporate leadership, had rebounded.[5]

After the recession of 1973–1975, the cities were rediscovered, and not just by segments of the middle class. Numerous large investors were also enticed. Once the 1981–1982 recession passed, a vast outpouring of investment flowed into the cities to build luxury housing, office buildings, retail malls, and waterfront complexes. Capital was literally returning to the city, rather than abandoning it for the suburbs.[6] The geographic switch was linked to the rise of financial and business services in the downtowns. These new employment centers replaced old-line manufacturing as these city's primary economic function, and the subsequent increase in central business district employment made inner-city locations attractive to the professional middle class. Moreover, a robust economy was boosting the discretionary income of middle- and upper-income urbanites.

Blake Fleetwood's celebratory comment about New York City in 1979 could just as easily have been applied to Boston, Baltimore, Cincinnati, Washington (D.C.), Philadelphia, Chicago, and other places that had recently been on the list of large cities in decline: "Indeed, the evidence of the later '70s suggests that New York of the '80s and '90s will no longer be a magnet for the poor and the homeless, but a city primarily for the ambitious and educated—an urban elite."[7] This new urban elite would be employed in high-wage corporate and banking firms as financial consultants, insurance executives, stock brokers, lawyers, upper-level managers, and real estate professionals. They would work in the new office buildings that, it seemed, had appeared overnight, dramatically reshaping skylines.

Newsweek pointed to a "new hope abroad in the cities—a sense that the older cities of the Northeast and Midwest are staging a Big Comeback from the urban crisis of the 1960s." One aspect of this was "a vision of commercial resurgence, of booming retail sales downtown and corporations gobbling up every square foot of office space in new towers."[8] Reinvestment was evidence that the heart of decayed cities could be revived. The president of the Williams Realty Corporation in Tulsa resuscitated an earlier urban metaphor: "The core of the cities is the figurehead or central image. If you let it deteriorate or die, it has a bad effect on the total community."[9] Redeveloping that core and polishing that image was a major objective for investors during the 1980s.

Chicago, for example, was on the verge of "what may become the greatest corporate expansion in its history," noted the reporters of *Newsweek:* "It includes almost two dozen new skyscrapers costing $1 billion now planned or under construction."[10] An urban building boom was underway. "Fueled by massive capital infusions from around the world," two commentators wrote, "office buildings and shopping centers are rising from the rubble of ruins that seemed, only a few years ago, to foretell the death of great municipal centers."[11] Office expansion, moreover, meant construction jobs and increased tax revenues. It was also an indication that formerly manufacturing cities had found a new economic function—business, financial, and corporate services—that would pull them off the path of decline and place them on a trajectory of growth.

Equally visible and as symbolically important for the sense of revival was the growth in downtown retail activities. In the 1980s, numerous cities—Philadelphia and White Plains (New York) to name just two—constructed large retail malls that imitated their suburban counterparts, while other cities—Baltimore, Boston, New York, and Toledo—built what came to be called "festival marketplaces." The business editor of *Builder* magazine wrote that "single-handedly, these downtown development projects, with their distinctive architecture, unusual settings, special mix of shops, restaurants and entertainment and unique urban style, rekindled sparks of life in their cities and, in turn, became celebrations of the vibrancy and diversity of city life."[12] They were sited along waterfronts and in historic districts and were designed to lure middle-income residents and tourists. Their goal was a "shopping experience" that combined luxury purchases, impulse buying, ethnic foods and fine dining, nightclubs, and street entertainment. In the 1990s, national and international chains—The Gap, Williams Sonoma, Benetton, Borders—developed stores on once-moribund retail streets. Together, festival marketplaces and revived shopping districts engendered a vibrant, upscale urban ambience that redefined the image of the city, making it attractive, safe, and pleasantly consumable.

No one earned more credit in the 1980s for the revival of once-decayed downtown retailing than James Rouse, a developer of shopping malls. Using governmental subsidies and the festival marketplace concept, Rouse found a way to make investment in downtown development profitable. He had his first successes with Boston's Fanueil Hall and Baltimore's Harborplace complex and went on to repeat these efforts in St. Louis, Milwaukee, New York City, San Francisco, and Atlanta (among other cities). For Rouse, "a city is hollow without a lively, effective retail core." Gurney Breckenfeld, writing about Rouse in *Fortune,* praised Rouse's retail projects for "recaptur[ing] the timeless delights to be found in the marketplace, the historic reason for cities."[13]

City governments and local elites were quick to grasp the significance of redefining the city as a place to shop and be entertained rather than as a site for making flour, brewing beer, or writing insurance. They pursued developers like Rouse who understood that one became "urban" by "experiencing" the city. "City" magazines—*Philadelphia Magazine,* for one—touted the new urban lifestyle, sports teams became necessary ingredients of a city's image, and television shows featured specific cities (*WKRP in Cincinnati,* for example, and later *L.A. Law* and *NYPD Blue* as brand-name logos). The American city was a commodity to be marketed, not a place in decline to be ignored. Karl Meyer, writing in *Saturday Review,* captured both sides of this turn of events when he wrote that

> [t]he big city, *our* city, is now indispensible to our self-esteem, so much so that we take a chauvinist delight in luring a
> Peter Rose to our baseball team, or a Zubin Mehta to our symphonic podium. In some ways, we are becoming very like the original Greek city-staters, in that our thirst for urban display is

overriding the less glamorous priorities of health, welfare, and education.[14]

This image of the rejuvenated city as a place of upscale consumption had its origins in the expansion of corporate and financial services. The highly publicized lifestyle that the city now represented was closely tied to the ostensible return of the middle-class to gentrified neighborhoods, and that movement was dependent on the expansion of high-wage, white-collar jobs in the city's core.

Key to this new image of urbanity were the gentrifiers—young, urban professionals known colloquially as yuppies. *Business Week* reported in 1977 that "young middle-class couples, many of them the children of parents who led the flight to the suburbs a generation ago, are leading the deslumming movement."[15]

In search of an active, urban lifestyle, young professionals were spurring a back-to-the-city movement. "While many experts sound the death knell for cities," one national magazine noted, "an increasing number of people—many of them refugees from the suburbs— are snapping up block after block of urban property, convinced the city offers a better way of life."[16]

Typically, "the urban pioneers move to an old declining neighborhood, populated mainly by blacks and varied ethnic groups, adjacent to downtown or within easy commuting distance. As the new owners fix up, paint and improve their houses, others join in. Property values rise. Sometimes, speculators move in, too, but most often the activity is by owner-occupants."[17] Gentrifiers were even found entering neighborhoods previously ripped apart by riots and still frequented by prostitutes and drug dealers. Mayor Coleman Young of Detroit told *Nation's Cities* that "for the first time in years, you find white middle-class people mingling with blacks shopping for houses in better neighborhoods."[18] The phenomenon, despite doubts about its scale and persistence, stunned commentators accustomed to urban decline.

This new urban elite wanted renovated neighborhoods stocked with like-minded people, along with shopping and entertainment opportunities. Joseph Baum, president of a Hilton Corporation subsidiary, pointed to a desire for a "sensuality of place"—urban areas of diverse and vibrant activities in which the urban gentry could satisfy their need for conspicuous consumption.[19] Gentrified neighborhoods became defined by the "power to spend" rather than any racial and ethnic characteristics. Ethnically diverse urban neighborhoods had been replaced by neighborhoods that were more like suburban shopping malls. "I don't have to move back to the suburbs . . . [t]he suburbs have moved to me," one observer noted.[20]

Writing in *American Scholar,* Aristedes (the *nom de plume* of Joseph Epstein) parodied the rise of upscale retailing in the cities and the proliferation of stores with names like Rag-Time Boutique (rather than Howard Street Secondhand Clothing) and Moveable Feast. He labeled this Boutique America—"the new urban renewal"—and linked it to the decline of immigration and the expansion of the middle class. He aptly summarized the lifestyle of these young, urban professionals: "To live in Boutique America is to live in a state of permanent transitoriness, a tourist in one's own neighborhood."[21]

These urban dwellers seemed to be rejecting the old suburban lifestyle. Sutton noted that "the underlying reasons [for this monumental renaissance] can be traced to the disenchantment with the suburbs on the part of individuals who began a massive diaspora from urban centers to the country in the years following the Second World War and on the part of large corporations who [sic] followed them there."[22] Regardless, such a return was seen as highly selective. As Lewis Bolan, vice president of the Real Estate Research Corporation, suggested, "The cities will probably never get back the typical couple with two or more children that moved to the suburbs to raise their family." Ironically, this typical household was not all that desirable: "There is a question whether the core city really wants these people. No community, in terms of revenue, makes a profit on a family with many children."[23]

By the second urban renaissance of the 1990s, this issue was still unresolved. The historian Kenneth Jackson noted in 2001 that cities had revived due to an influx of immigrants and of young childless professionals who were abandoning the suburbia of their formative years. But, Jackson was doubtful that these new residents, and the sharp drop in crime, were enough to assure complete success: "Unfortunately, immigrants without options and yuppies without children cannot by themselves revitalize cities. Only ordinary families with ordinary incomes can do that."[24] Stable, tax-paying households with a long-term commitment to the city—the ever-elusive urban middle class—were preferable.

In the late 1970s and 1980s, the decreasing desirability of suburban life was connected to a host of factors that made cities more attractive. The energy crisis of the mid-1970s had driven up gasoline prices and thus commuting costs, the sales prices of single-family homes in suburbia had risen dramatically relative to incomes, and the costs of renovation in the city were competitive with new construction. The riots had subsided and violent crime remained under control. Moreover, the fiscal problems of the cities seemed to be subsiding.[25] On the other hand, newcomers to the suburbs brought "city problems" with them. The city was being rediscovered because it offered something different and better than the suburbs: a range of opportunities and amenities that appealed to young, urban professionals and affluent households of all ages.

The views of skeptics and critics hardly dampened the celebration of revival. They pointed to the comparatively small scale of the gentrification movement and the more robust forces of decline relative to those driving new investment and middle-class in-migration. Richard Nathan of Princeton University observed in 1980 how some cities (Houston, San Diego) were becoming richer but others (Detroit, St. Louis, Cleveland) were becoming poorer. The danger, he warned, was in "being lulled into a false sense of complacency about . . . cities. We are inclined to think that their problems are abating and that conditions aren't as serious as they were."[26] Nathan could claim vindication seven years later when the historian Jon Teaford provided testimonial evidence. "For all the ballyhoo about the back-to-the-city movement and publicity about glittering new downtown office-hotel-apartment complexes," he wrote, "the hard figures still indicate decline and decay."[27]

The predominant flight of people and capital to the suburbs had not ended, despite migration in the other direction. A syndicated columnist admonished his readers: "Read Census Bureau reports alone, and you'd never believe a revival was underway."[28] Aggregate statistics hardly registered the rebirth that seemed so visually obvious and anecdotally real. "In cold fact," the editors of *Newsweek* wrote, "most long-term indicators are still gloomy in nearly all the older Snow Belt cities." It seemed as if decline was endemic and chronic: "[T]he same old problems remain—from budget deficits and deteriorating water mains to troubled schools and a large welfare class."[29] Even in the early 1990s, after the prosperity of the previous decade and during another period of revival, commentators were skeptical of any reversal of urban fortunes. As one wrote, "Some of America's largest urban centers continue to deteriorate."[30]

This was a familiar list, and few commentators wanted to return to it. The promise of reinvestment was much more attractive than the reality of decay. Many commentators, though, could not give themselves fully to celebration. A special report in *The Progressive* put this unease in rhetorical form: "What happened to the victims of the great urban crisis of the 1960s? Did they get well? Did they go away? Or do they speak now in voices that can no longer be heard?"[31]

Critics were generally concerned with the increasing bifurcation of the city into enclaves of rich and poor. Most immediately bothersome about gentrification was the displacement of previous residents. Writing in *The Christian Century,* the director of communications for the United Methodist Church commented on the irony that while the new urban gentry were attracted to the ethnic and racial pluralism of inner-city neighborhoods, their presence subverted that diversity. The "increased rents and property values and a new elitism . . . drive the poor and lower income workers into suburban areas" or into adjacent and still undiscovered neighborhoods. Once again, the poor "are pawns in a game controlled by those with money."[32]

In essence, the poor were subsidizing the revitalization of the cities.[33] Not only were wealth and poverty inextricably linked, with the poor frequently serving the rich in return for low wages, poor housing, inadequate health care, and poor quality education, but the exchange was terribly one-sided. In fact, for the poor, gentrification was always and every place a bad deal.

Others were less sensitive to the costs of urban revival. Or, were they simply more realistic about the long-term prospects for the city? Everett Ortner, managing editor of *Popular Science Monthly*, was blunt: Displacement "is a small social price, compared to the large social price to be paid if these neighborhoods are destroyed. We are helping to stabilize the cities."[34] The "we" in Ortner's comments harkened back to an earlier belief in the pivotal contribution of the middle class to vibrant cities. Fleetwood expressed this less elliptically: "Urban experts and politicians are beginning to understand that only the middle and upper classes—not the poor—can rebuild the cities."[35] Fleetwood's observation thus pointed to one of the factors that had made this particular form of reinvestment so attractive during the late 1970s and 1980s: Ostensibly, it occurred with little of the massive governmental assistance that had previously been touted as the solution to urban decay.

City governments were still reeling from the fiscal difficulties of the mid-1970s even as urban revival was under way in the 1980s. Property taxes remained high when compared with those of the suburbs, and tax bases were still anemic.[36] In addition, proposed federal government budget cuts were about to reduce aid to cities even further. Hope for more federal assistance had been aroused in 1978 when President Carter's advisors publicly debated the possibility of a national urban policy. Mary Jo Huth, a professor of sociology, aptly captured the hope that while federal programs had heretofore and implicitly been anti-city, a new "urban ethic" had emerged. She wrote, "If the new optimism persists, we may be at the beginning of a new direction in domestic policy which will provide livable cities for the future."[37] The dream was not to be realized.

Warning that "federally-administered cures have often had consequences worse than the original diseases," the journalist Helen Leavitt joined the critics of prior governmental efforts. Her comments reflected a widely held doubt about the efficacy of a national urban policy. Even the 1977 report of the president's Urban and Regional Policy Group had pointed out how interstate highways had given rise to suburban sprawl and undermined mass transit while federally financed home mortgage assistance had encouraged mass urban exodus. Moreover, Leavitt observed that "[President] Carter is skeptical of the idea that money can solve everything."[38] Leavitt, in effect, repeated the policy position of the federal government: "Federal programs should not be viewed as panaceas for the ills of cities. . . . The most essential ingredients of urban progress are local and state leadership in concert with private-sector resources."[39]

Regrettably, Carter's national urban policy proved not to be a serious commitment to the channeling of more resources to the cities. Nevertheless, its major initiative, the Urban Development Action Grant, soon became a symbol of and contributor to revival; cities used it to subsidize the new hotels and commercial developments that were keystones of their redevelopment schemes. Overall, however, the new urban agenda was mainly geared to encouraging local efforts that combined the resources and energies of the private sector, government, and community groups.

In recognition of this spreading of responsibility, Mayor George Voinovich of Cleveland asserted that "the new urban agenda demands a scrappy, independent city," one able to survive despite the diminution of federal aid.[40] The reality was that cities had lost legislative representation both at the federal and state levels as their populations shrank. Being independent was not a choice but a consequence. Marshall Kaplan of the University of Colorado posed this problem more broadly: "The question is what types of policies can help when urbanism isn't politically popular."[41]

In fact, the extolling of gentrification, festival marketplaces, and office development all could be viewed in political terms. Sidney Blumenthal, writing in the socialist newspaper *In These Times,* observed a "Social Darwinist cant" to the revival hyperbole. "[N]eoconservative ideologues," he wrote, "are trying to make political capital, blaming the victims, and lauding the victors."[42] This particular form of conservatism rejected the notion that the city should be hospitable to all classes and races. Instead, the city had come to be viewed as a business enterprise: "as a capital conserving, income generating center which will retain its vitality only through adherence to sound management procedures and a rational structure of economic incentives."[43] Those groups that could not contribute were not welcomed.

The returning middle class helped to expand office and retail activity, and both together enhanced the tax base and local tax revenues. The poor, it was generally believed, did neither.

The fact that revitalization was taking place without massive infusions of federal, state, or local governmental funds made it extremely attractive to elected officials. For many observers, not only had urban decline been abated and reversed, but the process was self-sustaining, operating without the need for politically contentious and often inadequate public intervention. Commentators of all political persuasions heaped praise on historic preservation, gentrification, and working-class efforts to resist the abandonment of neighborhoods by capital and governments—"fragile blossoms of hope scattered across [a] barren valley."[44] For decades, the decline of cities had occupied an ignoble place on the public agenda and had anguished and perplexed elected officials and urban experts. Simply put, revival removed it. Toward the end of the 1980s, urban decay seemed history, as it would throughout most of the 1990s. If not totally recovered, the cities had notably advanced in the quest for renewed prosperity.

GLITTER AND SQUALOR

The urban reinvestment of the 1980s and 1990s produced a peculiar postwar representation of the city. On the one hand, revitalization displaced decline as the central theme of urban commentary. On the other hand, renewed investment and the cessation of massive population loss, not to mention a rediscovered in-migration of middle-class households, brought to the fore many long-forgotten consequences of growth. Additionally, numerous commentators found it difficult to overlook an increasingly visible, bothersome, and deepening bifurcation of the city into rich and poor. A fascination with ranking cities on their "livability," however, blurred widening inequalities and thereby rescued revival from its critics. Critical commentary, regardless of its severity, could not dislodge the discourse from its hopefulness.

In 1989, *U.S. News & World Report* sent reporters around the country to assess the recent progress made by cities such as New York,

Berkeley, Bayonne (New Jersey), and Natchez (Mississippi). The resultant article was titled "Coming Home." Like so much travel writing, it mixed nostalgia and surprise to contrast what was now to what had once been. William Allman, the reporter sent to St. Louis, wrote in a particularly evocative manner. First, he reflected on what it had been like in the 1970s when, as a suburbanite, he attended baseball games in the city: "Returning from the city after a Cardinals' game at Busch Stadium, I would drive slowly homeward through the night, marveling at blocks upon blocks of empty lots and buildings of steel and concrete and brick unmarked by any human presence." Only in retrospect did his visit take on meaning: "Coming back to St. Louis after many years . . . the city's surface has changed considerably. The downtown area has been spruced up, the old train station is now a glitzy shopping mall and a few of the once stately but dilapidated downtown neighborhoods are being rehabilitated by pioneering former urbanites." Still, as far as Allman could tell, the city had not been saved: "[T]hese changes, while putting a shine on the old city, are mostly cosmetic. The downtown areas seemed designed primarily for tourists."[45]

A similar mix of optimism and realism characterized Robert Price's article, "The Good News about New York City." "There are positive things happening in the city," he wrote, "along with the bad." This former deputy mayor found employment growth and new housing outside Manhattan, particularly in the Bronx. He remarked that the poor "seek aggressively to become part of the middle class," cited improvements made to the city's public school system, and commented on how Mayor Edward Koch had turned a deficit of a billion dollars into a surplus. But, in closing, Price's incredulity seeped into his prose: "I went in search of positive signs—signs of economic growth, of vibrancy, of hope. I found them; that is hardly surprising. What is surprising is how *easily* I found them, and how abundant they are."[46]

Throughout the 1980s and thereafter, one did not have to search far for positive signs and vibrant cities. "[A]fter 50 years of discarded opportunities," D. J. Waldie wrote in 2001, "there are now new and hopeful signs that city life in Los Angeles has a chance of being revived."[47] A new concert hall, a new convention center, hotel expansion, and the renovation of Broadway, once the downtown's main shopping street, served as evidence. In Nashville, a city that had not caught the wave of the early 1980s' revival, the end of the century brought an end to adult bookstores and seedy nightclubs along its Broadway. The state's tallest skyscraper, water taxis on the Cumberland River, renewed tourism, and the return of downtown entertainment all attested to the city's dramatic renaissance.[48]

Middle-class commentators wanted more than glitz, and they wanted livable cities. *Newsweek* in early 1989 attempted to identify the "growing cities that combine good jobs and affordable housing with livability and lack of pretension." Not surprisingly, it found mid-size cities that were "manageable enough to avoid urban blight." The "hot" cities were places like Portland (Oregon), Albuquerque, St. Paul, Charlotte, Orlando, and Providence. Technology, the fine arts, restored neighborhoods, downtown investment, an energetic labor force, and headway in solving racial problems characterized these born-again urban places.[49]

The larger cities in the "livable" category, though, were faced with the problems that came with rapid growth and concentrated investments. People in Seattle worried about the congestion of new skyscrapers—a potential Manhattanization—and threats to the city's unique market districts. In Philadelphia, a proposal to build an office building higher than the statue of William Penn atop City Hall led to a public controversy over the aesthetic consequences of growth. That building and those that followed radically changed the city's skyline. San Franciscans passed laws to preserve the vistas and views that make that city so visually exciting. In New York, certainly the most densely developed city in the country, the architectural critic of *The New York Times,* Paul Goldberger, lamented the frenzied investments in new and bigger buildings and the real estate philosophy that all sites had to be developed to their fullest. Air quality, sidewalk space, subway access, and general ambience were all sacrificed. "New York is supposed to be a crowded city," Goldberger wrote, "it is supposed to be a city constantly renewing itself, and it is a city that thrives on a certain degree of disorder." Nevertheless, "to approve of dense, congested cities in principle is hardly to applaud a city in which land has such inflated value that virtually any building that makes the mistake of being less than a monolith is under threat of extinction."[50]

In effect, Goldberger pointed to the undesirable consequences of growth, the same growth that other commentators were celebrating. He was not alone. Other critics observed that the popularity of the cities meant more and more crowds and that overcrowding was likely to contribute to suburban sprawl.[51] Of specific concern was the widening gap between rich and poor, not only as experienced in the dichotomy of city and suburb, but also as it appeared within the revitalized cities themselves. The affluent bathed in economic expansion and the impoverished remained, as it was still nastily put, unwashed.[52]

As early as 1979, observers began to comment on an emerging "dual city." Fergus Bordewich, writing in the "city" magazine *New York,* was one of the first to make use of the obvious Dickensian reference. He contrasted the gentrified to the displaced, exploited tenants to rapacious landlords, and educated labor to "a kind of lumpen proletariat that isn't tied into work because work isn't there." Bordewich blamed city planners and derided the foolishness of hoping that the poor, after being pushed from neighborhood to neighborhood by gentrification, would leave the city. The more likely result, he thought, was that a new poor would replace an old poor. The problem was much more basic: "The only bulwark against the establishment of a permanent underclass," he wrote, "is work."[53]

Two commentators encouraged their readers to "look past the new fashion shops, the book stores, the restaurants, and you will find the underground economy at work. The sewing rooms and loading docks and kitchens of such places are the sweat shops of the working poor."[54] Low-wage jobs were proliferating in the revitalized city and "[f]illing the bad jobs are the makings of a new city proletariat composed of women, illegal immigrants, youths and minorities."[55] To Neal Peirce, it seemed that "the United States [was] practicing capitalism tempered with darwinism." The sharp contrasts were unavoidable: "Poverty, crack, violence and disease afflict millions of America's inner-city residents," while "[i]mmense wealth pours into urban financial markets and selected chic city neighborhoods." Expensive townhouses and shabby slums, smart boutiques and discount outlets, downtown office towers and aging factories could also be added to the list of dualisms.[56]

Writing in the magazine *dollars & sense,* two academics quantified one of these stark distinctions. "In 1986," they wrote, "the richest 20% of New York City residents earned 19.5 times as much as the poorest 20%—a 25% increase since 1977."[57] Moreover, such inequalities were worsening. About 42 percent of the country's poor people lived in the central cities in 1990, compared with 30 percent in 1968, with black poverty becoming even more spatially concentrated: 59 percent of the black poor lived in cities in 1990, compared with 34 percent in 1968. One might conclude that nothing had changed in the thirty years since President Johnson's Great Society: "Then, as now, the breeding ground of economic misery is the American city."[58]

Amid the "beautiful people" were the homeless, more and more prevalent on downtown streets, and an incorrigible underclass in which was concentrated the social and economic problems of society. That underclass, in turn, was clustered in racially segregated neighborhoods. Slums reappeared in the discourse, for they seemed to be spreading and deepening in intensity. Although this "dual city" perspective might be considered a dramatic shift from the celebration of revival, it had been around throughout the euphoric eighties. Even in the late 1970s, an editor of the *Smithsonian* visited Dallas to write of the "contrast of glitter and squalor." What Richard Williams found in this shining example of Sunbelt prosperity was a slum—West Dallas. "And if up-to-date Dallas has a shantytown problem," he asked, "what American city doesn't?"[59]

Disparities widened in the ensuing decades. The syndicated columnist Richard Reeves took Vice President Dan Quayle to task for a remark he had made to a political gathering in Omaha. Quayle had said that "America is the envy of the world." From his perch in Paris, this looked to Reeves like an opportunity for European derision. "Life in lean, mean America," Reeves wrote, "is seen as savage by pro-American citizens of Stockholm or Milan and by energetic capitalists in Tokyo or Singapore. People who take for granted free medical care and free education and know nothing of fear on their own streets are not lining up anymore for immigrant visas to an America that sometimes seems wretched and tempest-tossed." It was America's cities that came in for greatest disdain. In overseas conversations, Reeves noted, these cities, "spectacularly rich and frightenly impoverished, particularly New York, have often been compared these last few years to Third World cities."[60]

While one group of commentators was highlighting the contrasts and contradictions of urban revival, modern-day civic boosters turned their attention to city comparisons. In doing so, they contributed to the sense that urban decline had not been abolished. *Look*'s All-American cities and the "best cities in which to live" touted by numerous popular magazines evolved into a strategy for ranking cities from most to least livable. Using a multitude of indices, the strategy produced a single score that differentiated between the first and second most livable city and among all those that followed. Most importantly, it blurred the social and economic disparities within cities.

In 1975, *Time* magazine reported on a study conducted by the Midwest Research Institute that had ranked 243 metropolitan areas on the basis of their performance on 123 quantifiable variables. Statistical values, rather than emotional appeal, was the objective. Portland (Oregon), Sacramento, and Seattle, of the metropolitan areas with greater than fifty thousand population, emerged as outstanding, while Tampa, Philadelphia, and Memphis were classified as substandard.[61]

During the 1980s, Rand-McNally began producing its *Places Rated Almanac*. Achieving a high ranking became cause for local jubilation, and receiving a low ranking often elicited protest. In 1982, Atlanta and Washington, D.C., led the list. In 1985, it was Pittsburgh and Boston. The rankings were highly volatile from year to year; being the most livable city was a transitory status.[62]

As part of the American obsession with winning, ranking schemes proliferated. *Black Enterprise* magazine created a list of the "American cities that have become centers of success and opportunity for black professionals." Economic opportunities were a primary criterion, but Atlanta, with its good political atmosphere for black politicians, led the rankings.[63]

One was hard-pressed to find in these rankings the great disparities in wealth and opportunity that other commentators had used to characterized the revitalized city of the 1980s. Pittsburgh was a prime example. Despite a significant minority population, large public housing projects, concentrated poverty, and a regional economy devastated by the downsizing of the steel industry, it ranked number 1 in 1985 by being acceptable, but not outstanding, on most of the key indicators. Its low crime rate, reasonable housing costs, equitable climate, access to recreational facilities, and arts raised its score despite lingering problems of a prerevival era.[64] Pittsburgh was a "model of survival against high odds," a city that had "industrialized first . . . became obsolescent first, and . . . overcame obsolescence first." As Brendan Gill wrote, "The greater the prosperity [the Industrial Revolution] provided, the more repellent were the physical consequences." Thus, "Pittsburgh at the height of its success . . . [was at] . . . the nadir of its livability."[65]

Gill went on to praise the medium-size city and to relate large size with urban extinction. Despite revival, the big city was still suspect, enough so that the editors of *Changing Times* magazine in 1990 could still appeal to their readers by extolling, though somewhat equivocally, small-time life over life in the big city. "Breathes there an urbanite," they asked rhetorically, "who hasn't dreamed of [kissing the big city goodbye]?"[66]

This fascination with ranking cities, and thus trying to decide in which cities people should live and invest, continued during the urban prosperity of the 1990s. In innumerable articles, cities were ranked on whether they were the best places to raise families, healthiest for women to work, most segregated, worst for pedestrian safety, best for cycling and running, best for business, and most underrated.[67] Such rankings literally shouted out the ambivalence Americans have for their cities—recognizing that cities were doing well but still deeply concerned about those that were not, and thus about making the wrong choices. Yet, they were also an indicator that anti-urbanism was less virulent.

CALLOUS DISREGARD

Earl Graves, the publisher and editor of *Black Enterprise,* observed as early as 1979 that "[t]he worst hasn't happened to American cities." His skepticism became palpable as he went on to say that "[n]one has been consumed by riot or conflagration. . . . The advertised cataclysm didn't materialize and so now an equally absurd picture of recovery and rebirth is being painted."[68] Was the gloom that had characterized the discourse of the mid-1970s simply to be dismissed as myopic and insufficiently hopeful? Were the optimistic commentators of the 1980s and 1990s the fickle ones?

In the late summer of 1990, Ze'ev Chafets, a novelist and newspaper editor, published an account of conditions in Detroit. In describing its tragedy, Chafets evokes the 1967 riots, the flight of the white middle class, the collapse of the auto industry, the rise in unemployment and poverty, the erosion of the tax base, and high crime rates and drug abuse. He further notes the lingering consequences of these events and the immutability of their conditions: "Detroit today is a genuinely fearsome-looking place. Most of the neighborhoods appear to be the victims of bombardment . . . [and] . . . downtown Detroit is now pretty much empty."[69]

Race is at the center of Chafets' report, even as he strives to present a picture that balances crime and poverty with racial discrimination and race-driven politics. At one point, he observes tellingly that "in most parts of town, most of the time," Detroit is as black as Nairobi. Money, he proposed, was part of the solution, but would not improve matters unless an emotional reconciliation enabled "the black polis to rejoin the American family and to accept help without feeling humiliated or being robbed of its political gains." Displaying little optimism, the article ends with the thought that without such generosity and good will, America's first black metropolis and its white suburbs will fall to the flames of anger and depravity.[70]

Suburbanization was still "working to intensify the geographic separation of the races, particularly of whites from poor blacks." Moreover, race remained a core issue in a variety of debates about social welfare, fiscal conditions, housing, education, and taxes, even as it was suppressed rhetorically. Indeed, it had become one of the most powerful symbols in U.S. political discourse, one used to great advantage by the Republican Party throughout the 1980s and 1990s. National politics embraced the suburbs over the cities, the middle class over the underclass, and individual initiative over group advancement. Each of these choices exacerbated racial divisions.[71]

Kenneth Lipper, a former deputy mayor of New York City, was less appalled by urban tragedy than Chafets had been a year earlier. But, Lipper was still concerned that the city had not yet eradicated the roots of urban decline. Drugs were everywhere and crime abundant, he lamented. Homelessness was a crushing problem and, overall, the quality of life was deteriorating, a condition that encouraged the flight of corporations and well-to-do households. "Middle-class New York is sliding into decline," Lipper wrote, and absent its upper-middle and wealthy classes, "the city will flounder, without human and financial resources to right itself." His conclusion was alarmist and apocalyptic: "It would be a blow to civilization if we let this world-class city, this fragile organic creation, succumb to the ravages of urban barbarism."[72]

As the building boom of the 1980s dissipated and government officials began to uncover the shaky financial machinations that had fueled it, more and more commentators, like Lipper, returned to earlier refrains. *Newsweek* in 1990 noted that "[w]hile no municipal government is worse off than Philadelphia, cities throughout the northeast area are in tough economic straits." This included a New York City that was once again facing fiscal difficulties and possible bankruptcy.[73] Such commentary evoked remembrances of the discourse of the mid-1970s and earlier. A good comparison is this excerpt from a speech delivered before the Cleveland City Club in 1977 by Henry Reuss, chairman of the House Committee on Banking, Finance, and Urban Affairs. Congressman Reuss provided a concise description of the then current conditions: "Many of our great cities are sick—losing population, losing jobs, losing fiscal solvency, losing the experience of neighborhood and community, safety and attractiveness which are the reasons for their existence in the first place."[74]

Any respite from pessimism and foreboding slowly dissipated by the early 1990s as a recession, rising crime, homelessness, AIDS, drugs, and gang violence rose to public prominence. The discourse seemed to be back on its historical trajectory; its imagery, though, was somewhat stale. A number of commentators, if their observations were any indication, forgot that an urban renaissance had even occurred.[75] What would re-energize the discourse? Would the 1990s produce another crisis or a return to reinvestment and revitalization?

The answer was not far in the future. Only hours after the "not guilty" verdict in the Rodney King trial was made public on April 29, 1992, south-central Los Angeles, one of the poorest sections of the city, erupted in civil disobedience. Although the extended beating of King by Los Angeles police officers had been captured on videotape, a beating in which King offered minimal resistance, an all-white jury decided against the black victim and for the four white officers. The public reaction was one of disbelief and shock. Latinos, blacks, and whites—mostly men, but not all—took to the streets in part to protest, in part to express long-suppressed anger, and in part to engage in looting, arson, and violence. A reporter for *U.S. News & World Report* wrote that "[i]n south-central Los Angeles, as in many blighted urban communities, poverty and criminality are worse; anger has metastasized beyond the white vs. black engagements of the past to the growing variety of ethnic cultures that live in tense proximity; feral youth gangs have taken root and have at their disposal a mind-boggling arsenal of fire power."[76]

The toll was staggering; one reporter could not resist hyperbole—it was "the worst riot since the Civil War."[77] The insurrection went on for nearly three days, and at the end, fifty-eight people were dead and nearly 2,400 officially counted as injured. Property damage was estimated at $1 billion, with Korean store owners being particularly hard-hit. As estimated one hundred Asian-owned stores were burned, and, in total, twelve hundred businesses destroyed. Nearly fifteen thousand police and troops were eventually deployed and over seven thousand people arrested, with Latinos comprising 50 percent of the total and blacks 36 percent.[78]

Mortimer Zuckerman, the editor in chief of *U.S. News & World Report,* proclaimed that "Los Angeles writ large is a symptom of a domestic agenda too long unattended."[79] References to the race riots of the sixties, few as veiled as Zuckerman's, were abundant. Yet, the anger and alienation of Los Angeles did not materialize in comparable ways in other cities as it had a quarter of a century earlier. Atlanta, Seattle, and San Francisco experienced unrest, but New York, Newark, Philadelphia, and Detroit registered hardly any verdict-induced violence or public demonstrations. Moreover, racial unrest had continued after the prime riot years of the 1960s. Miami's Liberty City in 1980 and its Overtown section in 1982 and 1989 had witnessed bouts of public violence. The racial problems of the cities had not been resolved by national leaders; they had been ignored.

Visits to south-central Los Angeles by President George Bush and presidential candidate Bill Clinton, and a widespread public outpouring of concern and resolve, led one national magazine to assert that "the rioting in Los Angeles galvanized Americans to worry again about the state of their cities and, more importantly, about how to improve race relations."[80] The Bush Administration and leaders of Congress pledged financial assistance, and civic leaders in Los Angeles set up a nonprofit corporation to rebuild the south-central area. Federal lawmakers produced an omnibus emergency aid package for cities, and government disaster agencies offered immediate relief. By late 1992, the new urban aid bill had been vetoed by President Bush, Rebuild L.A. had merely produced a music video, and disaster aid had been stalled. Writing in Cleveland's *The Plain Dealer,* Neal Peirce offered a challenge: "[I]magine anything worse than the indifference, the political jockeying, the callous disregard of America's urban future, which official Washington is now demonstrating. I can't."[81]

For a brief moment, as if each new urban crisis boosted the discourse to a new peak (only to quickly subside to a pessimistic normalcy), commentators waxed eloquently and passionately about the need to address the fate of the cities and their importance to American prosperity. A few weeks after the riots, the editors of *Business Week* spoke boldly and without conditions: "If we fail to act," they wrote, "we will all be the poorer. Morally and economically."[82]

The conservative editor-in-chief of *The American Spectator,* R. Emmett Tyrrell, assessed blame: "Before the liberal Democrats took over the cities, life for the urban poor was hard but steadily improving. Then the federal government began its ministrations, costing $2.6 trillion since 1965."[83] Harold Meyerson, a member of the editorial board of the socialist journal *Dissent,* instead indicted the Republicans: "[T]he downward spiral of the inner city is linked to the same Reagan–Bush policies of national neglect that in less drastic ways have injured the white middle class."[84]

The political bickering, the lack of consensus about what to do about the cities, the volatility of cities as symbols of American race relations, and the fixation on suburbs all combined to create political stalemate. The editor of *Harper's Magazine* took a more Olympian perspective. Lewis Lapham wrote, "The idea of a great city never has occupied a comfortable place in the American imagination . . . and . . . [u]ntil we learn to value the idea of the city, we can expect to see the streets paved with anger instead of gold."[85]

It was not only the American ambivalence toward cities that was at issue. Our inability to mount a compassionate response to urban problems was inseparable from our reluctance to confront the issue of race. Cornel West, the director of the Afro-American Studies program at Princeton University, recognized the sense of powerlessness signaled by south-central Los Angeles. He attributed this "multi-racial, trans-class and largely male display of justified social rage" to the "lethal linkage of economic decline, cultural decay and political lethargy in American life." For West, race was the "visible catalyst, not the underlying cause." The problems of black people would not be solved if we did not address the flaws of American society that generated these conditions. Public discussions, however, avoided both the contradictions and the racial divisions. Consequently, because we are unable to talk about race, we could not address the crisis of the cities. West ended his essay by predicting that "[e]ither we learn a new language of empathy and compassion, or the fire this time will consume us all."[86]

Almost ten years later, Cincinnati also experienced the consequences of deeply rooted racial antagonisms. Fifteen black males had been killed by police in the past five years and police–community relations were at a low point. In April 2001, street violence was the response to another fatal shooting of a young black man. People protested; vandals looted and destroyed property. Over one hundred arrests were made, and forty people were injured. The usual handwringing took place, but with a federal and state response even more subdued than that which followed the 1992 Los Angeles riots. More than a single city had to erupt for a nation, now inured to racial unrest, to mobilize.[87]

The upheaval in Los Angeles brought to the surface of the discourse the domineering pessimism and unassailable realism that had characterized it throughout the 1960s and into the 1970s. The riots in Cincinnati returned us there, after nearly a decade of urban celebration. As always, though, such attitudes were tempered with a tenuous optimism and a cautious hopefulness. The revivalist discourse of the 1980s and 1990s had neither displaced nor foreshadowed the recentering of urban decline in the early 1990s. The euphoria of rebirth had displaced the fiscal crisis just as that crisis had, albeit temporarily, unseated "The Negro Problem," but the urban trauma of April 1992 brought race back into the debate with a vengeance. Obviously, the massive reinvestment had not been successful and the decline and decay of cities had not been halted during the 1980s and late 1990s.

The terrorist destruction of the twin towers of the World Trade Center in New York City on September 11, 2001, only briefly derailed the relentless American ambivalence toward the cities. In the attack's immediate aftermath, all of America seemed to embrace New York City, and the national outpouring of sympathy and assistance was overwhelming. The city that one observer called "the lighting rod for national resentment" gained, at least for the moment, a whole new mythic status.[88]

Before the "war on terrorism" and the U.S. incursion in Afghanistan took center stage, commentators began to debate what the attack meant for cities. Decentralization of the city's core was one of the most commonly heard, read, and debated recommendations. Numerous commentators pointed to a possible intensification of middle-class flight. Consensus, though, formed only around the inadvisability of building 110-story skyscrapers. Certainly, the cities were now vulnerable in ways that many people had not fully appreciated, and subject to a wider variety of national and global forces. In the throes of resolve, architectural historian Robert Bruegmann announced that "the urban revival now underway will not falter in the aftermath of terrorism."[89] He was half-right; revival did falter, but it did so because of a deepening recession, not the terrorist attacks. The discourse on urban decline had been only temporarily detoured.

MEMORY IS BLURRED

The discourse of the late 1970s through to the first years of the twenty-first century hints of a cyclical pattern—the decay of the mid-1970s and early 1980s turned into the revitalization of the 1980s. That revival ended with the recession of the early 1990s but was followed by another period in which Americans toned down the anti-urbanism that dominated the discourse in the decades after World War II. The euphoria of the 1980s and 1990s suppressed broad recognition of the cities' fundamental problems. Selective amnesia erased the past and the city's current social disparities. The writer of a special report for the Pacific News Service captured this interplay of recollection and forgetfulness: "Today, the agony of the cities—and the deeper national illness it symptomized—is a receding memory for most Americans. The memory is blurred not only by the passage of time but also by the appearance of what many regard as signs of recovery. Old symptoms have given way to new, more ambiguous ones."[90]

An "unadorned" and unqualified optimism is rare in the discourse on urban decline. Consider the view of the U.S. Conference of

Mayors in 1986, a view that dismissed the decline of cities, their racial divisions, and a host of other problems: "[S]ufficient economic segregation [exists] in the United States so that, in the absence of rebellion of decades past, the majority of Americans are not excessively inconvenienced by declining urban conditions."[91] One could hardly be more politely circumspect. With apologies made for those years when prosperity reigned, optimism has always struggled with pessimism when Americans have reflected on their cities. Pessimism, though, has always been haunted by past glories and future possibilities.

Reading the Discourse

CHAPTER 10

Epilogue

For over five decades, images of urban decline have flamed across the covers of national magazines, illustrated numerous front-page stories by major newspapers, and become a staple in the speeches of city officials. The discovery of one or another loss—of jobs, tax revenues, white households, a professional sports team—generated a multitude of academic studies and spawned a small industry of consultant reports. Analysts endeavored to pinpoint the strengths and weaknesses of cities in decline, the reasons for population loss and business flight, and the actions that governments might take to entice growth back to their jurisdictions. Pictures of abandoned houses, children playing in glass-strewn lots, traffic-clogged streets, boarded-up storefronts, and large-scale demolitions have made for striking visuals to focus the wandering mind of the television viewer.

People directly experienced urban decline when they visited parks that were poorly maintained or walked through once-busy neighborhoods blighted by abandoned factories. The absence of employment opportunities was less obvious, an absence that compelled city residents to leave for places where jobs were more plentiful. Of course, the whole of urban decline is never fully accessible. No one can perceive at one time decline's many facets. As a composite of our experiences and understandings of the city, urban decline appears symbolically and representationally; it comes to us through an open-ended and tangled public debate.

The voices in the discourse are beguiling. Numerous differences of opinion exist, yet we (as readers and listeners) cannot help but think that there is an incontestable reality to which commentators refer. Commentators present their views with confidence; events and conditions cohere. The issue of city size dominated in the 1920s when cities were overflowing their boundaries, blight and slums as World War II ended, race during the riots of the 1960s, the fiscal crisis a few years later, and poverty and inequality when growth returned in the 1980s and 1990s. Substantive themes appear to reflect actual urban conditions, a discourse without pretense.

Wrapped in Census Bureau data and eyewitness accounts, the extent and depth of urban problems seem beyond debate. And, although prescriptions (as compared to conditions) are more contentious, the available options have a self-evident quality. Each commentator, each in his or her own way, is entirely convincing.

As I have tried to demonstrate throughout this book, though, the discourse is not as transparent as one might first assume. "Events do not just hit us on the head, provoking reactions as if by reflex," the social critic Barbara Ehrenreich once wrote, "they come to us already thickly swathed in layers of judgment and interpretation."[1] Woven within and hidden beneath its surface are numerous subtexts. The city has a gravitational pull that brings to it a variety of other concerns. Commentators, moreover, are hardly constrained by the weight of "the data" to adhere to a specific interpretation or to portray conditions in a particular way.

Consequently, and when the discourse is taken as a whole, no one set of choices is offered to the exclusion of all others. At any one point in time, some commentators might counsel flight to the suburbs (or to exurban small towns), while other commentators praise the tenacity and vibrancy of urban neighborhoods. Edge cities beckon, but central cities still thrive. Over time, the general tone vacillates, with ambivalence the common thread.

Still, the discourse has dominant tendencies. On the whole, commentators favor growth; it arrives in the form of office construction and new housing, new businesses, inflated property values, and rising tax revenues. They want the cities to be populated by the middle class. Jobs are important, particularly those that require a college education. Governments are to intervene to spur investment, but not to interfere too much or in any way that constrains the prerogatives of private investors.

Critics worry about the inequalities that growth exacerbates, the emphasis on downtown investment to the detriment of struggling neighborhoods, an insensitivity to race, the lack of attention to manufacturing jobs, and the deification of gentrifiers. Sadly, these critics are in the minority. Their voices are muted; their indignations deflated by a paucity of ideas that might mobilize society to, once and for all, rescue the cities.

Any discussion that focuses on cities and their history, of course, is likely to be filled with disagreements. To this extent, the discourse on urban decline favors specific responses and permits choice. It presents its readers with disputes about how they should live and with whom, where they should shop, the best and worst places to work or play and to bring up children, and the most desirable communities in which to invest and reside. The choices are conflicting; they are the possibilities one faces in an actual world.

Certainly, not so long ago, urban decline seemed inevitable. Cities were old, their factories obsolete, and manufacturing on a downward trajectory. Homes were shabby and neighborhoods crowded. Streets were congested. For a few decades, from the mid-1950s to the late 1970s, U.S. cities—as they had existed for a century—were apparently no longer viable. They had led useful lives, but now with maturity turning into senility, they were becoming relics. The country simply had to move on: to the suburbs, to suburban-style Sunbelt cities, to edge cities, and back to small towns.

Nonetheless, the United States today is no less an urban society than it was when World War II ended or when cities were straining their bounds in the 1920s. Rather, it is so profoundly an urban society that it draws on, even thrives on, the vibrancy and, ironically, the precariousness of its cities.

Without cities, we are a country without history. Though the cities' political weight has been waning since the 1960s, cities retain profound cultural and social significance. Moreover, they continue to propel regional economies, without which the national economy could not function. Despite more than a century of purported decline, cities have not actually disappeared. This does not mean that Americans love their cities, nor does decline imply that they hate them. It simply means that the phenomenon of urban decline is fundamental to an understanding of America as a nation.

Regardless of its pessimism and fears, its moral condemnation and outrage, and its insensitivities, the discourse proclaims that cities, those places of concentrated human energy and shared identity, will forever figure prominently in the country's development and occupy the core of debates about who Americans are and how they should live together. This is a discourse of accommodation; it operates to reconcile listeners and readers to the contradictory dynamics of urban development. Probing to its core reveals not that decay and deterioration are inherent to cities, but that destruction is essential to the creativity of a contradiction-filled political economy. Growth and decline, reward and sacrifice, celebration and disappointment are *the* dialectics of urban change.

The implications are profound. First, cities, as we came to understand them in the late nineteenth and early twentieth centuries, are expendable. Under capitalism, the country is highly differentiated and uneven development shows little preference for places where investment and people were once concentrated. What capitalism requires is agglomeration, and this can take many forms, only one of which is the industrial city. Even the global cities of the late twentieth century might well fade as capital circulates in new ways and novel mechanisms are developed to manage investment and disinvestment.

Second, U.S.-style capitalism requires decline. There is no growth without decline, and no investment without disinvestment. Even inner-ring suburbs, whose picturesque allure once offered a stark and attractive alternative to the congested and dangerous city, are facing the same conditions of decay their central cities once experienced.[2] It is the "decline"—real or otherwise—of society that is sited in the cities. Consequently, urban decline will endure as long as society's tensions and conflicts remain unresolved.

Anchored in a capitalist order insufficiently reined in by democracy and perplexed by the frictions inherent to multiculturalism, urban ambivalence persists. Tolerance for diversity clashes with an obsession with national identity, freedom of speech undermines shared norms and revered symbols, idealism infringes on American pragmatism, racism makes a lie out of equality, national compassion exists uneasily alongside the neglect of enduring poverty, and a peacekeeping image seems ludicrous, given militaristic excursions. Each of these tensions is grounded in the cities. Consequently, Americans have never been quite sure whether they wish cities well, whether they find them to be abominations or treasures, or whether they should resign themselves to living with their flaws.

Since the early 1800s, cities have served as the scapegoat for society's ills. Why did this happen? Why did cities become the national symbol of decay and perversion?

Any answer must begin with the way in which investors centralize activities in order to organize the flow of capital and governments act similarly to enhance their governing capacity.[3] Their actions concentrate geographically the sources of alienation and the consequences of exploitation. In this way, attention is directed to the cities, thereby shifting the object of blame from society more generally to cities more specifically. Our limited consciousness of capitalism's dynamics becomes conflated with the processes of urbanization to produce an ideological siting of decline.

This perspective is reinforced by the diverse social relations of cities, with their multiple subjectivities and fragmented social arrangements. Social bonds are loosened and reestablished, norms contested and redefined, and moral limits stretched and constricted. Innovation is rewarded and punished, and cultural differences condemned and celebrated. These tensions undermine the security of one or another group. They threaten, and they attract public attention.[4]

Such tensions likewise subvert cohesive and comprehensible representations. Representations are always unstable, with all the ontological and ideological dangers this entails. Moreover, they require constant attention as they shift in content and form over and over again.[5]

When Americans talk about the dire conditions and dismal fate of cities, it is not only because what has and is happening in cities churns up the frightening underside of society, a side many prefer to remain invisible. Nor is it simply because such discussion reveals the future as it might unfold, with its many unpredictable challenges to who we are and how we want to live. Cities are in decline because they threaten our security and identity, and because society itself is riven with contradictions whose presence we can neither accept nor eliminate. Urban decline exists because we have made it so.

The various unstable and divergent perspectives that comprise the discourse cannot be reconciled by studies claiming privileged access to what is really happening. Even the Bureau of the Census, on which many commentators hung their most dire warnings or looked to for signs of resurgence, can offer only circumstantial evidence. It is not just that the evidence is always voluminous, an abundance from which to choose: so many impressions, so many anecdotes, so much data, so many images, so many metaphors. Rather, no matter what information is selected, even if commentators attempt to include all types without prejudice, it still has to be interpreted and presented. Choices have to be made.

A major consequence of the discourse, then, is to feed anti-urbanism by connecting general fears and anxieties to conditions, events, and peoples within cities. Whether commentators mention traffic congestion or slums, soaring tax burdens or broken-down neighborhood swimming pools, Americans cannot but imagine that conditions might become worse or spread into communities heretofore unscathed. When commentators observe how people have responded, their audience cannot help but ask what they should have done or will do when decline deepens or when prosperity brings forth the resources to redress past sins. When commentators suggest the likely rewards of action and costs of inaction, Americans face choices that cannot be ignored. Reporters, elected officials, academic experts, and editorial writers compose the story of urban decline, and Americans study their words in search of guidance.[6]

For the advice to be adopted, commentators must offer credible explanations of why cities declined and convince readers that the processes by which some places prosper while others do not are natural and even desirable. One way to do this is to evade society's many contradictions. If people cannot be convinced that decline is inevitable, at least they might come to believe that it is tolerable; if not natural, at least reversible; if not curable, at least susceptible to containment.[7]

Commentators aim to create comprehensible stories that give meaning to urban decline without undermining widely shared beliefs or the ideological underpinnings that support dominant interests. Generally, they wish to tell a story of progress.[8] Their strategy is to displace people's deep-seated insecurities onto the cities. The city becomes the symbol and the scapegoat for the destitution, alienation, oppression, decay, and fears engendered by a flawed political economy. Commentators thereby stifle and rechannel the indignation and outrage that are the appropriate responses to the injustices and inequalities of urban America.

The observations and opinions of commentators provide both sense and security. The discourse offers explanations; it gives answers to the "why" of urban decline by, for example, linking the various "problems" of the cities to the "opportunities" in the suburbs, seemingly within the same coherent story. By providing a means to comprehend decline, anxiety and fear are reduced and people are reassured. The listeners and readers of the discourse achieve, albeit fleetingly, a sense of security. Commentators foster trust that reality exists as it appears to be. This also allows them to serve as a source of advice.

In this way, the discourse mediates the dissonances that people experience as they react to declining cities. But it also filters how they listen to the interpretations of their actions—the social trends. People "read" the discourse for reassurance that they are doing what is right, for evidence that their actions are defensible, and for validation of their status as victims or survivors. The discourse affirms anger and makes undesirable conditions tolerable. All of this helps to reconcile "what is" with "what might be."

To the extent that the discourse expresses the thoughts of those allowed to speak and be heard and functions to tame rather than erase the causes of what most threatens, it legitimates the world as it is. Americans are thereby inclined to be more accepting of the many disruptions and disparities that engulf them and to acquiesce more readily to society's dominant interests.[9]

By isolating decay and decline in the cities, the discourse additionally subverts a society-wide sharing of responsibility for the dire city conditions faced by those too poor or too powerless to flee. Moral obligations vanish. The plight of female-headed households in Harlem is disconnected from the affluent families in Scarsdale, the fiscal crisis of Philadelphia from newly built schools in suburban Lindenwold, the homeless of downtown Los Angeles from the boutiques of Beverly Hills. The failure to make these connections weakens a moral discourse centered on the development and underdevelopment of cities and regions, and suburbs and small towns.

People, now becalmed, leave moral choices aside as they ponder where and how to live and invest. The discourse allows them to live comfortably with their choices. These choices are easier when Americans are less burdened by personal uncertainties and misgivings and less bothered by the juxtaposition of growth and decline, affluence and poverty. As long as this continues, a just society will remain elusive.

By reading, listening to, and speaking the discourse on urban decline, Americans shrink the distances between individual experiences and join a public debate about how they should live their lives and in what manner of society. At the same time, they are burdened with a language of fear and loss, sacrifice, and purported progress. The discourse smothers the actual causes of discontent. It stifles an awareness of how cities might be different. As a result, Americans are unable to imagine cities in which shared prosperity, democratic engagement, and social tolerance are the norms rather than the exceptions. To allow cities to be the discursive sites for society's contradictions is to be imprisoned in the cynicism of decline.

No matter how Americans read the discourse on urban decline, no matter what point of view they take, they cannot escape the contradictions that make large cities both fearful and alluring. Ambivalence prevails.

Notes

NOTES TO PREFACE

1. For local variation, see Jon C. Teaford's *The Rough Road to Renaissance* (Baltimore, MD: Johns Hopkins University Press, 1990). Teaford's focus, though, is urban redevelopment (in twelve large central cities), not urban decline.
2. One exception is Dana F. White's *The Urbanists, 1865–1915* (New York: Greenwood Press, 1989). His theme is the public perception of the evolving urban culture of the modern city. He draws on magazines and journals to tell the story.
3. See Gunther Barth, *City People: The Rise of Modern City Culture in Nineteenth-Century America* (New York: Oxford University Press, 1980); William Cronon, *Nature's Metropolis: Chicago and the Great West* (New York: W. W. Norton & Company, 1991); Peter Fritzsche, *Reading Berlin 1900* (Cambridge, MA: Harvard University Press, 1996); David Schuyler, *The New Urban Landscape* (Baltimore, MD: Johns Hopkins University Press, 1986); and Daphne Spain, *How Women Saved the City* (Minneapolis: University of Minnesota Press, 2001).
4. Among numerous book-length, synthetic narratives are Carl Abbott, *Urban America in the Modern Age* (Arlington Heights, IL: Harlan Davidson, 1987); Howard P. Chudacoff, *The Evolution of American*

Urban Society (Englewood Cliffs, NJ: Prentice-Hall, 1975); Peter R. Gluck and Richard J. Meister, *Cities in Transition* (New York: New Viewpoints, 1979); Blake McKelvey, *The Emergence of Metropolitan America, 1915–1966* (New Brunswick, NJ: Rutgers University Press, 1963); Zane L. Miller, *The Urbanization of Modern America* (New York: Harcourt Brace Jovanovich, 1973); Jon C. Teaford, *The Twentieth Century American City* (Baltimore, MD: Johns Hopkins University Press, 1986); Jon C. Teaford, *Cities of the Heartland: The Rise and Fall of the Industrial Midwest* (Bloomington: Indiana University Press, 1993); and Sam Bass Warner, *The Urban Wilderness* (New York: Harper & Row, 1972). Numerous city biographies could also be cited, including Carol E. Hoffecker, *Corporate Capital: Wilmington in the Twentieth Century* (Philadelphia: Temple University Press, 1983), and Mark Goldman, *High Hopes: The Rise and Decline of Buffalo, NY* (Albany: SUNY Press, 1983).

5. Examples include John T. Cumbler, *A Social History of Economic Decline* (New Brunswick, NJ: Rutgers University Press, 1989); Arnold R. Hirsch, *Making the Second Ghetto* (Cambridge: Cambridge University Press, 1983); Thomas J. Sugrue, *The Origins of the Urban Crisis* (Princeton, NJ: Princeton University Press, 1996); Jon C. Teaford, *The Rough Road to Renaissance;* and Lawrence J. Vale, *From the Puritans to the Projects: Public Housing and Public Neighbors* (Cambridge, MA: Harvard University Press, 2000).

6. Since the first edition was completed in the early 1990s, a number of quite good books on the city have considered the importance of representation. To name just a few: Mike Davis, *Ecology of Fear* (New York: Metropolitan Books, 1998); James Donald, *Imagining the Modern City* (Minneapolis: University of Minnesota Press, 1999); Brian Ladd, *The Ghosts of Berlin* (Chicago: University of Chicago Press, 1997); Jan Lin, *Reconstructing Chinatown* (Minneapolis: University of Minnesota Press, 1998); Peter Preston and Paul Simpson-Houstey, eds., *Writing the City* (London: Routledge, 1994); and Alex Reichl, *Reconstructing Times Square* (Lawrence: University Press of Kansas, 1999). See also James S. Duncan, "Me(trope)olis: Or Hayden White among the urbanists," in Anthony D. King, ed., *Re-Presenting the City* (New York: New York University Press, 1996), pp. 253–268; Liam Kennedy, "'It's the third world down there!': Urban decline and (post)national mythologies in *Bonfire of the Vanities*," *Modern Fiction Stud-*

ies 43 (Spring, 1997), pp. 93–111; and Steve Macek, "Places of hor-
ror: Fincher's 'Seven' and the fear of the city in recent Hollywood
films," *College Literature* 26 (Winter, 1999), pp. 80–97. The need to
theorize representation, of course, was extant in the early 1990s; see,
for example, the writings of Christine Boyer, Jerry Herron, and
Anthony King, among others.

7. For this edition, I stripped away most of the postmodern reflections
   and interpretive interventions that began and ended the first edition.
   The result is more of a history book than a cultural studies text. There
   are also slight changes in style of presentation.

NOTES TO CHAPTER 1

1. Harland Bartholomew, "The American city: Disintegration is taking
   place," *Vital Speeches of the Day* 7 (November 1, 1940), p. 61.
2. Louis Wirth, "The cities' most serious crisis," *The American City* 59
   (November, 1944), p. 5.
3. See Arthur Herman, *The Idea of Decline in Western History* (New York:
   The Free Press, 1997) for this distinction. On the theme of decline in
   historical writings, see Randolph Starn, "Meaning-levels in the theme
   of historical decline," *History and Theory* 14 (1975), pp. 1–31; and
   Hayden White, "The tropes of history: The deep structure of the new
   science," *Tropics of Discourse* (Baltimore, MD: Johns Hopkins University Press, 1978), pp. 197–217.
4. See Starn, "Meaning-levels in the theme of historical decline," p. 3. On
   urban decline as loss, see Witold Rybczynski, "Losers," *The New York
   Review of Books* 43 (1996), pp. 34–36. On the relation of decline to
   utopian thought, see Ruth Glass, *Cliches of Doom* (Oxford: Basil
   Blackwell, 1989), especially pp. 125–128.
5. For an introduction to this debate, see Paul Kennedy, *The Rise and Fall
   of Great Powers* (New York: Random House, 1987); David S. Landes,
   The Wealth and Poverty of Nations (New York: W. W. Norton and
   Company, 1998); and Kenneth W. Thompson, "The literature of
   decline," *Ethics and International Affairs* 3 (1989), pp. 303–315. A literature also exists on the global competitiveness of cities. See John Mollenkopf, "Cities in the new global economy," *The American Prospect* 13
   (Spring, 1993), pp. 132–141; and David Wilson, ed., "Globalization

and the changing U.S. city," *The Annals of the American Academy of Political and Social Science,* 551 (May, 1997).

6. For the urban histories I have in mind, see note 4 in the Preface. On urban history and theory, see Timothy J. Gilfoyle, "United States urban history: Theoretical graveyard or interpretive paradise," in Hans Krabbendam, Marja Roholl, and Tity de Vries, eds., *The American Metropolis: Image and Inspiration* (Amsterdam: VU University Press, 2001), pp. 13–26.

7. Jon C. Teaford, *The Road to Renaissance* (Baltimore, MD: Johns Hopkins University Press, 1990).

8. As implied, the life-cycle metaphor infects histories with the teleological sense that what came after explains what came before.

9. Joseph A. Schumpeter, *Capitalism, Socialism and Democracy* (New York: Harper & Row, 1942), pp. 81–86. See also Marshall Berman, *All That Is Solid Melts into Air* (New York: Penguin, 1988).

10. Malcolm Bradbury, "The cities of modernism," in Malcolm Bradbury and James McFarlane, eds., *Modernism: 1890–1930* (Sussex, UK: The Harvester Press, 1978), pp. 96–104; Lewis Mumford, *The Culture of Cities* (New York: Harcourt, Brace, 1938); William Sharpe and Leonard Wallock (ed.), *Visions of the Modern City* (Baltimore, MD: Johns Hopkins University Press, 1987); Stephen Toulmin, *Cosmopolis: The Hidden Agenda of Modernity* (Chicago: University of Chicago Press, 1990); and Raymond Williams, "Metropolitan perceptions and the emergence of modernism," *The Politics of Modernism* (London: Verso, 1989), pp. 37–48.

11. See, for example, Blake McKelvey, *The Urbanization of America, 1860–1915* (New Brunswick, NJ: Rutgers University Press, 1967) and Eric H. Monkkonen, *America Becomes Urban* (Berkeley: University of California Press, 1988).

12. The demise of community was a central concern of early sociologists. See Thomas Bender, *Community and Social Change in America* (Baltimore, MD: Johns Hopkins University Press, 1982) and Richard Sennett, ed., *Classic Essays on the Culture of Cities* (New York: Appleton-Century-Crofts, 1969).

13. Berman, *All That Is Solid Melts into Air,* p. 15.

14. The phrase "urban village" draws its academic salience from Herbert Gans's *The Urban Villagers* (New York: Free Press, 1962) and Jane Jacobs's *The Death and Life of American Cities* (New York: Vintage, 1961). On small town nostalgia, see Alan Ehrenhalt, *The Lost City: Dis-*

covering the Forgotten Virtues of Community in Chicago in the 1950s (New York: Basic Books, 1995). For an introduction to the history of suburbia in the United States, see Rosalyn Baxendall and Elizabeth Ewen, *Picture Windows: How the Suburbs Happened* (New York: Basic Books, 2000); Robert Fishman, *Bourgeois Utopias* (New York: Basic Books, 1987); and Kenneth T. Jackson, *Crabgrass Frontier* (New York: Oxford University Press, 1985).

15. Carlo Rotella, *October Cities: The Redevelopment of Urban Literature* (Berkeley: University of California Press, 1998).

16. Discussions of postmodernism and the city can be found in Michael Dear, *The Postmodern Urban Condition* (Oxford: Blackwell, 2000); David Harvey, *The Condition of Postmodernity* (Oxford: Basil Blackwell, 1989); Fredric Jameson, "Post-modernism, or the cultural logic of late capitalism," *New Left Review* 146 (July/August, 1984), pp. 53–92; Paul L. Knox, "The restless urban landscape," *Annals of the Association of American Geographers* 81 (June, 1991), pp. 181–209; and Edward W. Soja, *Postmodern Geographies* (London: Verso, 1989), pp. 190–248. See also Mike Davis's wonderfully rich and compelling history of Los Angeles: *City of Quartz* (London: Verso, 1990).

17. David Harvey offers a critical perspective in his "Flexible accumulation through urbanization: Reflections on 'post-modernism' in the American city," *Antipode* 19 (December, 1987), pp. 260–286. Edward Relph's *The Modern Urban Landscape* (Baltimore, MD: Johns Hopkins University Press, 1987) and Nan Ellin's *Postmodern Urbanism* (Cambridge, MA: Blackwell, 1996) address these issues from an architectural and city-planning point of view.

18. Sharon Zukin, *Landscapes of Power* (Berkeley: University of California Press, 1991), p. 221.

19. Mike Davis, "Urban renaissance and the spirit of post-modernism," *New Left Review* 151 (May/June, 1985), pp. 106–113; Mike Davis, "*Chinatown,* part two? The 'internationalization' of downtown Los Angeles," *New Left Review* 164 (July/August, 1987), pp. 65–86; and Saskia Sassen, *The Global City* (Princeton: NJ: Princeton University Press, 1991).

20. John H. Mollenkopf and Manuel Castells, eds., *The Dual City* (New York: Russell Sage Foundation, 1991), pp. 405–418.

21. The quote is from Garry Wills, "American Adam," *The New York Review of Books* 44 (March 6, 1997), p. 30. Of a vast literature on anti-urbanism, see Thomas Bender, "Are cities American?" *CultureFront* 1 (1992), pp. 4–11; James B. Chapin, "Why Americans hate cities,"

Democratic Left 20 (July/August, 1992), pp. 14–16; Alfred Kazin, "Fear of the city: 1783–1983," *American Heritage* 34 (February/March, 1983), pp. 14–23; and Daniel Lazare, *America's Undeclared War: What's Killing Our Cities and How We Can Stop It* (New York: Harcourt, 2001). One of the well-exercised ironic revelations in this debate is the juxtaposition of government data showing that most Americans live within cities, whereas opinion polls indicate that most Americans wish to live in the suburbs or the countryside. For further consideration of this point, see Warren Susman, "The city in American culture," *Culture as History* (New York: Pantheon, 1984), pp. 237–251.

22. William Cronon grounds these themes in the emergence of Chicago as a national city. See his *Nature's Metropolis: Chicago and the Great West* (New York: W. W. Norton & Company, 1991), especially pp. 357–364.

23. Raymond Williams tells this story for England in his *The Country and the City* (New York: Oxford University Press, 1973). For the United States, see Leo Marx, *The Machine in the Garden* (New York: Oxford University Press, 1964).

24. For discussions of the role of nature in this discourse, see James L. Machor, *Pastoral Cities: Urban Ideals and the Symbolic Landscape of America* (Madison: University of Wisconsin Press, 1987); Marx, *The Machine in the Garden;* Michael Paul Rogin, "Nature as politics and nature as romance in America," in *Ronald Reagan, the Movie* (Berkeley: University of California Press, 1987), pp. 169–189; and Peter J. Schmidt, *Back to Nature: The Arcadia Myth in Urban America* (Baltimore, MD: Johns Hopkins University Press, 1990). On the origins of the pastoral in urban discourse, see George Shulman, "The myth of Cain: Fratricide, city building, and politics," *Political Theory* 14 (May, 1986), pp. 215–238.

25. Thomas Bender, "The end of the city?" *Democracy* 3 (Winter, 1983), pp. 8–20; and Walter Berns, "Thinking about the city," *Commentary* 56 (October, 1973), pp. 74–77.

26. Morton White and Lucia White, *The Intellectual versus the City* (New York: New American Library, 1962). The first quote is on page 16—note the use of *ambivalence*—and the second on page 221.

27. White and White, *The Intellectual versus the City,* p. 227. See also Susman, "The city in American culture."

28. Thomas Bender, *Toward an Urban Vision* (Baltimore, MD: Johns Hopkins University Press, 1982), p. xi.

29. Michael Kammen, *People of Paradox* (New York: Vintage, 1973), p. 290.

30. For an introduction to this perspective, see Manuel Castells, "The wild city," *Kapitalistate* 4–5 (Summer, 1976), pp. 2–30; Peter Dreier, John H. Mollenkopf, and Todd Swanstrom, *Place Matters: Metropolitics for the Twenty-first Century* (Lawrence: University Press of Kansas, 2001); Ira Katznelson, *City Trenches* (Chicago: University of Chicago Press, 1981); James O'Connor, *The Fiscal Crisis of the State* (New York: St. Martin's Press, 1973); and William Tabb and Larry Sawers, eds., *Marxism and the Metropolis* (New York: Oxford University Press, 1984, second edition). For a contrary view, see John A. Hall and Charles Lindholm, *Is America Breaking Apart?* (Princeton, NJ: Princeton University Press, 1999).

31. My comments are confined to internal conflicts. Moreover, they are not meant to devalue the multitude of oppositional movements and social protests that have occurred or to suppress the history of resistance carried out by Native Americans or the imperialism that extended the boundaries of the nation.

32. Joe R. Feagin and Robert Parker, *Building American Cities* (Englewood Cliffs, NJ: Prentice-Hall, 1990); John Logan and Harvey Molotch, *Urban Fortunes* (Berkeley: University of California Press, 1987); and Neil Smith, *Uneven Development* (Oxford: Basil Blackwell, 1984).

33. David Harvey, "The geography of capitalist accumulation," *The Urbanization of Capital* (Baltimore, MD: Johns Hopkins University Press, 1985), pp. 32–61.

34. Murray Edelman, *Constructing the Political Spectacle* (Chicago: University of Chicago Press, 1988), p. 119. See also Martin Bunzl, *Real History* (London: Routledge, 1997); Clifford Geertz, "Ideology as a cultural system," in David E. Apter, ed., *Ideology and Discontent* (New York: The Free Press, 1964); and Fred Weinstein, *History and Theory after the Fall* (Chicago: University of Chicago Press, 1990), pp. 38–44. My argument has a Habermasian flavor; it posits the importance of discourse in coordinating action and in producing normatively regulated action. See Stephen S. White, *The Recent Work of Jurgen Habermas* (Cambridge: Cambridge University Press, 1988), pp. 39–44; and Jurgen Habermas, *The Theory of Communicative Action* (Boston: Beacon Press, 1984), pp. 75–101. More broadly, see Robert N. Bellah, et al., *Habits of the Heart* (New York: Harper and Row, 1986) as regards Americans' search for a social philosophy. On choice and social respon-

sibility, see Isiah Berlin, "Determinism, relativism and historical judgement," in Patrick Gardiner, ed., *Theories of History* (New York: The Free Press, 1959), pp. 319–329.

35. An "objectivist" assessment of the discourse on urban decline is attempted by Gregory R. Weiher in his "Rumors of the demise of the urban crisis are exaggerated," *Journal of Urban Affairs* 11 (1989), pp. 225–242.

36. Peter L. Berger and Thomas Luckman, *The Social Construction of Reality* (New York: Anchor Books, 1967); Richard Harvey Brown, "Social science and the poetics of truth," *Sociological Forum* 5 (March, 1990), pp. 55–74; Hans Kellner, *Language and Historical Representation* (Madison: University of Wisconsin Press, 1989); Bruce London, *Discourse and the Construction of Society* (New York: Oxford University Press, 1989); Bryan D. Palmer, *Descent into Discourse* (Philadelphia: Temple University Press, 1990); Susan Wells, *The Dialectic of Representation* (Baltimore, MD: Johns Hopkins University Press, 1985); and Hayden White, *The Content of Form* (Baltimore, MD: Johns Hopkins University Press, 1987).

37. Denis Donoghue, "A guide to the revolution," *New York Review of Books* 30 (December 8, 1983), p. 45.

38. Kellner has written: "To get the story crooked is to understand that the straightness of a story is a rhetorical invention. . . ." See his *Language and Historical Representation* (Madison: University of Wisconsin Press, 1989), p. xi. On discourse as a collective representation, see Warren Susman, "Did success spoil the United States? Dual representations in postwar America," in Lary May, ed., *Recasting America* (Chicago: University of Chicago Press, 1989), pp. 19–37.

39. Leo Marx, "The puzzle of anti-urbanism in classic American literature," in *The Pilot and the Passenger* (Oxford: Oxford University Press, 1988), p. 210.

40. My premise is that societies are moral communities in which obligations and responsibilities are intrinsic components of all social relations.

41. "All of this results from the fact that people are rooted in multiple social locations and are characterized by multiple identities (as workers, parents, friends, neighbors, and members of ethnic, religious, linguistic, and other groups), and it is not possible to know prospectively, and it is difficult to know retrospectively, the basis on which people will respond or have responded, as workers or parents, or as workers one

time and as parents the next, and so on." See Weinstein, *History and Theory after the Fall*, p. 68.

NOTES TO CHAPTER 2

1. Throughout the book, I provide historical background drawing on both the urban histories listed in note 4 in the Preface and a number of general histories of the late twentieth century, including William H. Chafe, *The Unfinished Journey: America since World War II* (New York: Oxford University Press, 1986); Eric Hobsbawm, *The Age of Extremes* (New York: Vintage Books, 1996); James T. Patterson, *Grand Expectations: The United States, 1945–1974* (New York: Oxford University Press, 1996); and Donald H. White, *The American Century* (New Haven, CT: Yale University Press, 1996), among others.
2. Walter E. Weyl, "The brand of the city," *Harper's Magazine* 130 (1915), p. 774.
3. Editorial Comment, "Thriving cities," *Current Literature* 29 (December, 1900), p. 640.
4. Adna F. Weber, "Growth of cities in the United States: 1890–1900," *Municipal Affairs* 5 (June, 1901), p. 373.
5. Walter Wellman, "Rise of the American city," *McClure's Magazine* 17 (September, 1901), p. 470.
6. Josiah Strong, D. D. "The problem of the twentieth century city," *North American Review* 165 (September, 1897), p. 344.
7. Weyl, "The brand of the city," p. 771.
8. Strong, "The problem of the twentieth century city," p. 348.
9. Cited in Editorial Comment, "Thriving cities," p. 640. See also Wellman, "Rise of the American city."
10. Reported in "Why cities grow," *The Literary Digest* 58 (August 17, 1918), p. 22.
11. See Editor, "How big should a city be?" *The Literary Digest* 51 (August 28, 1915), p. 399.
12. G. S. Dickerman, "The drift to the cities," *The Atlantic Monthly* 112 (September, 1913), p. 350. In one of the few references to urban decline during this period, Dickerman points out that three of the 225 cities with over 25,000 inhabitants lost population between 1900 and 1910.

13. Mark Jefferson, "A hopeful view of the urban problem," *The Atlantic Monthly* 112 (September, 1913), p. 355. A similar argument is offered by Wellman, "Rise of the American city."

14. L. S. Rowe, "The social consequences of city growth," *The Yale Review* 10 (November, 1901), p. 298 and p. 299, respectively.

15. Dickerman, "The drift to the cities," p. 353.

16. Editor, "The problem of city life," *The Independent* 53 (1901), p. 1088. See also Wyle, "The brand of the city."

17. Busbey L. White, "The wicked town and the moral country," *The Unpopular Review* 10 (October-December, 1918), p. 386. See also Editor, "The growth of cities," *The Nation* 61 (August 8, 1895) for a similar rebuttal.

18. Weber, "Growth of the cities in the United States: 1890–1900," p. 375. See also Strong, "The problem of the twentieth century city," p. 344, and Benjamin C. Marsh, "Can land Be overloaded?" *The Annals of the American Academy of Political and Social Science* 51 (1914), pp. 54–58.

19. Bernard J. Newman, "Congestion and rents," *The Annals of the American Academy of Political and Social Science* 51 (1914), pp. 59–67.

20. Walter A. Wyckoff, "Incidents of the slums," *Scribner's Magazine* 30 (October, 1901), p. 486.

21. Lincoln Steffans, *The Shame of the Cities* (New York: Hill & Wang, 1957, originally published 1904).

22. Steffans, *The Shame of the Cities,* pages 11, 136, and 159, respectively.

23. Albert Shaw, "Our 'civic renaissance'," *The Review of Reviews* 11 (April, 1895), p. 427. On the relation of politics to business, Steffans noted that "[t]he politician is a businessman with a specialty." See Steffans, *The Shame of the Cities,* p. 4.

24. Frederick C. Howe, "The American and the British city—A comparison," *Scribner's Magazine* 41 (January, 1907), p. 114. Josiah Strong wrote in his book *The Twentieth Century City* (New York: The Baker and Taylor Co., 1898) that municipal affairs were a national scandal and "municipal democracy a stench in the nostrils of the civilized world" (p. 82).

25. Rudolph Blankenburg, "What is a city?" *The Independent* 85 (1916), p. 84.

26. Henry Oyen, "The awakening of cities—IV," *The World's Work* 22 (September, 1911), p. 14831.

27. Henry Oyen, "The awakening of cities—II," *The World's Work* 22 (July, 1911), p. 14612. Oyen's optimism should be put in context. Fifteen years earlier, Albert Shaw had written that "the American people are bestirring themselves to the cities wholesome and good." See Shaw, "Our 'civic renaissance',", p. 427.

28. Frederick C. Howe, "In defence of the American city," *Scribner's Magazine* 51 (April, 1912), p. 490.

29. Milo Roy Maltbie, "Municipal functions: A study of the development, scope and tendency of municipal socialism," *Municipal Affairs* 2 (December, 1898), pp. 587–799.

30. Editor, "Big American cities," *The World's Work* 21 (December, 1910), p. 13713.

31. Reported in Frank T. Carlton, "The civic ideal," *Current Literature* 32 (April, 1902), p. 418.

32. Randolph S. Bourne, "Our unplanned cities," *The New Republic* 3 (June, 1915), pages 202, 203, and 203, respectively.

33. See Bourne, "Our unplanned cities," and Charles H. Caffin, "The beautifying of cities," *The World's Work* 3 (November, 1901), pp. 1429–1435.

34. The Caffin quotation is from "The beautifying of cities," p. 1435. On this point, see also Horace Mcfarland, "The glory of the cities," *The Outlook* 85 (March 23, 1907), pp. 647–659; Charles Mulford Robinson, "New dreams for cities," *The Architectural Record* 17 (May, 1905), pp. 410–421; and Charles Mulford Robinson, "The remaking of our cities," *The World's Work* 12 (October, 1906), pp. 8046–8050.

35. Clinton Rodgers Woodruff, "The rebuilding of our cities," *The World To-Day* 16 (May, 1909), pages 493 and 500. See also Henry Oyen, "The awakening of cities—I," *The World's Work* 22 (June, 1911), pp. 14494–14506 and his "The awakening of cities—II."

36. Henry B. F. Macfarland, "The twentieth century city," *The American City* 5 (September, 1911), p. 138.

37. Macfarland, "The twentieth century city," pages 139 and 138, respectively. See also Amos Stote, "The ideal American city," *McBride's Magazine* 97 (April, 1916), pp. 89–99. A much smaller group of reformers saw the decentralization of the population to suburbs as prelude to a more appropriate solution; mainly, the potential for garden cities. See Frank T. Carlton, "Urban and rural life," *The Popular Science Monthly* 73 (March, 1906), pp. 255–260, and J. Russell Smith, "The recon-

structed city," *Annals of the American Academy of Political and Social Science* 59 (May, 1915), pp. 283–290.

38. Patrick Geddes, "The survey of cities," *The Sociological Review* 1 (January, 1908), pp. 74–79.

39. Albert Bushnell Hart, "The rise of American cities," *The Quarterly Journal of Economics* 4 (January, 1890), p. 148.

40. Richard M. Hurd, "The structure of cities," *Municipal Affairs* 6 (March, 1902), pp. 24–43.

41. Robert Park, "The city: Suggestions for the investigation of human behavior in the urban environment," *American Journal of Sociology* 20 (March, 1915), pp. 577–612.

42. Charles Richmond Henderson, "Are modern industry and city life unfavorable to the family?" *American Journal of Sociology* 14 (March, 1909), p. 674. Henderson proceeded to present his solution to the social problems of the city: a policy of eugenics and segregation to contain the "immigrants of a lower order" and allow "persons of normal life and civilized standards" to prosper.

43. Howard Vincent O'Brien, "The city," *The Forum* 54 (October, 1915), p. 390.

NOTES TO CHAPTER 3

1. George Soule, "Will the cities ever stop?" *The New Republic* 47 (June 16, 1926), pp. 105–107. The Census data are from "Changing rank of our cities," *The Literary Digest* 87 (November 7, 1925), p. 14.

2. "Changing rank of our cities," p. 14. By this time, immigration had slowed to a trickle as the United States entered a period of nativism and isolationism.

3. Harold Cox, "The overgrowth of cities," *The Forum* 68 (November, 1922), p. 933. Cox followed that sentence with the following: "Women in particular have a strong preference for town life. The town offers much greater facilities for women's special work of housekeeping. In addition, women like the gaiety of the crowded city, the increased liberty it gives them, the increased opportunities of enjoyment."

4. Soule, "Will the cities ever stop?" p. 105.

5. Frederick L. Ackerman, "Our stake in congestion," *The Survey* 54 (May 1, 1925), p. 141.

6. Soule, "Will the cities ever stop?" p. 106.

7. Cox, "The overgrowth of cities," p. 934.

8. Ackerman, "Our stake in congestion," p. 142.

9. Raymond Unwin, "The overgrown city," *The Survey* 49 (October 15, 1922), p. 85.

10. Clarence Stein, "Dinosaur cities," *The Survey* 54 (May 1, 1925), p. 134. On this point, see also Soule, "Will the cities ever stop?"

11. Cited in "Henry Ford dooms our great cities," *The Literary Digest* 83 (November 15, 1924), p. 13.

12. Soule, "Will the cities ever stop?" p. 105.

13. Lewis Mumford, "The intolerable city," *Harper's Magazine* 152 (February, 1926), pages 285 and 286, respectively.

14. Stuart Chase, "The future of the great city," *Harper's Magazine* 160 (December, 1929), pages 83 and 87 respectively. Chase then asserted that "[m]egalopolis will become so alien to normal living that even Jews, with two thousand years of urban adaptation in their inheritance will leave it" (p. 89).

15. Lewis Mumford, "The sacred city," *The New Republic* 45 (January 27, 1926), pp. 270–271.

16. Lewis Mumford, "Botched cities," *The American Mercury* 18 (October, 1929), pages 149 and 144, respectively.

17. Charles A. Beard, "The city's place in civilization," *The American City* 39 (November, 1928), p. 102.

18. Gerald W. Johnson, "The rise of the cities: A pessimistic note," *Harper's Magazine* 157 (July, 1928), p. 250.

19. "Great cities are declining in population," *Current Opinion* 75 (August, 1923), pages 207 and 208, respectively.

20. Lewis Mumford, "The fourth migration," *The Survey* 54 (May, 1925), pp. 130–133. Stein's "Dinosaur cities" was a response to Mumford's article.

21. Cited in "Pride and peril in city growth," *The Literary Digest* 96 (January 14, 1928), p. 10.

22. William L. Bailey, "The twentieth century city," *The American City Magazine* 31 (August, 1924), p. 143.

23. "Henry Ford dooms our great cities," p. 13. The same article cited The Jersey City *Journal* in disagreement: "[T]he urban population has shown no marked inclination to move *en masse* out into the suburbs. As a matter of fact, the cities are more than holding their own in the matter of population."

24. Beard, "The city's place in civilization," p. 102.

25. C. Leslie Lynch, "New cities for old," *Christian Science Monitor* (November 9, 1940), p. 7.

26. Warren S. Thompson, "On living in cities," *The American Mercury* 20 (June, 1930), p. 193.

27. Warren S. Thompson, "The future of the large city," *The American Mercury* 20 (July, 1930), pages 336 and 332, respectively.

28. Thompson, "On living in cities," p. 199.

29. Thompson, "The future of the large city," p. 337. Thompson was reacting to the fact that birth rates were lower in the cities as compared to outside of them.

30. Harold Ward, "Cities that consume men," *The Nation* 146 (January 22, 1938), p. 92.

31. "Our surging cities," *Collier's* 86 (July, 1926), p. 62.

32. "City growth and congestion as revealed by the 1930 Census," *The American City* 45 (November, 1931), p. 97.

33. "Growing cities grasp more power," *The Literary Digest* 105 (May 10, 1930), p. 11.

34. "Growing cities grasp more power," p. 11 for both quotes.

35. "City growth and congestion as revealed by the 1930 Census," p. 97. Note the phrase "central city," a label that becomes more and more common after 1920.

36. "Rebuilding the cities," *Business Week* 566 (July 6, 1940), p. 35.

37. Quoted in Mark Gelfand, *A Nation of Cities* (New York: Oxford University Press, 1975), p. 106.

38. Quoted in Mabel L. Walker, *Urban Blight and Slums* (Cambridge, Harvard University Press, 1938), p. 13. See also C. E. A. Winslow, "The post-war city," *American Journal of Public Health* 33 (November, 1943), pp. 1408–1413. One of the very few articles written during this period linking racial segregation and slums was Alonzo G. Moron's "Where shall they live?" *The American City* 57 (April, 1942), pp. 68–70. Moron was a manager of public housing in Atlanta, Georgia. For further reference, see J. Randolph Coolidge, Jr., "The problem of the blighted district," *Proceedings of the Fourth National Conference on City Planning,* May 27–29, 1912, Boston, Massachusetts, pp. 100–106.

39. National Resources Committee, "Our cities—their role in the national economy" (Washington, DC: Superintendent of Docu-

ments, 1937), pages 15 and 2, respectively. The survey was reprinted in "U.S. real property inventory I: The facts," *The Architectural Forum* 61 (November, 1934), pp. 320–329. For an overview of the condition of cities and their residents during this period, see Niles Carpenter and Clarence Quinn Berger, "Social adjustments in cities," *The American Journal of Sociology* 40 (May, 1935), pp. 729–736. See also M. A. Mikkelsen, "Have the cities reached maturity?" *Architectural Record* 82 (December, 1937), pp. 60–64.

40. Clarence A. Dykstra, "Problems which face American cities," *Vital Speeches* 6 (November 15, 1939), p. 83.

41. "Rebuilding the cities," p. 35.

42. Ibid., p. 38.

43. "The life and death curve of an American city," *Survey Graphic* 29 (February, 1940), pp. 58–59.

44. George H. Herrold, "Obsolescence in cities," *The Planner's Journal* 1 (November/December, 1935), p. 73. See also C. Louis Knight, "Blighted areas and their effects on urban land utilization," *The Annals of the American Academy of Political and Social Science* 148 (March, 1930), pp. 133–138.

45. Henry M. Propper, "Solving our blighted downtown areas," *Nation's Business* 28 (May, 1940), p. 94.

46. "Rebuilding the cities," p. 35.

47. Urban Land Institute, *Decentralization: What Is It Doing to Our Cities?* (Chicago: Urban Land Institute, 1940), p. 2.

48. Knight, "Blighted areas and their effects upon urban land utilization."

49. Lewis Mumford, "Wither the city?" *The American City* 11 (November, 1939), p. 60. A year earlier, Mumford had published his now-famous *The Culture of Cities*. In an obituary for Mumford (who died January 26, 1990), it was noted that "the book was a slow seller, perhaps because urban dwellers then were less occupied with problems of decay." See "Lewis Mumford, a visionary social critic, dies at 94," *The New York Times* (January 28, 1990), p. 30.

50. Boyden Sparkes, "Can the cities come back?" *The Saturday Evening Post* 217 (November 4, 1944), p. 42.

51. Walker, *Urban Blight and Slums*, p. 17.

52. Henry Wright, "Sinking slums," *Survey Graphic* 22 (August, 1933), pp. 417–419.

53. Walker, *Urban Blight and Slums*, p. 17.

54. Urban Land Institute, "Decentralization," p. 1. George Herrold agreed: "[A]lmost all cases of obsolescence may be laid at the door of exploitation." See his "Obsolescence in cities," p. 75.

55. Catherine Bauer, "Cities in flux," *The American Scholar* 13 (Winter, 1943–1944), p. 77.

56. Ibid., p. 77.

57. Robert Moses, "Slums and city planning," *The Atlantic* 175 (January, 1945), p. 64.

58. Propper, "Solving our blighted downtown areas," p. 92. The economist Guy Greer summed up: "Of all the sore spots of the cities and towns of the United States today, the best advertised are the slums and blighted areas." See Greer, *Your City Tomorrow* (New York: The Macmillan Company, 1947), p. 102. The architect Jose Luis Sert offered slums as the principal reason for the cities' bankruptcy in his "Can our cities survive?" *Science Digest* 13 (May, 1943), pp. 25–28.

59. Herrold, "Obsolescence in cities," p. 75. And, Thomas C. Desmond, "Blighted areas get a new chance," *National Municipal Review* 30 (November, 1941), pp. 629–632, 640; Lynch, "New cities for old"; and Joseph D. McGoldrick, "Can we rebuild our cities?" *National Municipal Review* 34 (January, 1945), pp. 5–9.

60. Wright, "Sinking slums," p. 419.

61. Thomas Adams, "The American community in fifty years," *Proceedings of National Conference on City Planning* (Philadelphia: Wm. F. Fell, Company, 1932), p. 63.

62. National Resources Committee, "Our cities—Their role in the national economy," p. 26. The Committee was a New Deal fact-gathering body whose ultimate goal was to address the relation between the federal government and urban society. See Gelfand, *A Nation of Cities*, pp. 71–104.

63. Harland Bartholomew, "The American city: Disintegration is taking place," *Vital Speeches* 7 (November 1, 1940), p. 61.

64. "Rebuilding the cities," p. 39.

65. Urban Land Institute, "Decentralization," p. 1.

66. Ibid., p. 2.

67. "Rebuilding the cities," p. 35.

68. "The problem of the cities and towns," p. 22.

69. National Resources Planning Board, *Better Cities* (Washington, DC: U.S. Government Printing Office, 1942), p. 4. The National

Resources Planning Board and the National Resources Committee were essentially the same entity at different points in time and with a different name.

70. Warren S. Thompson, "Our birth rate stops city growth," *Journal of the American Institute of Architects* 1 (April, 1944), p. 193.

71. National Resources Committee, "Our cities," pages 11 and 7, respectively.

72. J. C. Furnas, "What will happen to our problem towns?" *The Saturday Evening Post* 216 (March 18, 1944), p. 21. See also "Boom bonanzas swell pockets but boost community problems," *Newsweek* 17 (January 27, 1941), pp. 34, 36; and "Boom cities aided," *Business Week* 783 (September 2, 1944), pp. 31–32.

73. "The problem of the cities and towns," Conference on Urbanism (Cambridge, MA: Harvard University, 1942), p. 19.

74. Bauer, "Cities in flux," p. 82.

75. "Ghost cities of the future," *Science Digest* 13 (March, 1943), p. 2 for both quotes.

76. Rexford G. Tugwell, "San Francisco as seen from New York," *Proceedings of the National Conference on Planning* (Chicago: American Society of Planning Officials, 1940), p. 186.

77. At least one commentator believed that decentralization would not create suburbs but make it possible for the United States to be a nation of small towns. See David Cushman Coyle, "Back to the land?" *Survey Graphic* 29 (February 1940), pp. 115–118.

78. "Back to the land," *The Nation* 136 (February 8, 1933), p. 138.

79. "25 cities—17 up, 8 down," *Business Week* (August 10, 1940), p. 30.

80. Cited in Mel Scott, *American City Planning* (Berkeley: University of California Press, 1969), pp. 377–378.

81. Homer Hoyt, "The structure of American cities in the post-war era," *American Journal of Sociology* 48 (January, 1943), pages 475 and 477, respectively.

82. "25 cities—17 up, 8 down," p. 30. Providing circumstantial evidence in support was a New York City economist, Frank Fisher. Fisher pointed out that "[b]etween 1930 and 1940, the population in the outskirts of 140 metropolitan areas increased by 16.9 per cent, while the population of the central cities increased by only 6.1 per cent, and in some cases actually declined." See Frank Fisher, "Rebuilding our cities," *The Nation* 161 (August 11, 1945), p. 131.

83. T. H. Reed, "The metropolitan problem—1941," *National Municipal Review* 30 (July, 1941), pp. 400–408.

84. Bartholomew, "The American city," p. 63.

85. Urban Land Institute, "Decentralization," p. 5.

86. Sparkes, "Can the cities come back?" p. 43.

87. "Back to town," *Business Week* (April 7, 1934), p. 18.

88. Carol Aronovic, "Let the cities perish." *The Survey* 68 (October 1, 1932), p. 439.

89. "Back to the land," *The Nation* 136 (February 8, 1933), p. 138.

90. John A. Piquet, "The new frontier," *Survey Graphic* 22 (October, 1933), pages 510 and 511, respectively.

91. Louis Wirth, "Urban communities," *American Journal of Sociology* 47 (May, 1942), p. 833.

92. "How to cure the city," *Time* 40 (July 20, 1942), p. 48.

93. Eliel Saarinen, *The City* (New York: Reinhold Publishing Co., 1943), pages 147 and 149, respectively. For a similar organic perspective, this time by the architect Jose Luis Sert, see "Biology of cities," *Time* 40 (November 30, 1942), p. 78.

94. "Institute of Urbanism to be established at Columbia University," *The American City* 49 (May, 1934), p. 54.

95. Freeman Tilden, "Cities," *The World's Work* 60 (May, 1931), pages 48 and 47, respectively.

96. C. A. Dykstra, "The future of American cities," *The American City* 49 (October, 1934), p. 54.

97. C. A. Dykstra, "If the city fails, America fails," *Survey Graphic* 26 (December, 1937), p. 663.

98. "The American distrust of cities," *The Review of Reviews* 84 (October, 1931), p. 76.

99. Charles E. Merriam, "How far have we come and where do we go from here?" *National Municipal Review* 20 (January, 1931), p. 12. See also William Anderson, "The federal government and the cities," *National Municipal Review* 13 (May, 1924), pp. 288–293; and Charles E. Merriam, "The federal government recognizes the city," *National Municipal Review* 23 (February, 1934), pp. 107–109, 116.

100. "Postwar prospects for cities," *Business Week* 749 (January 8, 1944), p. 18.

101. The National Resources Planning Board offered a different assessment, one based more on the potential for human intervention than

the determinism of statistical trends: "The end of the war will offer the people of the United States the chance to rebuild American cities." See National Resources Planning Board, *Better Cities,* p. 1.

102. Louis Wirth, "The cities' most serious crisis," *The American City* 59 (November, 1944), p. 5. See also the speech by Charles T. Stewart, director of the Urban Land Institute, to the Cleveland Real Estate Board, reported in *The American City* 58 (April, 1943), pp. 63–64.

103. Charles S. Ascher, "What are cities for?" *The Annals of the American Academy of Political and Social Science* 242 (November, 1945), pages 1 and 6, respectively.

104. "The cities' job—Now that the war is won," *The American City* 60 (September, 1945), p. 94. See also Fisher, "Rebuilding our cities."

105. Hoyt, "The structure of American cities in the post-war era."

106. Charles S. Ascher, "Better cities after the war," *The American City* 57 (June, 1942), p. 55.

107. Alvin H. Hansen, "The city of the future," *National Municipal Review* 32 (February, 1943), pp. 68–72, 82.

NOTES TO CHAPTER 4

1. George Sessions Perry, "Cincinnati," *The Saturday Evening Post* 218 (April 20, 1946), p. 19.

2. "Cities take inventory," *Business Week* 905 (January 4, 1947), p. 22.

3. Louis B. Wetmore and Edward J. Milne, "Rebuilding our cities—Is there any progress?" *The American City* 63 (March, 1948), p. 94.

4. Lewis Mumford, "Cities fit to live in," *The Nation* 166 (May 15, 1948), pages 530 and 531, respectively.

5. Mabel L. Walker, "The American city is obsolescent," *Vital Speeches* 13 (September 1, 1947), pages 698 and 697, respectively.

6. Respectively, the quotes are from Joseph S. Clark, "A voice for the cities," *The Nation* 188 (March 7, 1959), pp. 199–201; Michael D. Reagan, "The urban vacuum," *The Nation* 189 (July 4, 1959), p. 12; and Eugene H. Klaber, "Urban exodus: A quandary for planners," *The American City* 63 (March, 1948), p. 104.

7. All of these quotations are from a three-part series titled "What next for our American Cities?" and published in *The American City* 64 (December, 1949), pp. 79–81, 159; 65 (January, 1950), pp. 75–78; and 65 (February, 1950), pp. 81–83.

8. Guy Greer, *Your City Tomorrow* (New York: Macmillan, 1947), p. vii.

9. "What next for our American cities?" *The American City* 65 (January, 1950), p. 78.

10. Fred K. Vigman, *Crisis of the Cities* (Washington, DC: Public Affairs Press, 1955), p. 6.

11. Doris Greenberg, "Civic embarrassment," *New York Times Magazine* (November 19, 1950), p. 20.

12. "U.S. sticks to cities," *Science News Letter* 65 (May 1, 1954), p. 285.

13. "Who can define 'urban' or 'city'?" *The American City* 69 (December, 1954), p. 100.

14. "Census Bureau urged to redefine urban areas," *The American City* 67 (July, 1952), p. 97.

15. "More people and problems," *Newsweek* 36 (August 28, 1950), p. 59.

16. "69,249,148 live in 157 urbanized areas," *The American City* 67 (February, 1952), p. 9.

17. "More people and problems," p. 63.

18. Bernard J. Frieden, *The Future of Old Neighborhoods* (Cambridge, MA: MIT Press, 1964), pp. 12–46.

19. Phillip M. Hauser, "The challenge of metropolitan growth," *Urban Land* 17 (December, 1958), p. 3. See also Coleman Woodbury, "Economic implications of urban growth," *Science* 129 (June 12, 1959), pp. 1585–1590.

20. "Our slow-growing cities," *Science Digest* 43 (June, 1958), p. 40.

21. "The suburbs grow . . . while New York rests. It's happening everywhere," *Business Week* 1293 (June 12, 1954), p. 68.

22. Walker, "The American city is obsolescent," p. 697.

23. Quoted in "Census Bureau urged to redefine urban areas," p. 97.

24. "The top 50," *Time* 76 (August 8, 1960), p. 18.

25. Walker, "The American city is obsolescent," p. 698.

26. "The top 50," p. 18.

27. Editorial, "Those Census figures," *The American City* 75 (October, 1960), p. 7.

28. "Rebirth of the cities," *Time* 66 (December 5, 1955), p. 26.

29. "More urban renewal plans to check urban decay at centers of cities," *The American City* 69 (September, 1954), p. 23.

30. Thomas H. Reed and Doris D. Reed, "Does your city suffer from SUBURBANITIS?" *Collier's* 130 (October 11, 1952), p. 20.

31. The data are from "1955 a banner year for annexations," *The American City* 71 (August, 1956), p. 17; and Jerome Ellison, "Relief for strangled cities," *The Saturday Evening Post* 229 (April 20, 1957), p. 38. See also "434 U.S. cities extend borders," *The American City* 69 (June, 1954), p. 9.

32. Ellison, "Relief for strangled cities," p. 38.

33. Reed and Reed, "Does your city suffer from SUBURBANITIS?" p. 18. For a similar perspective, see William Zeckendorf, "Cities versus suburbs," *The Atlantic Monthly* 190 (July, 1952), pp. 24–28.

34. "Flight to the suburbs," *Time* 63 (March 22, 1954), p. 102. The ratio data are from Hauser, "The challenge to metropolitan growth," p. 3.

35. "The suburbs grow while New York rests," p. 70.

36. Hal Burton, "Downtown isn't doomed! Part I," *The Saturday Evening Post* 226 (June 5, 1954), p. 22.

37. Vigman, *Crisis of the Cities,* p. 62.

38. "Suburbs cut cities down to size," *Business Week* 1607 (June 18, 1960), p. 64.

39. Special Correspondent, "Exploding cities," *The Economist* 186 (January 4, 1958), p. 35.

40. Hauser, "The challenge of metropolitan growth," p. 3.

41. Eugene H. Klaber, "Urban exodus: A quandary for planners," *The American City* 63 (March, 1948), p. 103.

42. Alfred Caldwell, "Atomic bombs and city planning," *Journal of the American Institute of Architects* 4 (December, 1945), p. 298.

43. "Moves are to cities," *Science News Letter* 64 (December 12, 1953), p. 373.

44. Mitchell Gordon, *Sick Cities* (New York, The Macmillan Company, 1963), pp. 1–13. For quarantine rather than war, see Catherine Bauer, "First job: Control central city sprawl," *Architectural Forum* 105 (September, 1956), pp. 105–111.

45. Harold H. Martin, "Our urban revolution, part one. Are we building a city 600 miles long?" *The Saturday Evening Post* 232 (January 2, 1960), p. 78.

46. Jean Gottman, *Megalopolis: The Urbanized Northeastern Seaboard of the United States* (New York: The Twentieth Century Fund, 1961), pages 7 and 11, respectively.

47. Christopher Tunnard, "America's super-cities," *Harper's Magazine* 217 (August, 1958), pp. 59–65.

48. "Cities as long as highways—That's America of the future," *U.S. News & World Report* 42 (April 5, 1957), p. 28. See also "Cities crowding—Countryside losing," *U.S. News & World Report* 52 (May 7, 1962), pp. 76–80.

49. "Cities as long as highways . . . ," p. 31. See also "The way the U.S. is growing—what it means," *U.S. News & World Report* 55 (January 13, 1964), pp. 82–85; and "Sprawling 'strip cities'—they're all over the U.S.," *U.S. News & World Report* 51 (September 18, 1961), pp. 73–75+.

50. Martin, "Our urban revolution, part one," p. 74.

51. Julian H. Levi, "Crisis of our cities," *Vital Speeches* 26 (February 1, 1960), pp. 254–256.

52. Clark, "A voice for the cities," p. 199. Hal Burton proclaimed that the "seepage of talent and leadership from city to suburb has become almost a torrent in the last few years." See Burton, "Downtown isn't doomed! Part I," p. 22.

53. Reed and Reed, "Does your city suffer from SUBURBANITIS?" p. 18. Tied to the loss of leaders was the loss of "productive" residents. See "Our changing cities."

54. "Rebirth of the cities," p. 26.

55. "The suburbs grow . . . while New York rests," p. 70.

56. "Big cities rank their worst problems," *The American City* 71 (April, 1956), p. 197.

57. Junius B. Wood, "Are cities headed for trouble?" *Nation's Business* 35 (October, 1947), p. 45.

58. See Ibid., and Sam Shulsky, "The financial plight of our cities," *The American Mercury* 66 (January, 1948), pp. 17–24.

59. Quoted in Subcommittee on Housing and Urban Affairs, *The Central City Problem and Urban Renewal* (Washington, DC: U.S. Government Printing Office, 1973), p. 163.

60. "Big cities' big future," *U.S. News & World Report* 33 (August, 1952), p. 28. See also "Can the big cities come back?" *U.S. News & World Report* 43 (July 19, 1957), pp. 72–73.

61. "How one big city is fighting for a comeback," *U.S. News & World Report* 43 (July 19, 1957), p. 86.

62. William H. Whyte, Jr., "Are cities un-American?" *Fortune* 55 (September, 1957), pages 226 and 125, respectively.

63. Woodbury, "Economic implications of urban growth," p. 1587.

64. Frieden, *The Future of Old Neighborhoods,* p. 1.
65. Harold H. Martin, "Our urban revolution, part II: Is downtown doomed?" *The Saturday Evening Post* 232 (January 9, 1960), p. 27.
66. Miles Colean, *Renewing Our Cities* (New York: The Twentieth Century Fund, 1953), p. 73.
67. Peter Wyden, et al., "Our changing cities," *Newsweek* 50 (September 2, 1957), p. 62. One might speculate that the demise of a vociferous moral condemnation of cities was a function not only of political realignments but also of the change in color of the typical rural migrant.
68. Frieden, *The Future of Old Neighborhoods,* p. 14.
69. Ibid., p. 25.
70. Whyte, "Are cities un-American?" p. 214.
71. Special Correspondent, "Exploding cities," p. 35.
72. Martin, "Our urban revolution, part one," p. 15.
73. Colean, *Renewing Our Cities,* p. 16.
74. "The suburbs grow . . . while New York rests," p. 72.
75. John Gunther, *Inside U.S.A.* (New York: Harper & Row, 1951 ed.), p. 1009.

NOTES TO CHAPTER 5

1. See Coleman Woodbury, *The Future of Cities and Urban Redevelopment* (Chicago: University of Chicago Press, 1953), and Louis B. Wetmore and Edward J. Milne, "Rebuilding our cities—is there any progress?" *The American City* 63 (March, 1948), pp. 94–96+.
2. Edward J. Logue, "Urban ruin—or urban renewal?" *New York Times Magazine* (November 9, 1958), p. 17. Logue mentioned industrial districts, but they never occupied a central position in the discourse.
3. Miles Colean, *Renewing Our Cities* (New York: The Twentieth Century Fund, 1953). Quotes are from pages 65, 41, 39, and 39, respectively.
4. Special Correspondent, "Exploding cities," *The Economist* 186 (January 4, 1958), p. 35.
5. See Coleman Woodbury, "Economic implications of urban growth," *Science* 129 (June 12, 1959), p. 1588. He attributed the ills of central business districts to three conditions: residential blight within and surrounding them, a high degree of congestion of buildings and people within the district, and traffic congestion throughout the center.

6. "How mayors rank their most urgent problems," *The American City* 70 (January, 1955), p. 112. The problem that received the most attention (55%) was "more and steadier employment in factories," while "more housing" was far down (17%) on the list.

7. Guy Greer, "Is your town fit to live in?" *The American Magazine* 146 (July, 1948), p. 50.

8. "What's happening to U.S. cities," *U.S. News & World Report* 48 (June 20, 1960), p. 84.

9. Hal Burton, "Downtown isn't doomed! Conclusion," *The Saturday Evening Post* 226 (June 19, 1954), p. 110.

10. "What's happening to U.S. cities?" p. 84.

11. "Rx for ailing cities," *Newsweek* 55 (May 23, 1960), pp. 111–112. This article includes one of the earliest references to the death of the cities, a theme that becomes prominent later.

12. "Cities in trouble—what can be done," *U.S. News and World Report* 48 (June 20, 1960), p. 86.

13. Henry S. Churchill, "Modern cities—now or never," *The Survey* 86 (January, 1950), p. 23.

14. Raymond Vernon, *The Changing Economic Function of the Central City* (New York: Committee for Economic Development, 1959).

15. Luther Gulick, "Five challenges in today's new urban world," *The American City* 71 (December, 1956), p. 149.

16. "Downtown rises above 'gray belt'," *Business Week* 1538 (February 21, 1959), p. 29.

17. Hal Burton, "Downtown isn't doomed! Part I," *The Saturday Evening Post* 226 (June 5, 1954), pages 102 and 99, respectively.

18. "How one big city is fighting for a comeback," *U.S. News & World Report* 43 (July 19, 1957), p. 86.

19. See Hal Burton, "Downtown isn't doomed! part II," *The Saturday Evening Post* 226 (June 12, 1954), pp. 38–39+; Henry S. Churchill, "Modern cities—now or never," *The Survey* 86 (January, 1950), pp. 23–26; "Logue, Urban ruin—or urban renewal?"; Wetmore and Milne, "Rebuilding our cities—is there any progress?"; and William Zeckendorf, "New cities for old," *The Atlantic* 188 (November, 1951), pp. 31–35.

20. The quotes, respectively, are from "What next for our American cities?" *The American City* (December, 1949), p. 81; and "New hearts for our cities," *Newsweek* 43 (March 29, 1954), p. 74.

21. "Rebirth of the cities," *Time* 66 (December 5, 1955), p. 25.

22. Phillip M. Hauser, "The challenge of metropolitan growth," *Urban Land* 17 (December, 1958), p. 4.

23. Hubert H. Humphrey, "What's wrong with our cities?" *The American City* 63 (July, 1948), p. 68.

24. Logue, "Urban ruin—or urban renewal?" p. 33.

25. Charles Abrams, *The Future of Housing* (New York: Harper & Row, 1946), p. 21.

26. "New hearts for our cities," p. 74. The quote points to a minor, but nonetheless important, national theme in the postwar period: the Cold War obsession with communism.

27. Junius B. Wood, "Clear slums? Yes! But how?" *Nation's Business* 35 (December, 1947), p. 43.

28. "Can the big cities come back?" *U.S. News & World Report* 43 (July 19, 1957), pp. 72–80+.

29. Eugene Raskin, "The unloved city," *The Nation* 188 (February 7, 1959), pages 120 and 119, respectively. Raskin's comment includes a not-so-subtle criticism of the architect Le Corbusier's vision of the ideal house as a machine for living.

30. Frieden, *The Future of Old Neighborhoods* (Cambridge, MA: MIT Press, 1964), p. 14.

31. "Cities aren't 'social jungles'," *Science Digest* 42 (August, 1957), p. 27.

32. Wetmore and Milne, "Rebuilding our cities—is there any progress?" p. 120.

33. Fred K. Vigman, *Crisis of the Cities* (Washington, DC: Public Affairs Press, 1955), p. 52.

34. Committee on Land Policy, "Statement of policy on urban development and expansion," *Journal of the American Institute of Planners* 16 (Spring, 1950), p. 97.

35. Zeckendorf, "New cities for old," pages 31 and 35, respectively.

36. Julian H. Levi, "Crisis of our cities," *Vital Speeches of the Day* 26 (February, 1960), p. 255. See also David O'Shea, "The urban evolution," *America* 101 (July 25, 1959), p. 552.

37. Joseph S. Clark, "A voice for the cities," *The Nation* 188 (March, 1959), p. 121.

38. Both quotes are on p. 44 in "A country of crowded clusters," *Newsweek* 54 (December 14, 1959).

39. "Metropolitan cities," *The American City* 72 (August, 1957), p. 163. See also "How to build tomorrow's city," *Nation's Business* 47 (January, 1959), p. 58.

40. Edward T. Chase, "Future of the city," *Commonweal* 67 (October 11, 1957), p. 39.
41. "Americans are mainly city dwellers," *Science Digest* 37 (June, 1955), p. 32.
42. Editorial, "Some urban trends for the 1960s—and beyond," *The American City* 75 (January, 1960), p. 7.
43. Woodbury, "Economic implications of urban growth," p. 1590.
44. Both quotes are from Mitchell Gordon, "Doomed cities," *The Wall Street Journal* (October 16, 1962), p. 13.
45. Logue, "Urban ruin—or urban renewal?" p. 17.
46. Paul N. Ylvisaker, "The miraculous city," *National Civic Review* 50 (December, 1961), p. 587.
47. "Can the big cities come back?" *U.S. News & World Report* 43 (July 19, 1957), p. 72.
48. Donald Campion, "Last mile for cities?" *America* 94 (October 15, 1955), p. 73.
49. "The suburbs grow . . . while New York rests: It's happening everywhere," *Business Week* 1293 (June 12, 1954), p. 70.
50. Herbert B. Dorau, "The big city must adjust itself," *The American City* 64 (February, 1949), p. 115.
51. Committee on Land Policy, "Statement of policy on urban development and expansion," p. 93. See also Gulick, "Five challenges in today's new urban world," p. 149.
52. Carl Feiss, "The architect and engineer in urban redevelopment," *Journal of the American Institute of Architects* 19 (June, 1953), p. 248.
53. Paul Windels, "How should our cities grow," *Journal of the American Institute of Architects* 14 (October, 1950), p. 149.
54. Henry Churchill, "What shall we do with our cities?" *Journal of the American Institute of Architects* 4 (August, 1945), p. 63.
55. Ibid., p. 64.
56. Victor Gruen, "Who is to save our cities?" *Harvard Business Review* 41 (May/June, 1963), p. 109.
57. "How one big city is fighting for a comeback," p. 90.
58. "A country of crowded clusters," p. 45.
59. "Suburbs cut cities down to size," *Business Week* 1607 (June 18, 1960), p. 72.
60. William H. Whyte, Jr., "Are cities un-American?" *Fortune* 55 (September, 1957), p. 124.

61. Martin Meyerson and Barbara Terrett, "Metropolis lost, metropolis regained," *Annals of the American Academy of Political and Social Science* 314 (November, 1957), p. 9.

62. Ibid., p. 2.

63. "Crisis in the city," *Senior Scholastic* 77 (October 5, 1960), p. 9.

64. Hauser, "The challenge of metropolitan growth," p. 4.

NOTES TO CHAPTER 6

1. Quoted in William H. Chafe, *The Unfinished Journey* (New York, Oxford University Press, 1986), p. 376.

2. Quoted in Nathan Glazer, *Cities in Trouble* (Chicago: Quadrangle Books, 1970), p. 24.

3. Ibid., p. 9.

4. "The cities: Waging a battle for survival," *Newsweek* 73 (March 17, 1969), p. 41. The Foster quote is from an editorial titled "1963—The brightening morning of the golden urban age," *The American City* 78 (January, 1963), p. 7.

5. "Three mayors speak of their cities," *Ebony* 29 (February, 1974), p. 35.

6. "Is flight from suburbs starting?" *U.S. News & World Report* 52 (June 11, 1962), pp. 86–89.

7. "End of rush to America's big cities?" *U.S. News & World Report* 75 (October 8, 1973), p. 72.

8. William S. Foster, "Central-city upsurge," *The American City* 79 (November, 1964), p. 7.

9. Quotes are from "Return to the cities—a trend that's picking up speed," *U.S. News & World Report* 75 (December 10, 1973), p. 68. See also "A trek back to the cities," *U.S. News & World Report* 76 (April 8, 1974), pp. 52–53.

10. Quoted in "What the big cities must do to stay alive," *U.S. News & World Report* 64 (January 8, 1968), p. 66.

11. The first quote is from "After 160 billions to rescue cities—," *U.S. News & World Report* 72 (April 10, 1972), p. 44; the second quote is from "A trek back to the cities," p. 53.

12. James V. Cunningham, "The indispensable city," *Commonweal* 74 (September 22, 1961), p. 511.

13. Ira Mothner, "Our cities: The uptight life," *Look* 32 (June 11, 1968), p. 27. While population grew 1 percent in the central cities from 1960

to 1968, growth in the suburbs was significantly greater at 28 percent. Between 1966 and 1968, central cities lost population at a rate of 381,000 per year versus gains of 271,000 per year from 1960 to 1966. See "Still more changes in central cities," *U.S. News & World Report* 66 (June 30, 1969), p. 52.

14. "Fastest-growing cities," *U.S. News & World Report* 66 (March 31, 1969), pp. 55–57.
15. "The rural exodus: New Census report," *U.S. News & World Report* 70 (February 22, 1971), p. 37.
16. Six of the top fifty metropolitan areas—New York, Los Angeles, St. Louis, Pittsburgh, Cleveland, Seattle-Everett—had lost population between 1970 and 1972. See "End of rush to America's cities," p. 72; see also "Drift away from big cities goes on," *U.S. News & World Report* 81 (November 15, 1976), p. 94.
17. "Rural & urban growth," *The New Republic* 165 (September 25, 1971), pp. 12–13.
18. "New towns—answer to urban sprawl?" *U.S. News & World Report* 60 (February 14, 1966), p. 116.
19. "Tomorrow's cities: Go up, spread out or start over?" *Changing Times* 24 (April, 1970), pages 19 and 20, respectively.
20. Max Ways, "The deeper shame of the cities," *Fortune* 77 (January, 1968), p. 133. For a similar assessment see Daniel Patrick Moynihan, "Is there really an urban crisis?" *Challenge* 15 (November/December, 1966), pp. 20–22+.
21. Editorial, "The mayor's exciting view from city hall," *Life* 59 (December 29, 1965), p. 6.
22. "Future of big cities—whites in minority?" *U.S. News & World Report* 53 (August 27, 1962), p. 73.
23. Charles E. Silberman, "The city and the negro," *Fortune* 65 (March, 1962), p. 90.
24. All the above data are from "Migration of negroes—here is real story," *U.S. News & World Report* 52 (May 7, 1962), pp. 54–56. In Newark, New Jersey, the head of the city's housing authority estimated in 1968 that since 1950, some 200,000 whites had moved out of Newark and 85,000 Negroes had moved in. See "We just can't make it any more," *U.S. News & World Report* 64 (June 24, 1968), p. 62, and "Migration of negroes—."

25. "Still more changes in central cities," *U.S. News & World Report* 66 (June 30, 1969), p. 52.
26. William V. Shannon, "Crisis of the cities," *Commonweal* 83 (December 3, 1965), p. 264.
27. "Negro cities, white suburbs—it's the prospect for the year 2000," *U.S. News & World Report* 60 (February 21, 1966), pp. 72–73.
28. "Our cities—are they really doomed?" *Senior Scholastic* 96 (February 16, 1970), p. 8.
29. "What's wrong with cities," *Senior Scholastic* 93 (November 22, 1968), p. 22. See also National Advisory Commission on Civil Disorders, *Report of the National Advisory Commission on Civil Disorders* (New York: Bantam Books, 1968), pp. 253–254.
30. Ibid., pp. 258–259.
31. "A 'liberal' mayor's advice to blacks: 'Think white'," *U.S. News & World Report* 71 (November 1, 1971), p. 94.
32. Daniel Patrick Moynihan, "Poverty in cities," in James Q. Wilson, ed., *The Metropolitan Enigma* (New York: Anchor Books, 1970), p. 369.
33. "Danger facing big cities," *U.S. News & World Report* 59 (September 6, 1965), p. 31.
34. Quoted in "Danger facing big cities," p. 30.
35. Editorial, "The mayor's exciting view from city hall," p. 7.
36. John F. Kain and Joseph J. Persky, "Alternatives to the gilded ghetto," *The Public Interest* 14 (Winter, 1969), p. 75.
37. Edmund K. Faltermayer, "What it takes to make great cities," *Fortune* 75 (January, 1967), p. 122.
38. John Peter, "Everybody's going to town," *Look* (September 21, 1965), p. 32.
39. National Advisory Commission on Civil Disorders, p. 204.
40. Ibid., p. 204.
41. Kenneth B. Clark, *The Dark Ghetto* (New York: Harper & Row, 1965), p. 11.
42. William V. Shannon, "Crisis of the cities," *Commonweal* 83 (December 3, 1965), p. 264.
43. See Charles A. Valentine, *The Culture of Poverty* (Chicago: University of Chicago Press, 1968), pp. 18–77.
44. U.S. Department of Labor, *The Negro Family* (Washington, DC: U.S. Government Printing Office, 1965), p. 5.

45. Edward C. Banfield, *The Unheavenly City* (Boston: Little, Brown and Company, 1968), p. 229.
46. "The cities: What next?" *Time* 90 (August 11, 1967), quote and data on p. 11.
47. "Looting, burning—new guerrilla war," *U.S. News & World Report* 63 (August 7, 1967), pp. 23–27. See also "Scars still are there," *U.S. News & World Report* 64 (April 22, 1968), p. 31.
48. See National Advisory Commission on Civil Disorders, pp. 84–108; "Looting, burning—now guerrilla war"; and "Scars still are there."
49. "Anarchy growing threat to big cities," *U.S. News & World Report* 63 (August 7, 1967), p. 28.
50. "Not all this country is tense, troubled," *U.S. News & World Report* 63 (August 7, 1967), p. 37. See also, from a few years earlier, another celebration of small towns: "Pleasant places to live in U.S.—where they are," *U.S. News & World Report* 58 (March 29, 1965), pp. 50–55+.
51. "In a week of riots: The toll," *U.S. News & World Report* 64 (April 22, 1968), p. 37.
52. "More violence and race war?" *U.S. News & World Report* 64 (April 15, 1968), p. 32. Radicals like Stokely Carmichael and Malcolm X and organizations such as SNCC and the Black Panthers were instrumental in changing the discourse on race from one that privileged the term *Negro,* a label they felt had been conferred upon them by white society and that represented an accommodating pose, to one that privileged the term *black,* a more explicit political statement and a label they willingly adopted despite its earlier historical connotations.
53. "The cities: Forecast for summer," *Time* 97 (May 31, 1971), p. 12.
54. National Advisory Commission on Civil Disorders, p. 410.
55. Ibid., p. 203.
56. "The cities: What next?" p. 11.
57. "Cities: The bonfire of discontent," *Time* 88 (August 26, 1966), p. 10.
58. "The cities: Forecast for summer," p. 12.
59. Clark, *Dark Ghetto,* p. 21.
60. Alex Poinsett, "Black takeover of U.S. cities?" *Ebony* 26 (November, 1970), p. 86. See also "Ten best cities for blacks," *Ebony* 29 (November, 1973), pp. 152–154+.
61. Mary McGrory, "What to do about the cities," *America* 115 (August 27, 1966), p. 203.

62. Silberman, "The city and the negro," p. 91. See also Robert A. Futterman, *The Future of Our Cities* (New York: Doubleday & Company, 1961), p. 78.
63. "The cities: What next?" p. 12.
64. The developer William Zeckendorf offered his own eccentric and certainly fearful prognosis of how we would overcome the problem of the ghetto. It "will have been completely solved, because we'll be [in 75 to 100 years] a nation of mulattos." See "As I see it," *Forbes* 103 (March 1, 1969), p. 55.
65. Norton E. Long, "The city as reservation," *The Public Interest* 25 (Fall, 1971), p. 32.
66. George Sternlieb, "The city as sandbox," *The Public Interest* 25 (Fall, 1971), pp. 14–21. See also George Sternlieb, "Are cities obsolete?" *Trans-action* 7 (April, 1970), pp. 84–87, where he separates the issue of function from the issue of race.
67. "Are big cities worth saving?" *U.S. News & World Report* 71 (July 26, 1971), p. 49.
68. Murray Bookchin, *The Limits of the City* (New York: Harper & Row, 1974), p. 76.

NOTES TO CHAPTER 7

1. John F. Kain, "The distribution and movement of jobs and industry," in James Q. Wilson, ed., *The Metropolitan Enigma* (New York: Doubleday and Company, 1970), pp. 1–43.
2. Ibid., p. 5.
3. Alexander Ganz, "The future of the central city," *The American City* 85 (August, 1970), p. 57.
4. David L. Birch, *The Economic Future of City and Suburb* (New York: Committee for Economic Development, 1970). Quotes are from pages 2, 6, 14, and 13, respectively.
5. Charles Abrams, *The City Is the Frontier* (New York: Harper & Row, 1965), p. 6.
6. "Can the big cities ever come back?" *U.S. News & World Report* 63 (September 4, 1967), p. 28.
7. George Sternlieb, "Is business abandoning the big city?" *Harvard Business Review* 39 (January/February, 1961), pages 7 and 160, respectively.

8. "Big-city troubles—is there an answer?" *U.S. News & World Report* 60 (March 21, 1966), pp. 78–81.

9. "In the inner cities: Acres of abandoned buildings," *U.S. News & World Report* 68 (January 26, 1970), pp. 54–56. Sternlieb and others failed to mention the extent to which financial institutions created the decay that repulsed them. See Jane Jacobs, "How money can make or break our cities," *The Reporter* (October 12, 1961), pp. 38–40.

10. William S. Foster, "Urban misconceptions," *The American City* 84 (June, 1969), p. 75.

11. Ibid., pp. 73–75+. See also Raymond Moley, "Mendicant cities," *Newsweek* 67 (April 11, 1966), p. 116.

12. "A liberal mayor's advice to blacks: 'Think white'," *U.S. News & World Report* 71 (November 1, 1971), p. 94.

13. Bennett Harrison, *Urban Economic Development* (Washington, DC: The Urban Institute, 1974), p. 56.

14. Nathan Glazer, ed., *Cities in Trouble* (Chicago: Quadrangle Books, 1970), p. 11. This is what Ganz called the "fiscal squeeze" in his "The future of the central city," p. 58.

15. "Big city woes as the mayors see them," *U.S. News & World Report* 73 (July 3, 1972), p. 52.

16. William V. Shannon, "Crisis of the cities," *Commonweal* 83 (December 3, 1965), p. 265. See also "Is the big city problem hopeless?" *U.S. News & World Report* 64 (June 24, 1968), pages 60 and 61, respectively.

17. Bernard Weissbourd, "Are cities obsolete?" *Saturday Review* 47 (December 19, 1964), p. 15.

18. C. W. Griffin, Jr., "City slums and segregated suburbs," *Saturday Review* 49 (January 8, 1966), p. 85. Griffin went on to decry slumlords as "the vultures of capitalism" and to condemn realtors for their efforts to undermine fair housing laws.

19. The data are from "Still more changes in central cities," *U.S. News & World Report* 66 (June 30, 1969), p. 52. The quote is from "The plight of our cities," *Senior Scholastic* 89 (January 20, 1967), p. 6.

20. "Three mayors speak of their cities," *Ebony* 29 (February, 1974), p. 38.

21. Henry Maier, "Suburbia & the city: Flight, fight or apathy," *Vital Speeches of the Day* 36 (January 1, 1970), p. 184.

22. Herbert J. Gans, "The white exodus to suburbia steps up," in Glazer, ed., *Cities in Trouble*. Quotes on pages 45, 46, 46, and 48, respectively.

23. Maier, "Suburbia & the city," p. 185.

24. Edward C. Banfield, *The Unheavenly City* (Boston: Little Brown & Company, 1968), pp. 23–44.

25. Robert C. Weaver, *The Urban Complex* (New York: Anchor Books, 1966), p. 35.

26. Daniel Patrick Moynihan, "Is there really an urban crisis?" *Challenge* 15 (November/December, 1966), p. 21.

27. Gans, "The white exodus to suburbia steps up," p. 44.

28. "Big cities try for a comeback," *U.S. News & World Report* 57 (December 28, 1964), p. 34. See also Victor Gruen, "WHO is to save our cities?" *Harvard Business Review* 41 (May/June, 1963), pp. 107–115. A few years earlier, *Newsweek* had noted that "[a]cross the nation, the cities are rebuilding, refurbishing, marching ahead." See "A country of crowded clusters," *Newsweek* 54 (December 14, 1959), p. 45.

29. "A country of crowded clusters," p. 44.

30. Quoted in James O'Gara, "The ugly city," *Commonweal* 80 (June 19, 1964), p. 390.

31. Frank Getlein, "A dream of fair cities," *Commonweal* 85 (January 6, 1967), p. 366.

32. Leland Hazard, "Are we committing urban suicide?" *Harvard Business Review* 42 (July-August, 1964), p. 154.

33. The quotes are from "Revolt against tearing up cities," *U.S. News & World Report* 64 (March 11, 1968), pp. 68–70. The latter quote, of course, makes allusion to the sexual dimension of the U.S. discourse on race. See also Stephen N. Adubato and Richard J. Krickus, "Stable urban neighborhoods: A strategy for cities," *The Nation* 218 (May 18, 1974), pp. 623–628.

34. Joseph S. Clark, "To come to the aid of their cities," *The New York Times Magazine* (April 30, 1961), p. 90.

35. Clifford Case, "A cure for sick cities," *Saturday Review* 46 (February 9, 1963), pp. 12–14.

36. James Bailey, "Congress and the crisis in our cities," *Architectural Forum* 127 (September, 1967), pp. 54–57. See also Robert C. Weaver, "Rebuilding America's cities: An overview," *Current History* 55 (December, 1968), pp. 321–326+.

37. "Candidates view the urban crisis," *Business Week* 2042 (October 19, 1968), p. 66.

38. See "'New directions' for communities—Nixon's blueprint," *U.S. News & World Report* 74 (March 19, 1973), pp. 86–88+; and "What

Nixon plans to do," *Newsweek* 73 (March 17, 1969), pp. 49–50, 52. The quote is from "'New directions' for communities—," p. 86.

39. "After 160 billions to rescue cities—," *U.S. News & World Report* 72 (April 10, 1972), p. 42.

40. Richard M. Nixon, "Community development," *Vital Speeches of the Day* 39 (April 1, 1973), pp. 356–357.

41. "Claim city problems abandoned by Nixon; erosion of authority, confidence, cited," *The American City* 88 (November, 1973), p. 44. See also "Disappearing act," *Commonweal* 98 (March 30, 1973), pp. 75–76.

42. Kenneth E. Fry, "Central cities fight back," *Nation's Business* 57 (September, 1969), p. 60.

43. Adubato and Krickus, "Stable urban neighborhoods: A strategy for cities," and "Nixon's plans for future of U.S. cities and small towns," *U.S. News & World Report* 69 (July 6, 1970), pp. 30–32. For a libertarian version of this argument, see Edmund Contoski, "Government controls and urban renewal," *Reason* (May, 1975), pp. 23–27.

44. Commission on the Cities, *The State of the Cities* (New York: Praeger, 1972).

45. Ralph Lazarus, "Surviving the age of the city," *Saturday Review* 49 (January 8, 1966), p. 44. See also C. W. Griffin, Jr., "Specialists diagnose the stricken American city," *Saturday Review* 46 (August 3, 1963), p. 23.

46. Gruen, "WHO is to save our cities?" p. 108.

47. Donald Canty, "Architecture and the urban emergency," *Architectural Forum* 121 (August/September, 1964), p. 175.

48. "The cities: Waging a battle for survival," *Newsweek* 73 (March 17, 1969), p. 40.

49. All quotes are from "Big cities do have a future—the picture that city planners see," *U.S. News & World Report* 62 (June 26, 1967), pp. 46–50.

50. "City woes: Easing a bit, mayors say," *U.S. News & World Report* 70 (June 28, 1971), p. 32.

51. "America's cities . . ." *Senior Scholastic* 88 (April 22, 1966), p. 4.

52. George Sternlieb, "Are cities obsolete?" *Trans-action* 7 (April, 1970), pages 85 and 86, respectively.

53. Weissbourd, "Are cities obsolete?"

54. Jacobs, "How money can make or break our cities," p. 40.

55. Wolf Von Eckardt, *The Challenge of Megalopolis* (New York: The Macmillan Company, 1964), p. 43.

56. Stewart Alsop, "The cities are finished," *Newsweek* 77 (April 5, 1971), p. 100.

57. "We just can't make it any more," *U.S. News & World Report* 64 (June 24, 1968), p. 62.

58. Catherine Bauer Wurster, "Can cities compete?" *Architectural Record* 136 (December, 1964), p. 150. See also "Troubled cities—and their mayors," *Newsweek* 69 (March 13, 1967), pp. 38–43; and "Vast city breaking down into a jungle," *U.S. News & World Report* 72 (April 10, 1972), p. 46.

59. "Troubled cities . . . ," p. 43.

60. Arthur M. Louis, "The worst American city," *Harper's Magazine* 250 (January, 1975), pp. 67–71.

61. Samuel C. Jackson, "Are American cities obsolete?" *Vital Speeches* 36 (September 15, 1970), p. 709.

62. Lewis Mumford, "Trend is not destiny," *Architectural Record* 142 (December, 1967), p. 132.

63. Banfield, *The Unheavenly City*. See also Edward C. Banfield, "A critical view of the urban crisis," *The Annals of the American Academy of Political and Social Science* 405 (January, 1973), pp. 7–14, in which he blames the urban crisis on a public state of mind that no longer values honesty, truth, kindness, compassion, racial tolerance, respect for law, nonviolence, and respect for democratic rights.

64. Richard Sennett, "Survival of the fattest," *The New York Review of Books* 15 (August 13, 1970), pp. 23–26.

65. Ruth Beinart, "The unheavenly city: The nature and the future of our urban crisis," *Commonweal* 92 (September 18, 1970), p. 466.

66. For the comments by Naftalin, see "Banfield's *Unheavenly City:* A symposium and response," *Trans-action* 8 (March/April, 1971), pp. 69–72, 74–78.

67. This and the previous paragraph are based on Naftalin, "Banfield's *Unheavenly City*," pp. 77–78.

68. See Harvey Averch and Robert A. Levine, "Two models of the urban crisis," *Policy Sciences* 2 (June, 1971), pp. 143–158.

69. "Rethinking cities," *Time* 95 (June 1, 1970), pp. 64–65.

70. Both quotes are from ibid., p. 65.

71. T. R. Marmor, "Banfield's 'heresy'," *Commentary* 54 (July, 1972), pages 87 and 88, respectively. Marmor was professor of public affairs and law at the University of Minnesota.

72. Irving Kristol, "The cities: A tale of two classes," *Fortune* 81 (June, 1970), pages 197 and 198, respectively. Forrester was a professor of engineering at MIT who developed a computer model that showed that the consequences of urban policies were counterintuitive, thereby providing scientific support for their inherent intractability.

73. Irving Kristol, "Common sense about the 'urban crisis'," *Fortune* 76 (October 1967), p. 234. Denying the urban-ness of the nation is one way to dismiss the cities from public debate.

74. Irving Kristol, "It's not a bad crisis to live in," *The New York Times Magazine* (January 22, 1967), p. 67. A similar historical perspective is provided by James F. Richardson, "The historical roots of our urban crisis," *Current History* 59 (November, 1970), pp. 257–261+.

75. Editorial, "U.S. cities improving," *Science News* 90 (September, 1966), p. 170.

76. Moynihan, "Is there really an urban crisis?" pages 20 and 21, respectively.

77. Editorial, "Cities much the same," *America* 116 (February 18, 1967), pp. 238–239.

78. "It's not a bad crisis to live in," p. 72.

79. Jane Jacobs, *The Death and Life of Great American Cities* (New York: Random House, 1961).

80. "American cities: Dead or alive?—Two views," *Architectural Forum* 116 (March, 1962), p. 90.

81. Lewis Mumford, "Home remedies for urban cancer," in *The Urban Prospect* (New York: Harcourt, Brace and World, 1962), pp. 182–207; and Herbert J. Gans, "City planning and urban realities," *Commentary* 33 (February, 1962), pp. 170–175.

82. See "American cities: Dead or alive?—Two views," pp. 90–91.

83. John V. Lindsay, "The future of the American city," *Saturday Review* 49 (January 8, 1966), p. 70.

84. "Cities: The bonfire of discontent," *Time* 88 (August 26, 1966), p. 9.

85. Wilson, ed., *The Metropolitan Enigma,* p. 391.

86. John F. Kain and Joseph J. Persky, "Alternatives to the gilded ghetto," *The Public Interest* 14 (Winter, 1969), p. 75.

87. Quoted in "Can today's big cities survive?" *U.S. News & World Report* 63 (November 6, 1967), p. 56. See also Lloyd Rodwin, "The quest to save the central city," *Nations and Cities* (Boston: Houghton Mifflin, 1970), pp. 217–267. Rodwin says about the discourse that "the focus

shifted from housing to the problems of the central city, and then to the relationship between the central city and the suburbs, and finally to the seething resentment of the ghettos which involved all of these issues and more" (p. 239).

88. Jay W. Forrester, *Urban Dynamics* (Cambridge: MIT Press, 1969), p. 70. On counterintuitive solutions, see Daniel Patrick Moynihan, "Eliteland," *Psychology Today* (September, 1970), pp. 35+. See also Averch and Levine, "Two models of the urban crisis."

89. Kain and Persky, "Alternatives to the Gilded Ghetto," p. 86.

90. Forrester, *Urban Dynamics,* p. 129.

91. "Are big cities worth saving?" *U.S. News & World Report* 71 (July 26, 1971), p. 43.

92. Albert Mayer, *The Urgent Future* (New York: McGraw-Hill Book Company, 1967), p. 2.

93. John B. Breslin, "Save the city!" *America* 129 (December 1, 1973), p. 425. For an analysis of American urban ambivalence written during this period, see Walter Berns, "Thinking about the city," *Commentary* 56 (October, 1973), pp. 74–77. Note also that Morton White and Lucia White had published *The Intellectual Versus the City* (Cambridge: Harvard University Press, 1962) as this stage of the discourse began to emerge. Many read that book as evidence of the American hatred rather than ambivalence toward cities. See Elias S. Wilentz's review, "The city haters," *The Nation* 195 (December 8, 1962), pp. 408–409.

94. Jeanne R. Lowe, *Cities in a Race with Time* (New York: Random House, 1967), p. 3.

NOTES TO CHAPTER 8

1. "Any way you look at it: The worst slump since 1930s," *U.S. News & World Report* 78 (March 31, 1975), p. 27.

2. The quote is from "Shaping—and misshaping—the metropolis," *Search* 7 (Spring, 1977), p. 5. The Urban Institute observation can be found in "Fiscal woes multiply for large central cities," *Search* 5 (Winter, 1975), pp. 3–9.

3. "Fighting the unthinkable," *Time* 106 (September 8, 1975), p. 9.

4. Ken Auletta, "After the storm, the hurricane," *The Village Voice* 20 (September 1, 1975), p. 8. More generally, see Phil Tracy, "What will happen when the city defaults?" *The Village Voice* 20 (August 4, 1975),

p. 9; and Felix Rohatyn, "New York and the nation," *New York Review of Books* 28 (January 21, 1982), pp. 26–28.

5. Jack Newfield, "How the power brokers profit," *The Village Voice* 21 (April 26, 1976), pp. 9–13.

6. "Fighting the unthinkable," p. 9. See also, "New York: Let's make a deal," *Newsweek* 86 (November 24, 1975), pp. 40, 42.

7. Charles N. Kimball, "Renaissance or ruin? Options for the future of urban America," *Vital Speeches* 42 (January 15, 1976), p. 199. For bankruptcies, see "Cities in peril," *U.S. News & World Report* 78 (April 7, 1975), p. 29.

8. "Behind the growing crisis . . . facts and figures," *U.S. News & World Report* 80 (April 5, 1976), p. 51.

9. "Cities are becoming dumping grounds for poor people," *U.S. News & World Report* 80 (April 5, 1976), p. 54.

10. Abraham D. Beame, "Cities here to stay, with business help," *The American City* 91 (July, 1976), p. 69.

11. Jason Epstein, "The last days of New York," *The New York Review of Books* 23 (February 19, 1976), p. 22.

12. Roger Starr, "Making New York smaller," *The New York Times Magazine* (November 14, 1976), p. 32. Witold Rybcznski returned to this issue twenty years later but could not spark a debate. See his "Downsizing cities," *The Atlantic Monthly* 2764 (October, 1995), p. 36ff.

13. Starr, "Making New York smaller," pages 32 and 106, respectively. For one critic's views, see Fergus Bordewich, "The future of New York: A tale of two cities," *New York Magazine* 12 (July 23, 1979), pp. 32–40.

14. William C. Baer, "On the death of cities," *The Public Interest* 45 (Fall, 1976), pages 4 and 8, respectively.

15. Marvin Stone, "Let big cities die?" *U.S. News & World Report* 83 (August 8, 1977), p. 80.

16. Beame, "Cities here to stay, with business help," p. 69.

17. Jack Patterson, "The prospect of a nation with no important cities," *Business Week* 2417 (February 2, 1976), p. 66. Patterson was particularly concerned with the flight of corporate headquarters from major cities. See also Peter O. Muller, "Are cities obsolete?" *The Sciences* (March/April, 1986), p. 46.

18. Richard C. Wade, "America's cities are (mostly) better than ever," *American Heritage* 30 (February-March, 1979), p. 9.

19. Alexander Ganz and Thomas O'Brien, "New directions for our cities in the seventies," *Technology Review* 76 (June, 1974), p. 11.

20. Quoted in Michael Doan, "Cities that thrive despite recession," *U.S. News & World Report* 92 (May 3, 1982), p. 66. The Pittsburgh quote is from Matt Rothman and Peter Engardio, "Cities aren't giving up on the high-tech dream," *Business Week* 2928 (January 13, 1986), p. 123. See also Michael Doan, "Cities that lead the recovery parade," *U.S. News & World Report* 95 (November 7, 1983), pp. 70–73.

21. Ford S. Worthy, "Booming American cities," *Fortune* 116 (August 17, 1987), p. 30. Worthy went on to say that some cities had not been able to make the transition and thus continued to decline.

22. "As the cities seek a new role—," *U.S. News & World Report* 87 (October 15, 1979), pages 69 and 67, respectively. For academic substantiation of these shifts, see Elizabeth Corcoran and Paul Wallich. "The rise and fall of cities," *Scientific American* 265 (August, 1991), p. 103.

23. Kenneth Labich, "The best cities for knowledge workers," *Fortune* 128 (November 15, 1993), pp. 50–78.

24. Christopher Farrell, et al., "Brighter lights for the cities," *Business Week* 3576 (May 4, 1998), pp. 88–95.

25. Anne Faircloth, "North America's most improved cities," *Fortune* 136 (November 24, 1997), p. 170.

26. Kirkpatrick Sale, *Power Shift: The Rise of the Southern Rim and Its Challenge to the Eastern Establishment* (New York: Random House, 1974), p. 19.

27. Edward Kelly, "Corporate prosperity and urban decline," *Urban Concerns* 1 (February/March, 1980), p. 5. See also Patterson, "The prospect of a nation with no important cities."

28. Sarah Peterson, "Why many firms return to smaller cities," *U.S. News & World Report* 93 (April 2, 1984), p. 76.

29. Monroe W. Karmin, "America's boom towns," *U.S. News & World Report* 107 (November 13, 1989), p. 55. On that same page, one realist suggested that these centers would become old and be displaced in a "constant economic metamorphosis that is a sign of national strength." See also "America's new boomtowns," *U.S. News & World Report* 116 (April 11, 1994), p. 62ff; and Muller, "Are cities obsolete?"

30. Carey W. English, et al., "Suburbs have jobs, cities have jobless," *U.S. News & World Report* 99 (November 18, 1985), p. 84. See also "Our dinosaur cities," *USA Today* 108 (October, 1979), pp. 12–13.

31. English, "Suburbs have jobs, cities have jobless," p. 84.

32. Kenneth Labich, "The best cities for business," *Fortune* 120 (October 23, 1989), pp. 56–58ff.

33. Franz Schurmann and Sandy Close, "The emergence of global city USA," *The Progressive* 43 (January, 1979), pages 27 and 29, respectively.

34. Ganz and O'Brien, "New directions for our cities in the seventies."

35. U.S. Department of Housing and Urban Development, *The President's National Urban Policy Report* (Washington, DC: U.S. Government Printing Office, 1980), chapter 1, p. 10.

36. "Drift away from big cities goes on," *U.S. News & World Report* 81 (November 15, 1976), p. 94.

37. "Flight from big cities—but not in Sun Belt," *U.S. News & World Report* 85 (November 27, 1978), p. 71. The Snowbelt was also known as the Rustbelt, in reference to declining manufacturing.

38. George Sternlieb and James W. Hughes, "The changing demography of the central city," *Scientific American* 243 (August, 1980), p. 48. See also Lowell W. Culver, "America's troubled cities: Better times ahead," *The Futurist* 13 (August, 1979), p. 279.

39. "Tale of America's shrinking cities," *U.S. News & World Report* 90 (March 23, 1981), quotes from page 66. See also, "Facts and figures," *Black Enterprise* 13 (July, 1983), p. 31.

40. The phrase is from "Flight from the inner cities goes on," *U.S. News & World Report* 85 (September 11, 1978), p. 49.

41. Lawrence Malony and Donald L. Battle, "Comeback for cities, woes for suburbs," *U.S. News & World Report* 88 (March 24, 1980), p. 58.

42. "City flight and suburb blight," *The Futurist* 21 (July-August, 1987), p. 49.

43. "Out of the cities, back to the country—," *U.S. News & World Report* 78 (March 31, 1975), pp. 46–50; and "Facts and figures," p. 31.

44. "Out of the cities, back to the country—," p. 46.

45. Ibid., p. 50; and Peterson, "Why many firms return to smaller cities," p. 77.

46. John Herbers, "America's profile shift," *The New York Times Magazine* (September 28, 1986), p. 75.

47. Thomas Hine, "Back to Main Street," *New Jersey Monthly* 13 (February, 1988), p. 63. See also Christopher B. Leinberger and Charles Lock-

wood, "How business is reshaping America," *The Atlantic Monthly* 258 (October, 1986), p. 45.

48. Herbers, "America's profile shift," p. 64.

49. Joel Garreau, *Edge City: Life on the New Frontier* (New York: Doubleday, 1991). See also Richard Louv, *America II* (New York: Penguin, 1985), p. 65.

50. Miriam Wasserman, "Urban sprawl," *Regional Review* 10 (2000), pp. 9–16.

51. George Sternlieb and James W. Hughes, "Post-industrial America: Decline of the metropolis," *Nation's Cities* 13 (September, 1975), p. 17. One urbanologist noted that in the early 1970s there had been "a slowdown in white movement out of most cities, but an increase in the black exodus." See Culver, "America's troubled cities: Better times ahead," p. 280 and also Maloney and Battle "Comeback for cities, woes for suburbs," p. 54.

52. George E. Jones, "The North fights back," *U.S. News & World Report* 90 (June 15, 1981), p. 27. Still, Jones was optimistic that the "big and aging cities" could respond to the challenge. See also "Fresh look at drift from cities," *U.S. News & World Report* 82 (April 25, 1977), p. 71; "Flight from big cities—but not in Sun Belt," p. 71; and "On the way up: Four cities show how it can be done," *U.S. News & World Report* 80 (April 5, 1976), pp. 62–64.

53. Sarah A. Peterson, "Worries on the rise in the Sunbelt, too," *U.S. News & World Report* 90 (June 15, 1981), p. 30.

54. Discussed in "Westward ho," *Time* 126 (December 16, 1985), p. 20.

55. "Where supercities are growing fastest," *U.S. News & World Report* 88 (June 30, 1980), pp. 52–55.

56. Alvin P. Sanoff, "'Strip cities' still gobbling up land, people," *U.S. News & World Report* 95 (October 3, 1983), pages 55 and 54, respectively.

57. Brian J. L. Berry, "Urbanization and counterurbanization in the United States," *The Annals of the American Academy of Political and Social Science* 451 (September, 1980), pp. 13–20.

58. Larry Long and Diane DeAre, "The slowing of urbanization in the United States," *Scientific American* 249 (July, 1983), pp. 33–41, quote on page 41. See also Sternlieb and Hughes, "The changing demography of the central city," p. 48.

59. "Cities are becoming dumping grounds for poor people," *U.S. News & World Report* 80 (April 5, 1976), p. 54.

60. Kimball, "Renaissance or ruin?" p. 199.

61. Charles H. Trout, "America's long urban turmoil," *The Nation* 222 (May 8, 1976), p. 561. See also Sternlieb and Hughes, "The changing demography of the central city," p. 48.

62. Long and DeAre, "The slowing of urbanization in the United States," p. 41. The doughnut metaphor had replaced another metaphor more attuned to the racial crisis of the sixties. That latter metaphor was mentioned by city councilman Harvey B. Gantt in discussing Charlotte's ability to annex fringe areas. Annexation avoided the "white noose around the neck of the central city that's happened to a lot of Northern cities." See "On the way up: Four cities show how it can be done," p. 63. Doughnuts, nooses, and albatrosses all share a common discursive space.

63. "Biggest U.S. cities now," *U.S. News & World Report* 96 (April 16, 1984), p. 14; and "Biggest cities—latest rankings," *U.S. News & World Report* 98 (May 13, 1985), p. 12.

64. See "The cities that grew the most," *The New York Times* (January 23, 1991); and Public Information Office, "195 cities have population over 100,000, New York first; Los Angeles second; San Antonio joins top ten. Mesa, Arizona, fastest growing city," *U.S. Department of Commerce News* (January 25, 1991).

65. Peter Dreier, "Bush to cities: Drop dead," *The Progressive* 56 (July, 1992), p. 23.

66. "Flight from inner cities goes on," p. 49. As for the "13 percent," see "Are cities obsolete?" *Newsweek* 118 (September 9, 1991), p. 42.

67. Myron Magnet, "Behind the bad-news census," *Fortune* 103 (February 9, 1981), pages 93 and 88, respectively.

68. Quoted in "Storming over the census," *Time* 116 (August 4, 1980), p. 25. See also James Gleick, "The census: Why we can't count," *The New York Times Magazine* (July 15, 1990), pp. 22–26, 54. It probably would have been more accurate for that Census Bureau official to have said, "We did not make them up."

69. "Smaller cities, with no end to suburbanization," *Business Week* 2601 (September 3, 1979), pp. 204–206.

70. "Our dinosaur cities," p. 13.

71. "Cities in peril," p. 29. See also, "Big cities wasting away—what are they doing about it?" *U.S. News & World Report* 79 (September 1, 1975), pp. 64–66.

72. "Cities in peril," p. 29. See also Ellis Cose, "Can America's cities survive?" *Current* 201 (March, 1978), pp. 25–29. Cose links the fate of cities to the fate of America's black population.

73. Judah Stampfer, "The city as an urban wilderness," *The Nation* 221 (October 4, 1975), pp. 315 and 314, respectively.

74. Lowell W. Culver, "The undisciplined city: In a resource short world," *The Futurist* 9 (August, 1975), p. 206.

75. Cose, "Can America's cities survive?" pages 26 and 25, respectively. For a different perspective, see Richard L. Williams, "Our older cities are showing age but also showing signs of fight," *Smithsonian* 9 (January, 1979), p. 66; and the comments of architect William Pereira in "As cities recklessly attempt to cope with change," *U.S. News & World Report* 88 (May 19, 1980), p. 63.

76. Irving Howe, "The cities' secret," *The New Republic* 1176 (January 22, 1977), p. 55.

77. Charles H. Trout, "America's long urban turmoil," *The Nation* 222 (May 8, 1976), pages 562 and 564, respectively.

78. "Cities at bay—men on the firing line sum up problems," *U.S. News & World Report* 78 (April 7, 1975), p. 44.

79. Cose, "Can America's cities survive?" p. 29.

80. "Danger in the safety zone," *Time* 142 (August 23, 1993), pp. 29–32; and "The war at home: How to battle crime," *Newsweek* 117 (March 25, 1991), pp. 35–38.

81. "Dead zones," *U.S. News & World Report* 106 (April 10, 1989), p. 22.

82. "Cities in peril," p. 30.

83. Rene Dubos, "The despairing optimist . . . ," *American Scholar* 45 (Autumn, 1976), p. 489.

84. Quote from "Goodbye gritty city—hello urban utopia," *U.S. News & World Report* 94 (May 9, 1983), p. A15.

85. Malony and Battle, "Comeback for cities, woes for suburbs," p. 54.

86. David M. Alpern, "A city revival?" *Newsweek* 93 (January 15, 1979), p. 29.

87. Quoted in "Urban pioneers gamble on the inner city," *Business Week* 2493 (July 25, 1977), p. 144.

88. "Flight from inner cities goes on," p. 49.

89. Malony and Battle, "Comeback for cities, woes for suburbs," p. 53.

90. "America's changing face," *Newsweek* 116 (September 10, 1990), p. 47. See also, "America helps itself by helping others," *U.S. News & World Report* 107 (October 23, 1989), p. 47; and "Census shows profound change in racial makeup of the nation," *The New York Times* (March 11, 1991), pp. A1, A12.

91. Frederico Pena, "The challenge of immigration," *USA Today* 115 (January, 1987), p. 61.

92. "Census paints a picture of New York; foreign, young, educated," *The New York Times* (August 1, 1992); Phillip Kasinitz, "The city's new immigrants," *Dissent* 34 (Fall, 1987), pp. 497–506; and "U.S. shows sharp rise in amount of foreigners," *The New York Times* (December 20, 1992), p. 14.

93. See "The dawn of downtowns," *U.S. News & World Report* 125 (October 5, 1998); Tim Schneider, "Older inner cities making comeback," *San Francisco Chronicle* (May 21, 1991); and Eric Schmitt, "Most cities in U.S. expanded rapidly over last decade," *The New York Times* (May 7, 2001). On Buffalo, see Jay Rey, "City falls below 300,000," *The Buffalo News* (March 16, 2001).

94. Eric Schmitt, "Whites in minority in largest cities, the census shows," *The New York Times* (April 30, 2001).

95. Jerry Adler, "A return to the suburbs," *Newsweek* 104 (July 21, 1986), p. 52.

96. Quoted in Dennis Sanders, "Stemming the tide," *Rutgers Magazine* 67 (September/October, 1988), p. 16.

97. As the historian Jon Teaford noted, "We don't want to talk about our failures." See "Are American cities obsolete?" *USA Today* 116 (August, 1987), p. 7.

NOTES TO CHAPTER 9

1. David Broder, "Public's attention isn't on cities, but problems haven't gone away," *The Houston Chronicle* (July 18, 1994).

2. Horace Sutton, "America falls in love with its cities—again," *Saturday Review* 5 (August, 1978), pp. 16–21.

3. Lawrence Malony and Donald L. Battle, "Comeback for cities, woes for suburbs," *U.S. News & World Report* 88 (March 24, 1980), p. 53.

4. Quoted in Franz Schurmann and Sandy Close, "The Emergence of global city USA," *The Progressive* 43 (January, 1979), p. 27.

5. "Reversal of fortune," *Newsweek* 118 (September 9, 1991), pp. 44–45.

6. For the early years, see "Downtown is looking up," *Time* 108 (July 5, 1976), pp. 54–62. For later, see Penelope Lemov, "Celebrating the city," *Builder* 7 (February, 1984), pp. 90–97.

7. Blake Fleetwood, "The new elite and an urban renaissance," *The New York Times Magazine* (January 14, 1979), pp. 16–20ff.

8. David M. Alpern, et al., "A city revival?" *Newsweek* 93 (January 15, 1979), p. 28. See also, eight years later, William E. Schmidt, "Riding a boom, downtowns are no longer downtrodden," *The New York Times* (October 11, 1987), p. 28.

9. Malony and Battle, "Comeback for cities, woes for suburbs," p. 54.

10. Alpern, et al., "A city revival?" p. 33.

11. Schurmann and Close, "The emergence of global city USA," p. 27. See also Fleetwood, "The new elite and an urban renaissance," pp. 20, 22.

12. Lemov, "Celebrating the city," p. 90.

13. Gurney Breckenfeld, "The Rouse show goes national," *Fortune* 104 (July 27, 1981), p. 50. See also Lemov, "Celebrating the city."

14. Karl E. Meyer, "Love thy city: Marketing the American metropolis," *Saturday Review* 6 (April 28, 1979), p. 16.

15. "Urban pioneers gamble in the inner city," *Business Week* 2493 (July 25, 1977), p. 144.

16. "Why more and more people are coming back to cities," p. 69. See also Sutton, "America falls in love with its cities—again," p. 21.

17. "Recycling slums—a spark for revival in decaying areas," *U.S. News & World Report* 80 (April 5, 1976), p. 60. See also "Why more and more people are coming back to the cities," *U.S. News & World Report* 83 (August 8, 1977), p. 69.

18. Neal R. Peirce, "Nation's cities poised for a stunning comeback," *Nation's Cities* 6 (March, 1978), p. 12.

19. Sutton, "America falls in love with its cities—again," p. 19.

20. David Blum, "The evils of gentrification," *Newsweek* 101 (January 3, 1983), p. 7. A similar concern appears in the revival of the 1990s. The architectural critic Robert Campbell wonders if Boston will remain "a mosaic of separate ethnic neighborhoods" or become a "unified, cosmopolitan, global metropolis." Will the new Boston, he asks, be more like a city or more like a suburb? See Robert Campbell, "Letter from Boston: Frump is fine," *Metropolis* 20 (March, 2001), quotes on p. 52.

21. Aristedes, "Boutique America," *American Scholar* 44 (Autumn, 1975), p. 533.

22. Sutton, "America falls in love with its cities—again," p. 18.

23. Quoted in "Recycling slums—a spark of revival in decaying areas," p. 61.

24. Kenneth T. Jackson, "Once again the city beckons," *The New York Times* (March 20, 2001), p. A23. See also Brendan I. Koerner, "Cities that work," *U.S. News & World Report* 124 (June 8, 1998), pp. 26–36.

Koerner notes that despite falling crime rates and balanced municipal budgets, cities still faced a dismal trend—the continued out-migration of middle-class families.

25. For the usual litany of reasons for gentrification, see Fleetwood, "The new elite and an urban renaissance"; Charles Hoyt, "New perceptions of opportunities for cities," *Architectural Record* 166 (December, 1979), pp. 114–118; and Peirce, "Nation's cities posed for a stunning comeback."

26. "America's false sense of complacency about its cities," *U.S. News & World Report* 89 (December 8, 1980), p. 72.

27. "Are American cities becoming obsolete?" *USA Today* 116 (August, 1987), p. 7.

28. Peirce, "Nation's cities poised for stunning comeback," p. 12. See also "Why more and more people are coming back to cities," p. 69.

29. Both quotes are from Alpern, et al., "A city revival?" p. 28.

30. Warren Cohen, "Cities try to bring home the bacon," *U.S. News & World Report* 116 (January 31, 1994), p. 59.

31. "Urban 'renascence': The reality beneath the glitter," *The Progressive* 43 (January, 1979), p. 26.

32. Vernon L. Schmid, "Gentrification: Pushing out the poor," *The Christian Century* 96 (September 26, 1979), p. 908. See also "Cities' biggest issue," *Current* 206 (October, 1978), pp. 14–15; and Matthew L. Wald, "Managing gentrification: A challenge to the cities," *The New York Times,* Real Estate Report (September 13, 1987), p. 5.

33. James David Besser, "'Gentrifying' the ghetto," *The Progressive* 43 (January, 1979), p. 32.

34. "Urban pioneers gamble on the inner city," p. 146.

35. Fleetwood, "The new elite and an urban renaissance," p. 35.

36. Alpern, et al., "A city revival?" p. 28.

37. Mary Jo Huth, "New hope for revival of America's central cities," *The Annals of the Academy of Political and Social Science* 451 (September, 1980), p. 129. For a view from the previous Gerald Ford Administration, see David M. Muchnik, "Death warrant for the cities: The national urban policy," *Dissent* 23 (Winter, 1975), pp. 21–32.

38. Helen Leavitt, "In search of an urban policy," *The New Leader* 61 (January 30, 1978), pp. 10, 12.

39. Quoted in Marvin Stone, "Who can save our cities?" *U.S. News & World Report* 84 (March 6, 1978), p. 88. The comment was made by

Patricia Harris, then Secretary of the federal Department of Housing and Urban Development.

40. Quoted in Marilyn Marks, "The new urban agenda: The focus is on helping cities help themselves," *National Journal* 16 (August 11, 1984), p. 1513.

41. Quoted in Marks, "The new urban agenda," p. 1514. See also "America's false sense of complacency about its cities," p. 72.

42. Sidney Blumenthal, "Skyscrapers and ferns create new poor," *In These Times* 3 (February 14–20, 1979), p. 19.

43. Paul Levy and Dennis McGrath, "Saving cities for whom?" *Social Policy* 10 (November/December, 1979), p. 20.

44. Richard West, "Fighting to save a neighborhood," *New York Magazine* 14 (July 20, 1981), p. 35.

45. William F. Allman, "St. Louis," *U.S. News & World Report* 107 (December 18, 1989), pp. 49–50.

46. Robert Price, "The good news about New York City," *The New York Times Magazine* (September 28, 1986), pages 30, 49, and 60, respectively.

47. D. J. Waldie, "Catching the urban wave," *The New York Times* (November 27, 2001), p. A19.

48. Laurel Sharper Walters, "Nashville gets its act together after years of urban decline," *Christian Science Monitor* (September 14, 1994).

49. "America's hot cities," *Newsweek* 93 (February 6, 1989), p. 42.

50. Paul Goldberger, "The limits of urban growth," *The New York Times Magazine* (November 14, 1982), p. 60.

51. See "Crowds and more crowds—no end to the urban hassles," *U.S. News & World Report* 92 (April 5, 1982), pp. 47–48. On sprawl, see Neal Peirce, "Cities and suburbs need restructuring," *The Philadelphia Inquirer* (December 25, 1989), sect. A, p. 19; and Neal Peirce, "The region must be tomorrow's new city," *The Philadelphia Inquirer* (December 11, 1989), sect. A, p. 15.

52. "Cities are becoming dumping grounds for poor people," *U.S. News & World Report* 80 (April 5, 1976), pp. 54–56.

53. Fergus Bordewich, "The future of New York," *New York Magazine* 12 (July 23, 1979), pages 34 and 40, respectively. The quote regarding the lumpen proletariat was made by Robert Wagner, then chairman of the New York's City Planning Commission. Bordewich's liberalism clearly had its limits and foreshadowed the welfare reform of the 1990s that emphasized employment and deemphasized financial assistance.

54. Schumann and Close, "The emergence of global city USA," p. 28.

55. Blumenthal, "Skyscrapers and ferns create new poor," p. 19.

56. Neal Peirce, "Rich-poor gap grows in cities," *The Philadelphia Inquirer* (December 18, 1989), sect. A, p. 15. See also "As the cities seek a new role," *U.S. News & World Report* 87 (October 15, 1979), p. 67; and "Why some people leave—and some come back," *U.S. News & World Report* 80 (April 5, 1976), pp. 57–59.

57. Chris Tilly and Abel Valenzuela, "Down and out in the city," *dollars & sense* 155 (April, 1990), p. 6.

58. "The economic crises of urban America," *Business Week* 3266 (May 18, 1992), p. 38.

59. Richard L. Williams, "In Dallas, as in most American cities, the contrast of glitter and squalor," *Smithsonian* 9 (November, 1978), p. 66.

60. Richard Reeves, "America's image is no longer envied," *The Philadelphia Inquirer* (October 13, 1988), sect. A.

61. "Ranking the cities," *Time* 106 (September 29, 1975), pp. 83–84. For a ranking based on "emotional appeal," see William Marlin and Roland Gelatt, "America's most livable cities," *Saturday Review* 3 (August 21, 1976), p. 9, in which the authors rank cities based on the ones in which they would like to live. Ranking schemes can be used to convey many different impressions of desirability. For example, one study explored the relation between "living in the fast lane" and rates of heart disease. See Robert Levine, "The pace of life," *Psychology Today* 23 (October, 1989), pp. 42–46.

62. See "What makes home sweet," *Time* 119 (January 11, 1982), p. 87; "America's cities: Best and worst," *U.S. News & World Report* 92 (January 18, 1982), p. 8; and J. D. Reed, "All riled up about rankings," *Time* 125 (March 11, 1985), p. 76.

63. R. G. Collazo, "Ten cities that work for blacks," *Black Enterprise* 13 (July, 1983), pp. 32–37ff. See also the reader survey by Richard Eisenberg and Debra Wishik Englander, "The best places to live in America," *Money* 16 (August, 1987), pp. 34–42ff.

64. See "What makes home sweet."

65. Brendan Gill, "The malady of gigantism," *The New Yorker* 64 (January 9, 1989), pages 74, 75, and 74, respectively.

66. "Kissing the big city goodbye," *Changing Times* 44 (August, 1990), p. 27. The editors warned, though, that small towns often meant fewer job opportunities and lower incomes.

67. See, of many, "Best cities," *Forbes* 165 (May 29, 2000), pp. 136–162; "The fifteen safest and most dangerous cities," *Jet* 86 (June 20, 1994), pp. 12–13; and Anne Faircloth, "North America's most improved cities," *Fortune* 136 (November 24, 1997), pp. 170–172ff.

68. Earl G. Graves, "Urban crisis or urban renaissance," *Black Enterprise* 9 (July, 1979), p. 5.

69. Ze'ev Chafets, "The tragedy of Detroit," *The New York Times Magazine* (July 29, 1990), p. 23. See his *Devil's Night and Other True Tales of Detroit* (New York: Vintage, 1990), along with "Are cities obsolete?" *Newsweek* 118 (September 9, 1991), pp. 42–44.

70. Chafets, "The tragedy of Detroit," quotes on page 23.

71. Thomas Byrne Edsall and Mary D. Edsall, "Race," *The Atlantic Monthly* 267 (May, 1991), pp. 53–86. The quotation at the beginning of this paragraph is on page 84. Also see William Schneider, "The suburban century begins," *The Atlantic Monthly* 270 (July, 1992), pp. 33–44; and Cornel West, "Learning to talk of race," *The New York Times Magazine* (August 2, 1992), pp. 24, 26.

72. Kenneth Lipper, "What needs to be done?" *The New York Times Magazine* (December 31, 1989), quotations from pages 28, 45, and 46, respectively.

73. The quotation is from Bill Turque, "Cities on the brink," *Newsweek* 116 (November 19, 1990), p. 44. On New York City, see Peter D. Salins, "Jump-starting New York," *The New York Times Magazine* (November 3, 1991), p. 52ff.

74. Henry S. Reuss, "Reviewing the American city," *Vital Speeches* 43 (March 15, 1977), p. 401.

75. A good example is Witold Rybcznski, "Losers," *The New York Review of Books* 43 (1996), pp. 34–36.

76. Brian Duffy, "Days of rage," *U.S. News & World Report* 112 (May 11, 1992), p. 21.

77. Richard I. Kirkland, Jr., "What we can do now?" *Fortune* 125 (June 1, 1992), p. 41.

78. "The fire this time," *Time* 139 (May 11, 1992), pp. 18–25; Harrison Raines, et al., "Requiem for cities," *U.S. News & World Report* 112 (May 18, 1992), pp. 20–26; and "The siege of L.A.," *Newsweek* 119 (May 11, 1992), pp. 30–38.

79. Mortimer B. Zuckerman, "The new realism," *U.S. News & World Report* 112 (May 25, 1992), p. 94. See also "The economic crisis of urban America," *Business Week* 3266 (May 18, 1992), pp. 38–43.

80. Raines, "Requium for cities," p. 20.
81. Neal R. Peirce, "Congress to L.A.: Drop dead," *The Plain Dealer* (Cleveland) (September 26, 1992), p. 7B. See also Peter Dreier, "Bush to the cities: Drop dead," *The Progressive* 56 (July, 1992), pp. 20–23; and Mickey Kaus, "False hopes for the cities," *Newsweek* 120 (October 19, 1992), p. 35. As for Bill Clinton and the cities, see Diane Frances, "Bill Clinton's new headache: Urban decay," *Maclean's* 106 (1993), p. 13. A few years later, little had changed: See Nathan Glazer, "Life in the city," *The New Republic* 216 (August 19–26, 1996), p. 37.
82. "The economic crisis of urban America," p. 43.
83. R. Emmett Tyrrell, Jr., "Unheavenly cities," *The American Spectator* 25 (July, 1992), p. 10.
84. Harold Meyerson, "Fractured city," *The New Republic* 206 (May 25, 1992), p. 25. See also Komozi Woosars, "Cleaning up the Reagan-Bush disaster," *Democratic Left* 20 (July/August, 1992), pp. 3–4. Neglect, of course, was not politically partisan. See Tom Morganthau, "The price of neglect," *Newsweek* 119 (May 11, 1992), pp. 54–55.
85. Lewis H. Lapham, "City lights," *Harper's Magazine* 285 (July, 1992), pages 4 and 6, respectively.
86. West, "Learning to talk of race," p. 26.
87. Francis X. Clines, "Cincinnati's mayor imposes curfew to quell violence," *The New York Times* (April 13, 2001); and, for a view from afar, Ed Vulliamy, "Boiling point in the ghetto," *The Observer* (UK) (April 15, 2001). On the indifferent state of national urban policy—cities as the "neglected stepchildren of American politics"—see the special issue of the *Boston Review* 22 (February, 1997); and Deborah K. Dietsch, "Return cities to the agenda," *Architecture* 85 (October 1996), p. 15ff.
88. The quote is from Jonathan Franzen, "First city," *The New Yorker* 72 (February 19, 1996), p. 88. On the city's new status, see Philip Weiss, "The city resurgent shakes off dust," *The New York Observer* 15 (October 1, 2001), pp. 1, 7.
89. Robert Bruegmann, "The end of cities? An urban legend," *The Washington Post* (November 24, 2001). See also Kirk Johnson, "A city changed forever? Maybe not," *The New York Times* (October 7, 2001), pp. A39, A40.

90. "Urban 'renaissance': The reality beneath the glitter," p. 26.
91. Ernest N. Moriel, *Rebuilding America's Cities* (Cambridge, MA: Ballinger, 1986), p. 30.

NOTES TO CHAPTER 10

1. Barbara Ehrenreich, *Fear of Falling* (New York: Pantheon, 1989), p. 9.
2. On these early, now inner-ring, suburbs, see Robert Fishman, *Bourgeois Utopias* (New York: Basic Books, 1987). As regards inner-ring suburban decay, see Rosalyn Baxandal and Elizabeth Ewen, *Picture Windows: How the Suburbs Happened* (New York: Basic Books, 2000), pp. 227–250.
3. See James C. Scott, *Seeing Like a State* (New Haven, CT: Yale University Press, 1998).
4. Richard Sennett admonishes us to embrace diverse cities in which "experiencing the friction of differences and conflicts makes men [sic] personally aware of the milieu around their own lives . . . [thus] . . . achieving an adulthood whose freedom lies in its acceptance of disorder and painful dislocation." See his *The Uses of Disorder* (New York: Vintage Books, 1970), pages 139 and xvii. See also Iris Marion Young's notion of "together in difference" in both *Inclusion and Democracy* (Oxford: Oxford University Press, 2000), pp. 221–228; and "Residential segregation and differentiated citizenship," *Citizenship Studies* 3 (July, 1999), pp. 237–252.
5. Marianna Torgovnick writes about the "primitive," that its real secret in this century "has often been the same secret as always: the primitive can be—has been, will be (?)—whatever Euro-Americans want it to be." See her *Gone Primitive* (Chicago: University of Chicago Press, 1990), p. 9.
6. Susan Wells extends these thoughts when she writes that "[t]he text labors over the world and transforms it by representing it; the reader transforms the text by interpreting it." See her *The Dialectic of Representation* (Baltimore, MD: The Johns Hopkins University Press, 1985), p. 17.
7. The difficulty of tracing what commentators write to how readers react is captured in Albert O. Hirschman's phrase "action-arousing gloomy

vision." See his "The search for paradigms as a hindrance to understanding," *World Politics* 22 (April, 1970), pp. 336–338.

8. Fred Weinstein writes of the importance in public discourse of "reassur[ing] the audience that these things are really comprehensible and that they fit into a known scheme of one sort or another." See his *History and Theory after the Fall* (Chicago: University of Chicago Press, 1990), p. 39.

9. Terry Eagleton reminds us that "the unending 'dialogue' of human history is as often as not a monologue by the powerful to the powerless." See his *Literary Theory* (Minneapolis: University of Minnesota Press, 1983), p. 73.

Index